the photoshop® CS book

for digital photographers

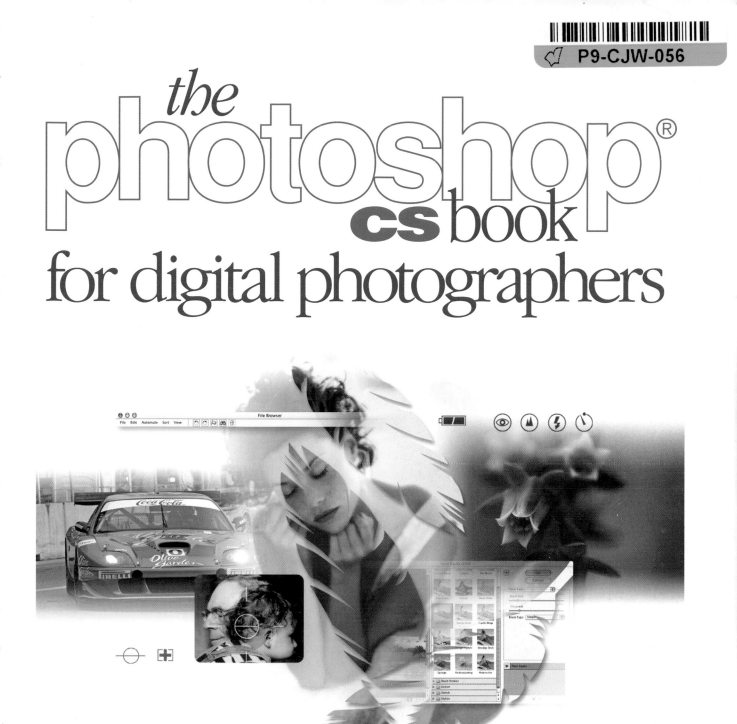

Scott Kelby

The Photoshop CS Book for
Digital Photographers Team

CREATIVE DIRECTOR
Felix Nelson

TECHNICAL EDITOR
Chris Main

EDITOR
Richard Theriault

PROOFREADER
Daphne Durkee

PRODUCTION DIRECTOR
Kim Gabriel

PRODUCTION LAYOUT
Dave Damstra
Dave Korman

PRODUCTION ART
Margie Rosenstein

COVER DESIGNED BY
Felix Nelson

COVER PHOTOS BY
**David Cuerdon, Julieanne
Kost, Dave Moser, and
Jeannie Theriault**

STOCK IMAGES
The royalty-free stock images
used in this book are courtesy of

NEW RIDERS PRODUCTION TEAM

ASSOCIATE PUBLISHER
Stephanie Wall

ACQUISITIONS EDITOR
Steve Weiss

PRODUCTION MANAGER
Gina Kanouse

SENIOR PROJECT EDITOR
Sarah Kearns

COMPOSITOR
Amy Hassos

PROOFREADER
Sheri Cain

Published by
New Riders Publishing

International Standard Book Number: 0-7357-1411-8

Library of Congress Catalog Card Number: 2003111673

07 06 05 04   7 6 5 4 3 2

Interpretation of the printing code: the rightmost double-digit number is the year of the book's
printing; the rightmost single-digit number is the number of the book's printing. For example,
the printing code 03-1 shows that the first printing of the book occurred in 2003.

Composed in Cronos and Helvetica by KW Media Group

Trademarks

Warning and Disclaimer

www.scottkelbybooks.com

For my wonderful wife Kalebra,
and my precious little boy Jordan.
It's amazing just how much joy and love
these two people bring into my life.

ACKNOWLEDGMENTS

First, I want to thank my amazing wife Kalebra. As I'm writing this, she's lying on the couch across from me reading a book (not one of mine, sadly), but I have to say that just looking at her makes my heart skip a beat, and again reminds me how much I adore her, how genuinely beautiful she is, and how I couldn't live without her. She's the type of woman love songs are written for, and I am, without a doubt, the luckiest man alive to have her as my wife.

Secondly, I want to thank my six-year-old son Jordan. God has blessed our family with so many wonderful gifts, and I can see them all reflected in his eyes. I'm so proud of him, so thrilled to be his dad, and I dearly love watching him grow to be such a wonderful little guy, with such a tender and loving heart. (You're the greatest, little buddy.)

I have to thank my wonderful, crazy, hilarious, and loving dad Jerry for filling me with childhood memories of nothing but fun, laughter, and love. His warmth, compassion, understanding, ethics, and sincerity have guided me my entire life, and I could never repay him for all that he's done for me. I love you, Dad.

I also want to thank my big brother Jeffrey for being such a positive influence in my life, for always taking the high road, for always knowing the right thing to say, and just the right time to say it, and for having so much of our dad in you. I'm honored to have you as my brother and my friend.

My heartfelt thanks go to the entire team at KW Media Group, who every day redefine what teamwork and dedication are all about. They are truly a special group of people, who come together to do some really amazing things (on really scary deadlines) and they do it with class, poise, and a can-do attitude that is truly inspiring. I'm so proud to be working with you all.

Thanks to my compadre Dave Moser, whose tireless dedication to making everything we do better than anything we've done before, is an inspiration to our whole team. He's an amazing individual, a great friend, and an awful lot of fun.

Special thanks to my layout and production crew. In particular, I want to thank my friend and Creative Director Felix Nelson for his limitless talent, boundless creativity, input, and just for his flat-out great ideas. To Kim Gabriel for doing for such an amazing job of keeping us all on track and organized—I can't thank you enough. To Margie Rosenstein for adding her special touch to the look of the book, and to Dave Damstra (the best layout guy in the business) for giving the book such a tight, clean layout, and to Dave Korman for his help in getting it out the door. To Daphne Durkee for stepping in at the last minute to help proof the book.

I'm very thankful to have Chris Main as the Tech Editor for all my books. He's a very dedicated person and tech-editing wizard who catches the little things that other tech editors might've missed. His comments, ideas, and input have improved every book I've written and I can't thank him enough.

Thanks to Jim Workman, Jean A. Kendra, and Pete Kratzenberg for their support, and for keeping a lot of plates in the air while I'm writing these books. A special thanks to my Executive Assistant Kathy Siler for keeping me on track and focused, and for doing such a wonderful job, all the while keeping such an amazingly upbeat attitude, even though her Redskins lost to my Buccaneers 35 to 13. (I'm going to pay for that one.)

I want to thank my longtime friend and first-class Editor Richard Theriault. This is the 12th book Dick has worked on with us, and we're totally hooked—we couldn't do it without him, and we wouldn't want to if we could.

I owe a special debt of gratitude to my friends Kevin Ames and Jim DiVitale for taking the time to share their ideas, techniques, concepts, and vision for a Photoshop book for digital photographers that would really make a difference. Extra special thanks to Kevin for spending hours with me sharing his retouching techniques.

I want to thank all the photographers, retouchers, and Photoshop experts who've taught me so much over the years, including Jack Davis, Deke McClelland, Ben Willmore, Julieanne Kost, David Cuerdon, Robert Dennis, Helene DeLillo, Felix Nelson, Jim Patterson, Doug Gornick, Manual Obordo, Dave Cross, Dan Margulis, Peter Bauer, Joe Glyda, and Russell Preston Brown.

Thanks to the brilliant and gifted digital photographers who graciously lent their talents to this book, including Carol Freeman, Todd Morrison, Jim Patterson, Dave Moser, Julieanne Kost, and Jeannie Theriault.

Also thanks to my friends at Adobe Systems, Barbara Rice, Terry "T-bone" White, Addy Roff, Gwyn Weisberg, John Nack, Kevin Connor, Tanguy Leborgne, Rye Livingston, Karen Gauthier, Russell Brady, Julieanne Kost, and Russell Brown.

Thanks to my Editor Steve Weiss for his unwavering commitment to "create great books," and my heartfelt thanks to Nancy Ruenzel, Scott Cowlin, and everyone at Peachpit Publishing—they're really great people who continually strive to produce very special books.

My personal thanks go to Jeffery Burke at Brand X Pictures for enabling me to use some of their wonderful images here in the book.

And most importantly, my deepest thanks to the Lord Jesus Christ for always hearing my prayers, for always being there when I need Him, for blessing me with a wonderful life I truly love, and such a warm loving family to share it with.

ABOUT THE AUTHOR

Scott Kelby

Scott is Editor-in-Chief and co-founder of *Photoshop User* magazine, Editor-in-Chief of Nikon's *Capture User* magazine, and Editor-in-Chief of *Mac Design Magazine.* He is President of the National Association of Photoshop Professionals (NAPP), the trade association for Adobe® Photoshop® users, and he's President of KW Media Group, Inc., a Florida-based software education and publishing firm.

Scott is the author of the best-selling books *Photoshop CS Down & Dirty Tricks, Photoshop Photo-Retouching Secrets,* and co-author of *Photoshop 7 Killer Tips,* and he's creator and series Editor for the *Killer Tips* series from New Riders Publishing. Scott has authored two best-selling Macintosh books: *Mac OS X Jaguar Killer Tips,* and the award-winning *Macintosh: The Naked Truth,* both also from New Riders, and the new *Mac OS X Conversion Kit: 9 to 10 side-by-side* from Peachpit Press.

Scott introduced his first software title in 2003 called "Kelby's Notes for Adobe Photoshop" which adds the answers to the 100 most-asked Photoshop questions, accessed from directly within Photoshop.

Scott is Training Director for the Adobe Photoshop Seminar Tour, Conference Technical Chair for the PhotoshopWorld Conference & Expo, and he is a speaker at graphics trade shows and events around the world. He is also featured in a series of Adobe Photoshop training videos and DVDs and has been training Adobe Photoshop users since 1993.

For more background info on Scott, visit www.scottkelby.com.

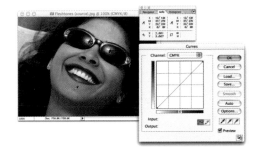

CHAPTER 8 227

Invasion of the Body Snatchers
Body Sculpting

CHAPTER 9 243

38 Special
Photographic Special Effects

I had no intentions of writing this book

So here it was, about four weeks before I would be flying up to New York City to teach a one-day seminar to more than 1,200 professional Photoshop junkies. (Okay, it was more like 1,160 pros, 42 people who just wanted a paid day off from work, and one total freak who kept asking me if I'd ever been in prison. I told him unequivocally, "Not as far as you know.")

Anyway, the seminar was just four weeks away, and there was one session that I still didn't have an outline for. It was called "Correcting Photos from Digital Cameras" (which is dramatically better than my original working title for the class, "Die, Traditional Camera User, Die!").

I knew what I needed to cover in the session because for the past ten years I've trained thousands of traditional photographers on how to use Photoshop. Most of them either have now gone digital or are in the process of going digital, and all these digital photographers generally seem to have the same type of Photoshop questions, which I'm actually thankful for, because now I can give them the answers. If they constantly asked different questions, I'd get stumped from time to time, and then I'd have to resort to "Plan B" (providing answers that sound good, but are in reality just wild-ass guesses).

So I knew what I had to cover, but I wanted to do some research first, to see if other people in the industry were addressing these questions the same way I was, or did they have a different take on them, different techniques or ideas? So I went out and bought every single book I could find about digital photography and Photoshop. I spent nearly $1.2 million. Okay, it wasn't quite that much, but let's just say for the next few months I would have to cut out some luxuries such as running water, trash collection, heat, etc.

I started reading through all these books, and the first thing I thought I'd look up was how they dealt with digital noise (High ISO noise, Blue channel noise, color aliasing, etc.), but as I went through them, I was amazed to find out that not one single book addressed it. Not a one. Honestly, I was shocked. I get asked this question many times at every single seminar, yet not one of these books even mentioned it. So then I started looking for how they work with 16-bit photos. Nothing. Well, one book mentioned it, but they basically said "it's not for you—it's for high-end pros with $15,000 cameras." I just couldn't believe it—I was stunned. So I kept up my search for more topics I'd been asked about again and again, with the same results.

Well, I went ahead with my New York session as planned, and by all accounts it was a big hit. I had photographer after photographer coming up to tell me, "Thank you so much—those are exactly the things I was hoping to learn." That's when I realized that there's a book missing—a book for people who already know how to shoot, they even know what they want to do in Photoshop; they just need somebody to show them how to do it. Somebody to show them how to deal with the special challenges (and amazing opportunities) of using digital photos with Photoshop. I was so excited because I knew in my heart, I could write that book.

So now I had intentions

The day after the seminar, I flew home and immediately called my Editor at New Riders (we'll call him "Steve" because, well…that's his name) and I said, "I know what I want my next book to be—a Photoshop book for digital photographers." There was a long uncomfortable pause. Steve's a great guy, and he really knows this industry, but I could tell he was choking a bit on this one. He politely said, "Really, a digital photography book, huh?" It was clear he wasn't nearly as excited about this concept as I was (and that's being kind). He finally said, "Ya know, there are already plenty of digital photography books

Continued

out there," and I agreed with him, because I just about went broke buying them all. So now I had to convince my Editor that not only was this a good idea, but that it was such a good idea that he should put our other book projects on hold so I could write this book, of which there are (as he put it), "already plenty of digital photography books out there."

Here's what I told my Editor that would be different about my digital photography book:

(1) It's not a digital photography book; it's a Photoshop book. One that's aimed at professional and high-end prosumer photographers who either have gone digital, or are just moving to digital. There'd be no discussion of film (gasp!), f-stops, lenses, or how to frame a photo. If they don't already know how to shoot, this book just won't be for them. (*Note: Editors hate it when you start listing the people the book won't be appropriate for. They want to hear, "It's perfect for everybody! From grandma right up to White House press photographers," but sadly, this book just isn't.*)

(2) I would skip the "Here's What a Digital Camera Is" section and the "Here's Which Printer to Buy" section, because they were in all those other books that I bought. Instead, I'd start the book at the moment the photo comes into Photoshop from the camera.

(3) It would work the way digital photographers really work—in the order they work—starting with sorting and categorizing photos from the shoot, dealing with common digital photography problems, color correcting the photos, selecting and masking parts of the photo, retouching critical areas, adding photographic special effects, sharpening their photos, and then showing the final work to the client for approval.

(4) It wouldn't be another Photoshop book that focuses on explaining every aspect of every dialog box. No sirree—instead, this book would do something different—it would show them how to do it! This is what makes it different. It would show photographers step-by-step how to do all those things they keep asking at my seminars, sending me e-mails about, and posting questions about in our forums—it would "show them how to do it!"

For example, I told Steve that about every Photoshop book out there includes info on the Unsharp Mask filter. They all talk about what the Amount, Radius, and Threshold sliders do, and how those settings affect the pixels. They all do that. But you know what they generally *don't* do? They don't give you any actual settings to use! Usually, not even a starting point. Some provide "numerical ranges to work within," but basically they explain how the filter works, and then leave it up to you to develop your own settings. I told him I wouldn't do that. I would flat-out give them some great Unsharp Mask filter settings—the same settings used by many professionals, even though I know some highfalutin Photoshop expert might take issue with them. I would come out and say, "Hey, use this setting when sharpening people. Use this setting to correct slightly out-of-focus photos. Use this setting on landscapes, etc." I give students in my live seminars these settings, why shouldn't I share them in my book? He agreed. I also told him that sharpening is much more than just using the Unsharp Mask filter, and it's much more important to photographers than the three or four pages every other book dedicates to it. I wanted to do an entire chapter showing all the different sharpening techniques, step-by-step, giving different solutions for different sharpening challenges.

I told him about the File Browser, and how there's so much to it (especially in Photoshop CS), it's just about a separate program unto itself, yet nobody's really covering the things photographers are telling me they need to know—like automatically renaming their digital camera photos with names that make sense. Other books mention that you can do that in the File Browser—I want to be the guy that "shows them how to do it!" I want a whole chapter just on the File Browser.

Steve was starting to come on board with the idea. What he didn't want was the same thing I didn't want—another digital photography book that rehashes what every other digital photography and Photoshop book has already done. Well, Steve went with the idea, and thanks to him, you're holding the book that I am so genuinely excited to be able to bring you. But the way the book was developed beyond that took it further than Steve or I had planned.

How the book was developed

When Steve gave me the final approval (it was more like, "Okay, but this better be good or we'll both be greeting people by saying, 'Would you like to try one of our Extra Value Meals today?'"), I sat down with two of the industry's top digital photographers—commercial product photographer Jim DiVitale and fashion photographer Kevin Ames—to get their input on the book. These two guys are amazing—they both split their time between shooting for some of the world's largest corporations and teaching other professional digital photographers how to pull off Photoshop miracles at events such as PhotoshopWorld, PPA/PEI's Digital Conference, and a host of other events around the world.

We spent hours hammering out which techniques would have to be included in the book, and I can't tell you how helpful and insightful their input was. This wasn't an easy task, because I wanted to include a range of techniques wide enough that it would be accessible to "prosumers" (the industry term to describe serious high-end amateurs who use serious cameras and take serious shots, yet don't do photography for a living), but at the same time, I wanted high-end professionals to feel right at home with techniques that are clearly just for them, at their stage of the game.

Does this make the book too advanced?

Absolutely not. That's because my goal is to present all these techniques in such a simple, easy-to-understand format that no matter where you are in your Photoshop skills, you'll read the technique and rather than thinking, "Oh, I could never pull that off," you'll think, "Hey, I can do that."

While it's true that this book includes many advanced techniques, just because a technique is advanced, doesn't mean it has to be complicated or "hard to pull off." It just means that you'll be further along in the learning process before you'd even know you need that technique.

For example, in the retouching chapter, I show how to use the Healing Brush to completely remove wrinkles, and that's what many photographers will do—completely remove all visible wrinkles. But an advanced Photoshop user might retouch the photo differently, because they know that a 79-year-old man's face shouldn't be as wrinkle-free as Ben Affleck's. When they do a similar retouch, they're not going to remove every wrinkle—instead they'll be looking for a way to just lower the intensity of the wrinkles, so the portrait looks more natural (and the photo appears unretouched). To do that, they'll need something beyond the basic Healing Brush technique—they'll need a more advanced technique that may require a few more steps along the way, but produces far better results.

So, how hard is it to do the advanced "healing" technique we just talked about? It's simple—duplicate the Background layer, remove all the wrinkles using the Healing Brush, then lower that layer's Opacity a bit to bring back some of the original wrinkles from the layer underneath (see page 190). It works like a charm, but really—how complicated is that? Heck, anyone that's used Photoshop for a week can duplicate a layer and lower the Opacity, right? Right. Yet few photographers know this simple, advanced technique. That's what this book is all about. If you understand that line of thinking, you'll really get a lot out of this book. You'll be able to perform every single technique—you'll be putting to use the same advanced correction and retouching techniques employed by some of today's leading digital photographers; yet you'll make it all look easy, because it really is easy, and it's a lot of fun—once somebody shows you how to do it.

Continued

Is there lots of new stuff for photographers in Photoshop CS?

You betcha! If there was ever a version of Photoshop that was made for digital photographers, Photoshop CS is it. In fact, they added so much to just the File Browser in Photoshop CS that I had to split it into two separate chapters (actually, you could probably do an entire book on just the File Browser alone. Of course, it would be a pretty thin book, and all the screen captures would look pretty much the same, and…okay, there's probably not enough there to make a whole book, but it would make a pamphlet. Of course, it would be a big pamphlet. Actually, it would be too thick to be a pamphlet. More like a guide. Maybe a guide book? It would either be a really thick pamphlet or a really thin guide book. Do you care? No. Because everything you want to know about the CS File Browser is already in the first two chapters of this book. See, you've already saved the cost of a thick guidebook-like pamphlet, which would sell for at least $200. In Canada).

So what's not in this book?

There are some things I intentionally didn't put in this book. Like punctuation marks (kidding). No, seriously, I tried not to put things in this book that are already in every other Photoshop book out there. For example, I don't have a chapter on the Layers palette, or a chapter on the painting tools, or a chapter showing how each of Photoshop's 102 filters looks when it's applied to the same photograph. I also didn't include a chapter on printing to your color inkjet because (a) every Photoshop book does that, and (b) every printer uses different printer driver software, and if I showed an Epson color inkjet workflow, you can bet you'd have an HP or a Canon printer (or vice versa) and then you'd just get mad at me. I also didn't include a chapter on color management because every Photoshop book has one (go look on your shelf and you'll see), but beyond that, a chapter on color management just doesn't cover it—that topic needs its own book (and if you want the best one on the subject, check out *Real World Color Management* by Bruce Fraser, Fred Bunting, and Chris Murphy, from Peachpit Press; ISBN: 0201773406).

What does this "For Pros Only" logo mean?

It means "Go away—this isn't for you!" (Kidding.) Actually, it's a "heads-up" to people who are further along in their skills, and are looking for more advanced techniques. What it *isn't* is a "this is hard" warning. It just means that as you get better in Photoshop, these are the techniques you're going to want to consider next, because although they usually include more steps and take a little longer, they provide more professional results (even though the difference may be subtle).

Is this book for you?

I can't tell you that for sure, so let's take a simple yet amazingly accurate test that determines without a doubt if this book is for you. Please answer the following questions:

(1) Are you a photographer?
(2) Do you now, or will you soon have a digital camera?
(3) Do you now, or will you soon have Adobe Photoshop CS?
(4) Do you now, or will you soon have $39.99 (the retail price of this book)?

Scoring: If you answered "Yes" to question #4 then yes, this book is for you. If you answered yes to questions 1, 2, or 3, that certainly is a good indicator, too.

Is this book for Windows users, Mac users, or both?

Because Photoshop is identical on Windows and on the Mac, the book is designed for both platforms. However, the keyboard on a PC is slightly different from the keyboard on a Mac, so any time I give a keyboard shortcut in the book, I give both the PC and Mac keyboard shortcuts. See, I care.

How should you use this book?

You can treat this as a "jump-in-anywhere" book because I didn't write it as a "build-on-what-you-learned-in-Chapter-1" type of book. For example, if you just bought this book, and you want to learn how to whiten someone's teeth for a portrait you're retouching, you can just turn to page 208, and you'll be able to follow along and do it immediately. That's because I spell everything out. Don't let that throw you if you're a longtime Photoshop user; I had to do it because although some of the people that will buy this book are gifted, talented, amazing traditional photographers, since they're just now "going digital," they may not know anything about Photoshop. I didn't want to leave them out, or make it hard for them, so I really spell things out like "Go under the Image menu, under Adjustments, and choose Curves" rather than just writing "Open Curves." However, I did put the chapters in an order that follows a typical correction, editing, and retouching process, so you might find it useful to start with Chapter 1 and move your way through the book in sequence.

The important thing is that wherever you start, have fun with it, and even more importantly, tell your friends about it so I can recoup the $1.2 million I spent on all those digital photography books.

Wait, one more thing! You can download the photos used in the book.

Thanks to the wonderful people at Brand X Pictures (www.brandx.com) you can download low-res versions of all the royalty-free stock photos used in the book so you can practice right along with the same photos (you can download these photos from the book's companion Web site at **www.scottkelbybooks.com/csbookphotos.html**). Of course, the whole idea is that you'd use these techniques on your own photos, but if you want to practice on these, I won't tell anybody. Now, you're probably wondering why I chose Brand X Pictures to provide the stock photos for this book? It's simple. Brand X Pictures' images rock. As soon as I saw them, I knew I wanted to use them in my book, and they graciously agreed to let you (the readers of this book) download some of their fantastic images, that are such a departure from most of the other royalty-free images available out there. I encourage you to visit their site (www.brandx.com) and check out their images for yourself. (If this sounds like a plug for Brand X—it is. They didn't ask me to do it, but I'm so tickled to be using their images, I wanted to let them, and you, know.)

Anything else?

Nah—now get to work!

At first, you might not think that Photoshop's File Browser deserves two chapters, but when you look at all the things it's done for the community (including taking meals to other software applica-

Start Me Up
file browser essentials

tions that are less fortunate), you realize it probably does deserve them after all. Especially when you take into consideration the fact that the File Browser all by itself is probably more powerful than many stand-alone products, like the Whopper (that computer in the movie *War Games* with Matthew Broderick) or Microsoft Office 2000. Sure, the Whopper could simulate a Soviet First Strike, but frankly, it was pretty lame at sorting and categorizing your photos (as is Microsoft Office). In fact, I'm not sure the Whopper could sort or categorize photos at all, which is probably why no Photoshop book to date has a chapter on the Whopper. You'd think that with all the cool things the File Browser does, surely at least one Photoshop book out there would dedicate a chapter to it, right? Well, not as far as I've found. So I set out to do just that—really dig into the meat of the Browser, uncover its hidden power, and see once and for all if it was really written by a man named Professor Faulken (this is precisely why they shouldn't let me write these chapter intros after 1:00 A.M.).

Saving Your Digital Negatives

Okay, I know this is the File Browser chapter, but there are just a couple of critically important things we have to do before we actually open Photoshop.

Step One:

Plug your card reader (Compact Flash card, Smartcard, etc.) into your computer and the images on the card appears on your hard drive (as shown). Before you do anything else, before you even open Photoshop, you need to burn these photos to a CD. Don't open the photos, adjust them, choose your favorites, and *then* burn them to a CD—burn them now—right off the bat. The reason this is so important is that these are your negatives—your digital negatives, which are no different from the negatives you'd get from a film lab after they process your film. By burning a CD now, before you enter Photoshop, you're creating a set of digital negatives that can never be accidentally erased or discarded—you'll always have these "digital negatives." Now, what if you don't have a CD burner? That's easy—buy one. It's that critical, and such a key part of your digital setup. Luckily, burning CDs has become so fast, inexpensive (you can buy blank, writable CDs for around 10¢ each), and easy-to-do that you can't afford to skip this step, especially if you're a professional photographer.

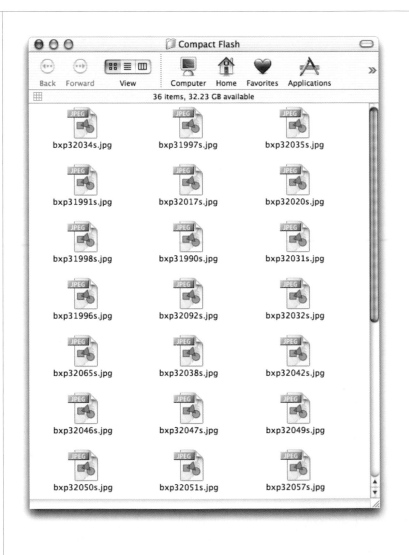

Step Two:

My personal favorite CD-burning software is Easy CD Creator for Windows or Roxio Toast Titanium for the Mac (its interface is shown here). It's become very popular, partially because its easy-to-use drag-and-drop interface is a real timesaver. Here's how it works: Select all the images from your card reader, then click-and-drag the whole bunch into the Toast Data window.

Step Three:

After your images appear in the Toast Data window, double-click the tiny CD icon in the window and give your disc a name (you can see the name highlighted in the example at left). Then, simply click the Record button and Toast does the rest, leaving you with a reliable, protected set of digital negatives. If you're the extra careful type (read as "paranoid"), you can burn yourself another copy to keep as a second backup. There's no loss of quality, so burn as many copies as you need to feel secure (remember, just because you're paranoid, doesn't mean they're not out to get you).

Creating a Contact Sheet for Your CD

All right, your CD of "digital negatives" is burned; but before you go any further, you can save yourself a lot of time and frustration down the road if you create a CD jewel-box-sized contact sheet now. That way, when you pick up the CD, you'll see exactly what's on the disc before you even insert it into your computer. Luckily, the process of creating this contact sheet is automated, and after you make a few decisions on how you want your contact sheet to look, Photoshop takes it from there.

Step One:

In Photoshop CS, you can access the Contact Sheet command by either going under the File menu, under Automate, and choosing Contact Sheet II, or by choosing it directly from the File Browser's "mini-menu" in the top left-hand corner under Automate (since this is the File Browser chapter, we'll assume you're going to choose it right from within the Browser). **NOTE:** People frequently ask me why it's called "Contact Sheet II," rather than just Contact Sheet. It's because it's the second version of Contact Sheet. When Adobe first introduced this feature back in Photoshop 5.5, it was, well...pretty lame (and that's being kind). So when they updated and improved it in the Photoshop 6 release, my guess is that Adobe was afraid people who had tried the previous Contact Sheet wouldn't try it again, so they added "II" to the name to let people know this was kind of like a version 2.0. By now, in Photoshop CS, it's been updated twice since Photoshop 6.0, so technically it should probably be called Contact Sheet IV. Personally, I'd prefer to see it named "Scott's Contact Sheet" but thus far, Adobe hasn't bought into that naming concept. Too bad—I think it has real potential.

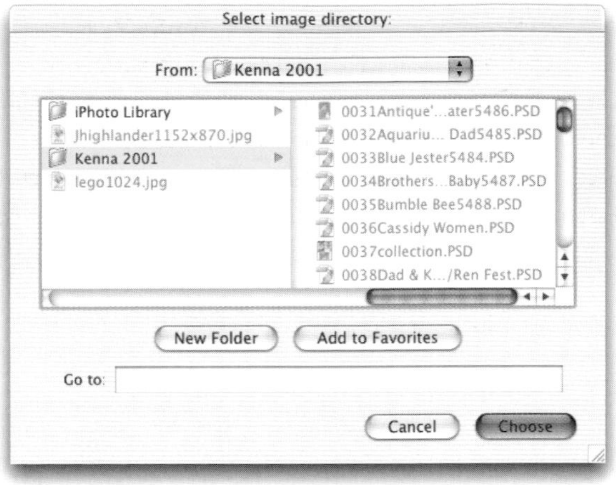

Select image directory:

From: Kenna 2001

iPhoto Library ▶	0031Antique'...ater5486.PSD
Jhighlander1152x870.jpg	0032Aquariu... Dad5485.PSD
Kenna 2001 ▶	0033Blue Jester5484.PSD
lego1024.jpg	0034Brothers...Baby5487.PSD
	0035Bumble Bee5488.PSD
	0036Cassidy Women.PSD
	0037collection.PSD
	0038Dad & K.../Ren Fest.PSD

New Folder   Add to Favorites

Go to:

Cancel   Choose

Step Two:

When the Contact Sheet II dialog appears (opposite page), under the Source Images section, select Folder in the Use pop-up menu, then click the Choose button and the standard Open dialog will appear (shown here). Navigate to your newly burned CD and click the Choose button in your Select dialog. This tells Photoshop to make your contact sheet from the images on your CD.

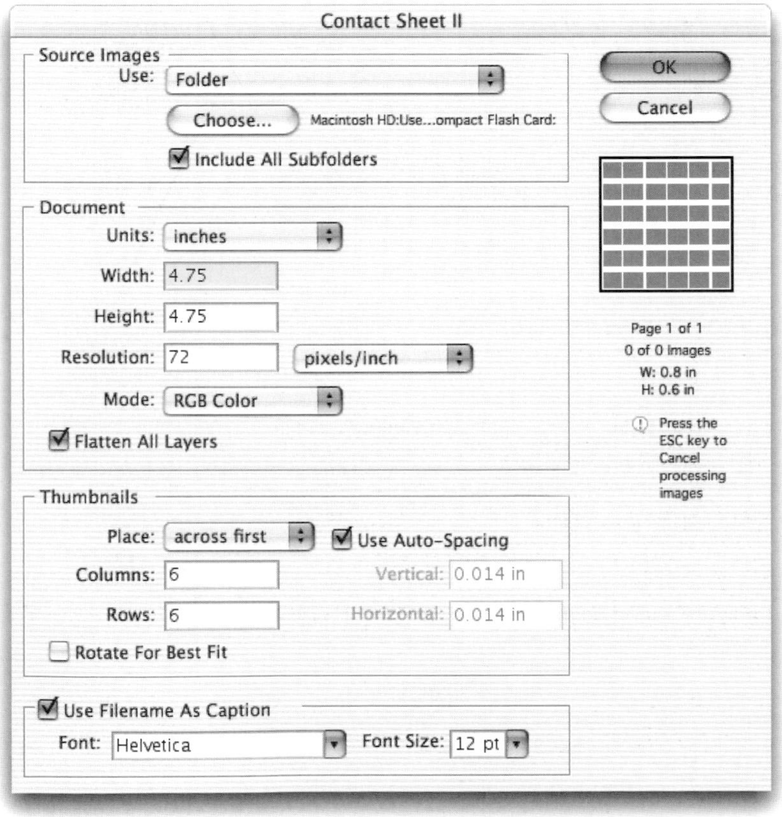

Contact Sheet II

Source Images
Use: Folder

Choose...   Macintosh HD:Use...ompact Flash Card:
☑ Include All Subfolders

Document
Units: inches
Width: 4.75
Height: 4.75
Resolution: 72   pixels/inch
Mode: RGB Color
☑ Flatten All Layers

Thumbnails
Place: across first   ☑ Use Auto-Spacing
Columns: 6   Vertical: 0.014 in
Rows: 6   Horizontal: 0.014 in
☐ Rotate For Best Fit

☑ Use Filename As Caption
Font: Helvetica   Font Size: 12 pt

OK
Cancel

Page 1 of 1
0 of 0 Images
W: 0.8 in
H: 0.6 in
ⓘ Press the ESC key to Cancel processing images

Step Three:

The rest of the dialog is for you to pick how you want your contact sheet to look. Under the Document section of the dialog, enter the Width and Height of your jewel box cover (the standard size is 4.75" x 4.75") and the Resolution for your images. (I usually choose a low resolution of 72 ppi because the thumbnails wind up being so small they don't need to be a high resolution; and Contact Sheet runs faster with low-res images.) I also leave the Mode as RGB Color (the default), and I choose to Flatten All Layers; that way, I don't end up with a large multilayered Photoshop document. I just want a document that I can print once and then delete. The Thumbnails section is perhaps the most important part of this dialog, because this is where you choose the layout for your contact sheet's thumbnails (Columns and Rows). Luckily, Adobe put a preview box on the far-right side of the

Continued

dialog, using little gray boxes to represent how your thumbnails will look. Change the number of Rows or Columns, and this live preview gives you an idea of how your layout will look.

Finally, at the bottom of the dialog, you can decide if you want to have Photoshop print the file's name below each thumbnail on your contact sheet. I strongly recommend leaving this feature turned on. Here's why:

One day you may have to go back to this CD to look for a photo. The thumbnail lets you see if the photo you're looking for is on this CD (so you've narrowed your search a bit), but if there's no name below the image, you'll have to launch Photoshop and use the Browser to search through every photo to locate the exact one you saw on the cover.

However, if you spot the photo on the cover *and* see its name, you just open Photoshop, and then open that file. Believe me, it's one of those things that will keep you from ripping your hair out by the roots, one by one. The capture here shows the font size being chosen from the Font Size pop-up menu.

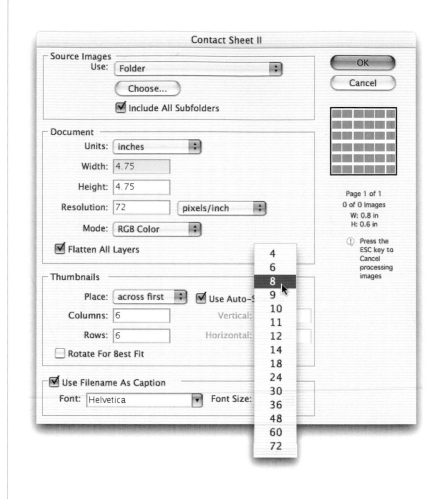

There's also a pop-up menu for choosing from a handful of fonts and font sizes for your thumbnail captions. The font choices are somewhat lame, but believe me, they're better than what was offered in the original Contact Sheet, so count your blessings.

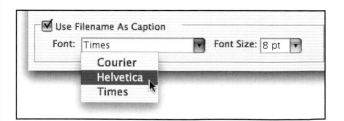

When you put a lot of thumbnails on your contact sheet, you need to make the font size smaller, or you'll see only the first few characters.

Here's the same contact sheet with a much smaller font size, enabling you to see the entire file name.

Font sizing:

When you're choosing a font size for your contact sheet thumbnail captions, make sure you decrease the default size of 12 to something significantly lower. You'll need to do this because of the long file names assigned to the images from your digital camera. In the example shown here, I used the default 12-point font size setting, and you see only the first 6 digits of the file name, making this contact sheet worthless.

I had to lower the font size to 6 to actually be able to read the entire file name under each thumbnail. So how small should you make your type? That depends. The more thumbnails you're fitting on your contact sheet, the smaller you'll need to make the font size.

Continued

Step Four:

Now all you have to do is click OK, sit back, and let Photoshop do its thing. (It may take up to two and half hours to create a single contact sheet. Kidding! Had you going there, didn't I?) It only takes a minute or so, and when you're done, you're left with a contact sheet like the one shown at right, with rows of thumbnails and each photo's file name appearing below it. (Note: I lowered the font size to 8, and could still see the full file name, but not the ".jpg" at the end; but since every file was a JPEG, no big loss).

Step Five:

This is more like a tip than a step, but a number of photographers add a second contact sheet to make it even easier to track down the exact image they're looking for. It's based on the premise that in every roll (digital or otherwise), there's usually one or two key shots—two really good "keepers" that will normally be the ones you'll go searching for on this disc. So what they do is make an additional contact sheet with just the two or three key shots on that CD (as shown here), to use either as the cover or the inside cover of their CD jewel case (the regular contact sheet is visible on the outside of the jewel case, and this additional contact sheet is on the inside). They include a description of the shots to make finding the right image even easier.

NOTE: If you're only using two or three images, you don't need to use Contact Sheet II—you can just create this second cover yourself.

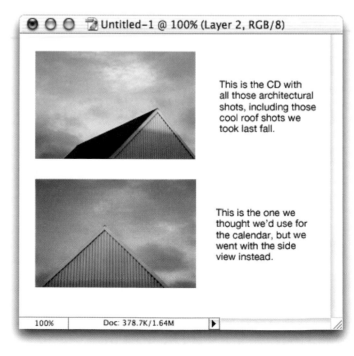

Step Six:
Here's the final result, after the contact sheet has been printed and fitted to your CD jewel case.

Browser Basics

Okay, we've burned our CD and we've created our contact sheet to keep track of all our images, so now we're going to open the images right from the CD using the File Browser (which is what we use to sort and categorize our digital-camera images).

There are three ways to access Photoshop CS's File Browser: (1) Back in Photoshop 7, the File Browser used to be docked up in the Palette Well by default, but the new enhanced File Browser in Photoshop CS won't fit there anymore; so now there's just a button near its old home that lets you toggle the File Browser open or closed by clicking it. This button is found on the far right of the Options Bar, immediately to the left of where the Palette Well starts (it's circled in red above); (2) You can go under the File menu and choose Browse; (3) You can bring it up with the keyboard shortcut Shift-Command-O (PC: Shift-Control-O).

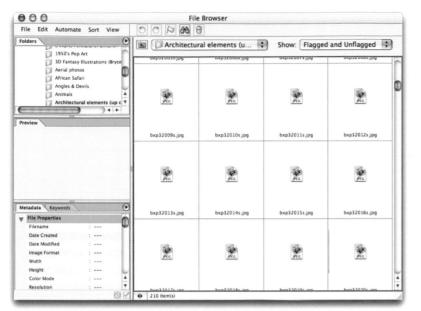

The File Browser takes the lame default icons and transforms them into...

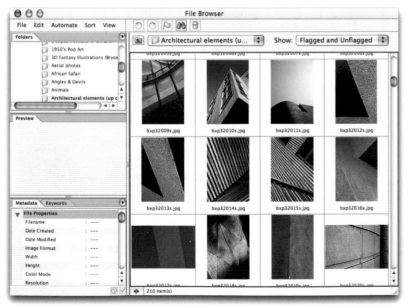

...full-color thumbnails. Ahhhhh, that's better!

A thumbnail factory:

One of the features that I love about the File Browser is that it does something wonderful to digital-camera images—it automatically creates full-color thumbnails of any photos you open within it. For example, when you open a folder, a CD of images, or a memory card from your digital camera, for just a moment, you'll see the generic icons (as shown here). As you can see, when it comes to finding an image, these generic icons are basically worthless.

However, in just a couple of seconds, Photoshop automatically generates gorgeous thumbnails in their place (as shown below). Photoshop is generally pretty quick about it too, but obviously the more images you have, the longer it will take. But, believe me—it's worth the wait. Also, it builds thumbnails from the top down, so even though you see thumbnails in your main window, if you scroll down, the thumbnails further down could still be drawing—just be patient and they'll appear (coming soon to a Browser window near you!).

Navigating to Your Photos Using the File Browser

The Browser is divided into two main areas: the main window, which displays thumbnail versions of your photos (once you find them) and the Palette area. The palettes include one for navigating to your photo, one that shows a larger preview of your currently selected thumbnail, and one that lets you see information about the currently selected photo. We'll start with the Navigation palette (after all, if you can't find your photos, the rest of the File Browser will look pretty, um…blank.)

Navigating to your photos:

The left side of the File Browser is the Palette area (although they're palettes, they're not "floating palettes" like the rest of the palettes in Photoshop CS, because they have to stay within the File Browser). The top-left palette (called Folders) gives you direct access to the photos on your digital camera's memory card, on your hard drive, on a CD of images, a network drive—you name it. The idea behind this is simple: It gives you access to your digital-camera images without having to leave Photoshop. To access the photos inside a folder from here, just click once on the folder (as shown).

Saving your Favorite folders:

If you find yourself going to a particular folder fairly often, you can save that folder as a Favorite. Just go under the File Browser's mini-menu, under File, and choose Add Folder to Favorites (as shown here). That folder now appears under the heading Favorite Folders in the pop-down navigation menu that appears directly above the main window. To delete a folder from your Favorites list, go under that File menu again and choose Remove Folder from Favorites.

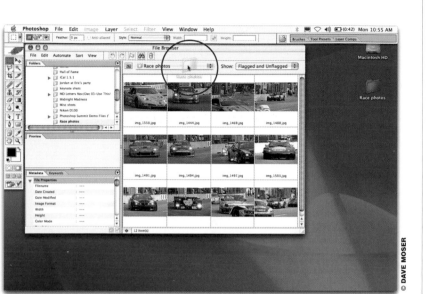

Getting to your folder fast!

Photoshop CS gives you another quick way to get right to the folder you want—just drag-and-drop a folder right from your desktop onto the navigation pop-up menu (as shown here) and the File Browser immediately displays the contents of that folder, just as if you had navigated to it from within the Folders palette of the File Browser.

Here, we're clicking the yellow car and dragging it to the D100 folder on the left.

Moving photos from folder to folder:

Another nice navigation feature of the File Browser is that you can use it to move photos from one folder to another. You do this by dragging the thumbnail of the photo you want to move, then dropping that photo into any folder that appears in the Folders palette (when you move the dragged photo over a folder, a highlight rectangle appears letting you know that you've targeted that folder). That photo is now removed from the currently selected folder and placed into the folder you dragged-and-dropped it into.

TIP: If you hold Option (PC: Alt) as you drag, instead of moving your photo, the File Browser will place a duplicate of your photo into that folder, rather than the original.

After dragging the yellow car to a different folder, it is removed from this folder.

Previewing Your Images

The second palette down on the left side of the Browser is designed to give you a larger preview of the thumbnail images that you click on in the main window. Although the Preview palette looks like a one-trick pony, here are a few hidden little features that can make it a much more useful tool.

Bigger previews are just a double-click away:

The default size for the Preview palette is fairly small, but you can make it much larger by double-clicking—not on the tab labeled Preview, but instead on the little tab labeled Folders. This collapses (hides) the Folders palette so that only its tab is visible, expanding the viewing area of the Preview palette automatically (as seen in the middle capture). If you need the preview even bigger, then double-click on the Metadata tab at the bottom left of the File Browser to collapse it, expanding the Preview palette even more (as shown far right). This works particularly well when you're viewing a portrait-oriented photo (tall rather than wide). However, when you have a photo in landscape orientation, to get the preview much larger, you also have to expand the width of the Preview palette by clicking anywhere along the divider bar between it and the main thumbnail window and dragging to the right.

NOTE: To make any collapsed palette visible again, just double-click directly on its name tab.

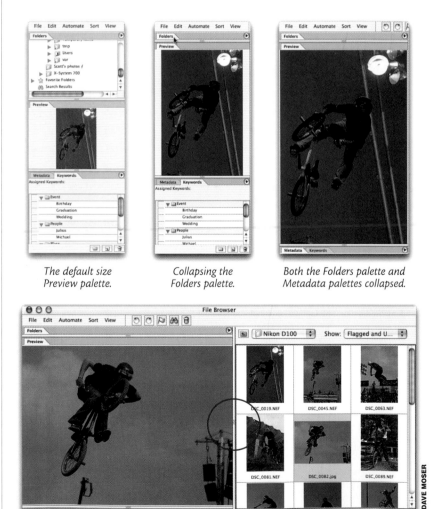

The default size Preview palette.

Collapsing the Folders palette.

Both the Folders palette and Metadata palettes collapsed.

© DAVE MOSER

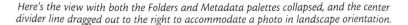

Here's the view with both the Folders and Metadata palettes collapsed, and the center divider line dragged out to the right to accommodate a photo in landscape orientation.

The third palette down in the Palette area is the Metadata palette. It gives you access to information that's embedded into your photo by the digital camera at the moment you take the shot. Nested with the Metadata palette is the Keywords palette, which enables you to search for specific images by assigning keywords (that may sound complicated, but it's actually pretty simple). We'll start here with a simple look at how to access the embedded background information on your photo by using the Metadata palette. The next chapter has more in-depth info on using and editing metadata.

Getting Info On Your Photos (Called Metadata)

Metadata	Keywords	
▼ **File Properties**		
Filename	: img_1521.jpg	
Date Created	: 10/14/03 3:26:47 AM	
Date Modified	: 10/14/03 3:26:47 AM	
Image Format	: JPEG	
Width	: 3072	
Height	: 2048	
Color Mode	: RGB	
Resolution	: 180.0	
File Size	: 1.26M	
Color Profile	: Adobe RGB (1998)	
Bit Depth	: 8	
DocumentID	: adobe:docid:photoshop:54065f08...	
Creator	: Adobe Photoshop CS Macintosh	
▶ **IPTC**		
▼ **Camera Data (Exif)**		
Make	: Canon	
Model	: Canon EOS 10D	
Date Time	: 2003-10-13T23:26:47-04:00	
Date Time Original	: 2003-09-26T08:29:28-04:00	
Date Time Digitized	: 2003-09-26T08:29:28-04:00	
Exposure Time	: 1/350 sec	
Shutter Speed	: 1/350 sec	
F-Stop	: f/5.6	
Aperture Value	: f/5.6	
Max Aperture Value	: f/4.0	
ISO Speed Ratings	: 200	
Focal Length	: 200.0 mm	
Flash	: Did not fire	
Metering Mode	: Pattern	
Pixel X Dimension	: 3072	
Pixel Y Dimension	: 2048	
Orientation	: Normal	
X Resolution	: 180.0	
Y Resolution	: 180.0	
Resolution Unit	: Inches	
Compressed Bits Per Pixel	: 3.0	
EXIF Color Space	: Uncalibrated	
File Source	: DSC	
ExifVersion	: 0220	
Exposure Bias Value	: 0.00	
FlashPix Version	: 0100	
Custom Rendered	: Normal Process	
Exposure Mode	: Auto	
White Balance	: Manual	
Scene Capture Type	: Standard	
Sensing Method	: One-chip color area sensor	
Software	: Adobe Photoshop CS Macintosh	
Artist	: David Moser	
yCbCr Positioning	: Centered	
Focal Plane X Resolution	: 3443.946	
Focal Plane Y Resolution	: 3442.017	
Focal Plane Resolution Unit	: Inches	

Background info on your photo:
When you take a photo with today's digital cameras, at the moment you take the shot, the camera automatically embeds loads of information about what just took place. Things like the make and model of the camera, the time the photo was taken, the exposure setting, the f-stop, shutter speed, etc. Then, once you bring the digital photo into Photoshop, Photoshop embeds more information into the photo (stuff like the file name, when it was last edited, which file format the file was saved in, its physical dimensions, color mode, etc.). All this embedded info comes under the heading Metadata and that's why it appears in the Metadata palette (shown here). At the top of the palette is the info Photoshop embeds into your file, under the heading File Properties. The next field down is IPTC metadata, which is where you can embed your own customized info (stuff like copyright info, credits, etc.) into the photo (this is covered in detail in the next chapter). The next field down displays the Camera EXIF Data (the background info embedded by your camera). You may never use this, but it's nice to know it's there in case of a pop-quiz.

Searching for Photos by Adding Keywords

Right next to the Metadata palette is the Keywords palette. Keywords are new in Photoshop CS, and they are more important than they appear because this is what enables you to search for photos by topic. Basically, you assign a descriptive keyword to a photo (for example, you could assign the word Sunsets to all your sunset photos), then when you need a sunset shot, you're not opening hundreds of photos—you just do a quick search and all your sunset photos appear in seconds.

Step One:

Go to the bottom left side of the File Browser and click on the Keywords tab to make the Keywords palette visible (shown here). You'll see a list of default keywords put there by Adobe that are segmented into folders. If you don't like the default choices, you can either collapse them (by clicking on the little gray down-facing triangles) or delete them forever by first clicking on the folder you want to delete, then clicking once on the Trash icon at the bottom of the Keywords palette.

Step Two:

You'll usually start by creating a category of photos (that's what a keyword really is, a category name that you'll use to search for your photos). To do that, click on the New Keyword icon at the bottom of the palette (it looks like the New Layer icon in the Layers palette). A new field appears at the top of the keyword list (above the Event folder). Type "Red Cars" and then press the Enter key. Once you press Enter, your new keyword appears alphabetically in the keyword list.

NOTE: Make sure you don't have any keywords highlighted when you create a new keyword, because it will add the new keyword to that folder.

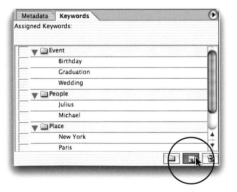

© DAVE MOSER

Step Three:

Next, hold the Command key (PC: Control key) and click on all the photos that have red cars in them. Then, go over to the list of keywords and double-click on the keyword Red Cars. You'll get one of those annoying "You have selected multiple files. Are you out of your mind?" type of warning dialogs. Just click Yes and that's it—those photos with red cars in them are now searchable using the keyword Red Cars. Let's test it (just in case I'm lying and made the whole keyword thing up as a cruel joke).

Step Four:

Click the Search icon at the top of the File Browser (as shown here) to bring up the Search dialog.

Step Five:

You can search by a host of methods (file name, size, etc.), but since you added a keyword—it's simple. Choose Keywords from the Criteria pop-up list, then in the search field type in your keyword "Red Cars," and then click the Search button. In seconds, only photos tagged with the keyword Red Cars will appear in the main thumbnail window.

Step Six:

If you create a keyword, and then want to delete it, just Control-click (PC: right-click) directly on the keyword in the list, and choose Delete from the pop-up menu (as shown).

Setting Up How You View Your Photos

Before you start sorting your photos, it helps to get a handle on how to view your images. In Photoshop CS, you have a decent amount of control over how this is done, so I'm going to show you what your options are, and then how to set up the File Browser to display photos in a way that's most comfortable to you.

Working in the main window:

The main window displays the thumbnail views of your photos. If you click on a thumbnail within this window, the photo highlights to let you know it's selected (as shown here), and a preview of the photo is displayed in the Preview palette to its left. If you want to open the full-size image in Photoshop, just double-click on the thumbnail in the main window. (Note: You can also double-click on the Preview to open the photo.)

You can select multiple photos to open at the same time by clicking on the first photo you want to open, holding the Command key (PC: Control key), and then clicking on any other photos. You can select entire rows by clicking on the first thumbnail in a row, holding the Shift key, and clicking on the last photo in that row.

You can also navigate from thumbnail to thumbnail by using the arrow keys on your keyboard.

TIP: If you want to open a photo and have the File Browser close automatically, don't just double-click on the preview of the photo, instead Option-double-click (PC: Alt-double-click). The photo opens and the Browser closes.

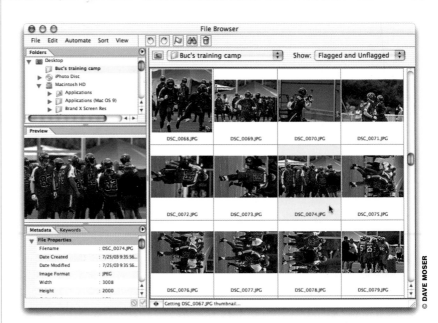

Here's the standard default layout with the Palette area on the left, and the main window to its right.

© DAVE MOSER

By clicking the Expanded View icon (circled in red), you now get six rows across in the same amount of space.

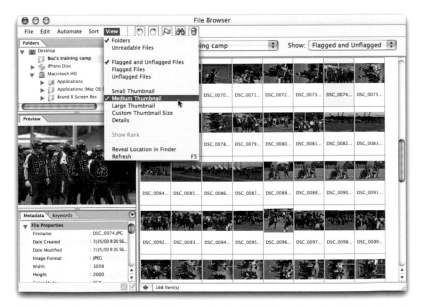

Here's the Medium Thumbnail view. Okay, pop-quiz time: Which photo shows just #83? Who knows? The thumbnails are so tiny, you can't tell if you're looking at football or farm equipment.

Viewing things your way:

The default setup for the File Browser has the Palettes area on the left and the main window on the right. However, once you locate the folder with the images you'll be working with, you might want to do what many pros do at this point and choose the Expanded View (which hides the Palettes area altogether, enabling you to see significantly more thumbnails at one time). You do that by clicking on the two-headed arrow icon at the very bottom of the File Browser, to the immediate right of the divider bar that separates the Palettes area from the main window (it's circled here so you can see what the icon looks like). If you want to get back to the standard view, click the same icon again.

Changing the view size of your thumbnails:

In Photoshop CS, there are four different thumbnail view sizes to choose from: Small, Medium, Large, and Custom. You choose which view you'd like from the File Browser's View menu (as shown here). Here's my handy tip on how to determine which view is right for you: Small is way too small. Ants use small and they complain. Medium is still too small to see what's going on (believe it or not, that's the Medium view shown here). Large should probably be called Small but it's the first thumbnail view that's big enough so you can actually tell what's going on in the photo. I used Large almost exclusively back in Photoshop 7. But in Photoshop CS, something wonderful happened....

Continued

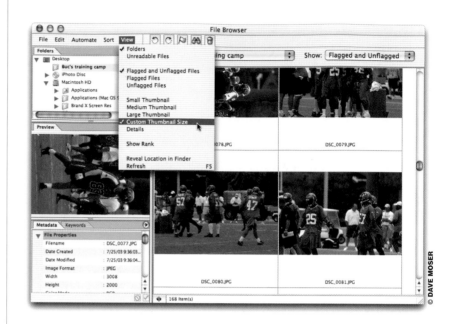

The wonderful world of custom views:

In Photoshop CS, Adobe introduced the view of your dreams—a custom view where you decide how big you want your thumbnails to be. To access this view, just go under the View menu and choose Custom Thumbnail Size (as shown here) and your thumbnails adjust to a size that's perhaps even larger than the default size in the Preview palette. This is one sweet view! Oh, but it gets better, because you're not stuck at this size—remember this is called "Custom Thumbnail Size" so you can customize it.

Customizing the custom size:

To create your own custom-sized thumbnails, go to the File Browser's mini-menu, under Edit, and choose Preferences (as shown here). This is just a shortcut to Photoshop's main Preferences dialog, so you can also get there by going under the Photoshop menu (PC: Edit menu), under Preferences, and choosing File Browser (as shown below right). It brings up the same dialog, and does the same thing, but since you're already in the File Browser, why not use the shortcut, eh?

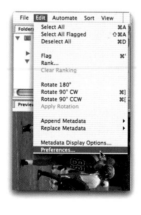

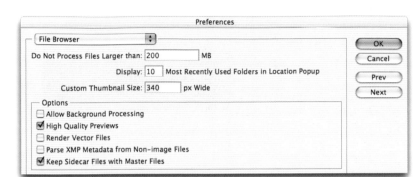

Changing the default size:

When the Preferences dialog appears, there's a field called Custom Thumbnail Size. By default, it's set to 256 pixels wide. Highlight that 256 and type in your own preferred size (I chose 340 pixels wide, but choose whatever you like), then click OK to set this size as your new Custom Thumbnail Size.

Ahhhh, that's more like it!

Here's the 340-pixel custom thumbnail view, and I clicked the Expanded View icon to hide the Palettes area so I can get two of these large thumbnails side by side. (Hey, there's Joe—#83!)

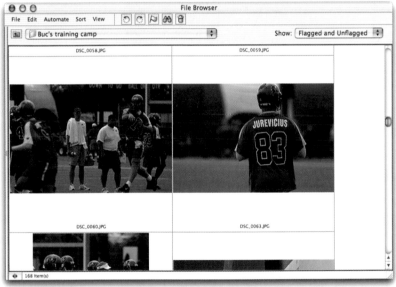

Here's a Custom Thumbnail View at 340 pixels wide, using the Expanded Viewing area.

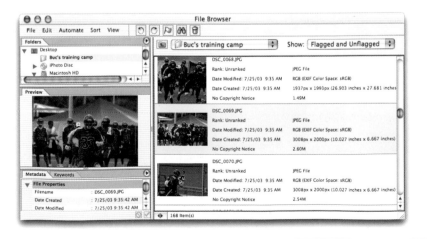

Getting the details:

There's another layout view for your Browser window called Details. This particular view option is very popular with professional photographers because not only does it display the thumbnail at a decent size, but it also displays some of the file properties to the right of the thumbnail. The Details view is found under the View menu, listed right below Custom Thumbnail Size.

Renaming Individual Photos

If you want to rename an individual photo, it's fairly straightforward. Now there is a way to actually rename every photo at once with names that make sense (to you, anyway); but that, my friends, is in the next chapter. For now, here's how to rename one thumbnail image at a time (this is a great technique to employ if you charge by the hour).

Step One:

It's hard to imagine why someone wouldn't like such a descriptive name as "DSC_0029.jpg," but if you're one of those people who enjoys names that actually describe what's happening in the photo, here's how it's done. When you move your cursor over the name of a thumbnail, you'll notice that your cursor changes into a Text cursor (an "I-beam"). All you have to do is click that I-beam once on that text and a text entry field appears with the old name already highlighted.

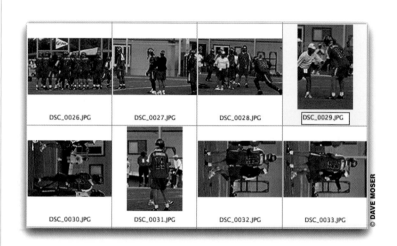

Step Two:

Now, type in a new name, then press the Enter key. The thumbnail now carries your new and improved name. Here, I changed the name of the file "DSC_0029.jpg" to "Brad warming up 1.jpg."

NOTE: There is yet another way to rename a photo from within the File Browser: You can Control-click (PC: right-click) on the thumbnail and a pop-up list appears. Choose Rename and it highlights the naming field for you. Isn't that more complicated than just clicking on the name field? Yep.

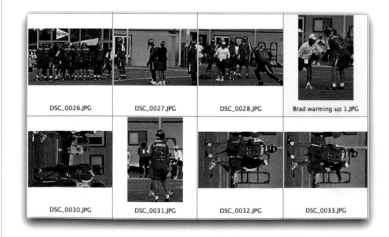

Rotating Photos (It's Different in CS)

Rotating photos within the File Browser is as easy as clicking one button. However, when you rotate photos within the File Browser itself, it's only really rotating the thumbnail. This is handy, because when you're sorting photos and you have some photos with a portrait orientation (they're tall rather than wide), you want to be able to see them upright to make a sorting judgment call; but you have a separate decision to make if you want the actual photo rotated—not just the thumbnail. Here's how to do both.

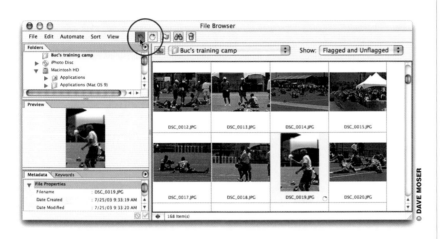

© DAVE MOSER

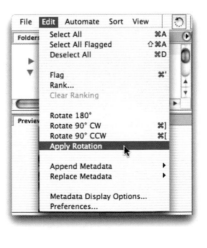

Rotating thumbnails:

Rotating a thumbnail is a total no-brainer: Just click on the thumnail you want to rotate, then click on one of the circular rotation icons (circled in red here) in the File Browser's Toolbar. The left icon rotates counterclockwise, the right icon rotates clockwise. You can also use the shortcut Command-[(PC: Control-[) to rotate counterclockwise, and Command-] (PC: Control-]) to rotate clockwise. When you rotate a thumbnail, a Rotate icon appears in its lower right-hand corner.

Rotating the actual photo:

When you rotate a thumbnail, you're doing just that—the photo doesn't really get rotated until you actually open it in Photoshop (go look in the folder on your drive, and you'll see—the photo isn't rotated). However, in Photoshop CS, you can apply the same rotation to the photo itself (not just the thumbnail) by going under the File Browser's Edit menu and choosing Apply Rotation (as shown here). You get a warning dialog telling you this will degrade the image a bit (rotating does that, ya know). Click OK to apply the rotation (since it's rotating the real photo, it'll take a minute or so).

Sorting and Arranging Your Photos

Ah, finally, we get to the fun part—actually sorting and arranging photos. Sorting photos in Photoshop 7 was kind of complicated. You had to rank each photo, and even then you didn't necessarily get them in the exact order you wanted. Luckily in CS, that's all changed, but sorting is still based on the simple premise that in every roll of digital film, you have some good shots, some "just okay" shots, and some that stink. You want to stack the good shots up top (at the top of your Browser's main window), the "okay" shots below those, and the bad shots at the bottom (or delete them altogether).

Method One: Drag-and-drop

In Photoshop CS, if you want a particular photo in a particular spot in your main window, you just click on that photo and drag it to that spot. For example, in the capture shown here, if you want the green car (the selected car) to appear in the second position from the top left, just click on its thumbnail and drag it to that spot. That thick black vertical bar (shown here) lets you know where the dragged thumbnail will land. You can treat the main window like your own personal light box, dragging photos into the exact order you want them.

This "dragging-them-where-you-want-them" scheme works great when you're working with a small number of photos (like 24 or fewer), but when you start to sort 80 or 100 photos, dragging them around gets incredibly cumbersome, and that's why now there's "flagging."

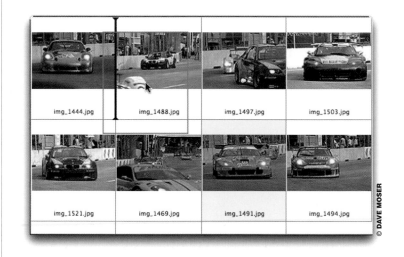

© DAVE MOSER

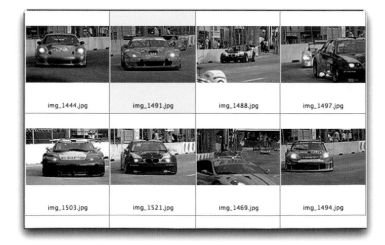

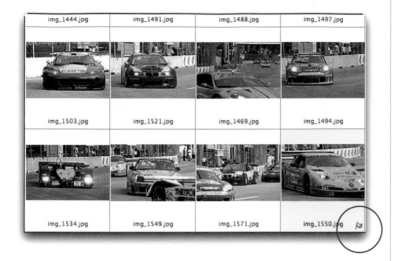

Method Two: Flagging

When you're sorting a large number of images, you might prefer the "flagging" method, at least as an initial step. Basically, you flag the good photos and leave the bad ones unflagged. You can then view just the flagged images separately (which will normally be a much smaller group of photos), and then you can use the drag-and-drop sorting method to get them in the exact order you want.

To flag an image, you just click on it and then click the Flag button at the top of the File Browser in the Toolbar (right next to the Rotation buttons)–although it's probably faster to click on a thumbnail you want to flag, then press Command-' (PC: Control-'). If you're charging by the hour, slower ways to flag include Control-clicking (PC: right-clicking) on a thumbnail and choosing Flag from the pop-up menu, or going under the File Browser's Edit menu and choosing Flag. When you flag an image, a tiny Flag icon appears in the bottom-right corner of the thumbnail area (circled in red above).

To flag multiple images (which is what you'll probably wind up doing most), just Command-click (PC: Control-click) on the photos you want to flag as you work your way through all the thumbnails. When you reach the end, just click the Flag button and they'll all be flagged at once (as shown here). Once you flag your photos, you're on to the next step.

Continued

Sorting the flagged from the unflagged:

Once you flag your photos, you can separate them from the rest of the bunch by going to the Show pop-up menu and choosing Flagged Files (circled here). Now, only the flagged thumbnails will be visible, and with this reduced number of thumbnails, you can easily use the drag-and-drop sorting method to get them in the exact order you want. (Incidentally, to "un-flag" a file, you just click on the file and click the Flag button again, or use the flag keyboard shortcut.)

Here's another place flag sorting helps: Go up to the Show pop-up menu and choose Unflagged Files (as shown here). That way, you can quickly scan the "leftovers" and see if you missed any photos you should have flagged the first time around.

Flagging your photos using this method simply puts them into two groups: Keepers (flagged) and Losers (unflagged). If you want a greater level of differentiation, you can use the sorting method from Photoshop 7 called Ranking (which many people have become fond of. These people are freaks, but nonetheless, they like it).

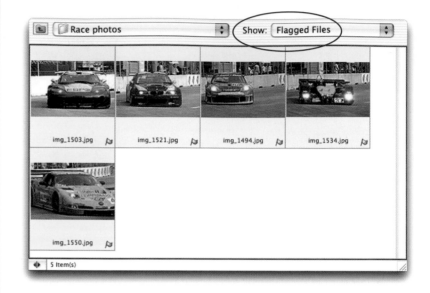

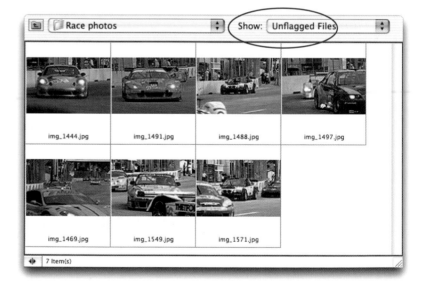

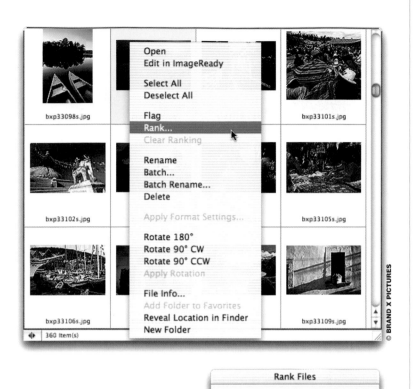

© BRAND X PICTURES

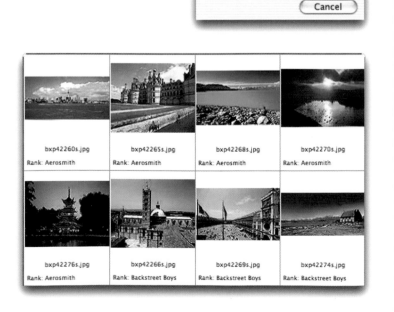

Method Three: Ranking

This method of sorting lets you decide the order by ranking your photos alphabetically or numerically. (Photoshop 7's default ranking used A, B, C, and D. Photos ranked "A" would appear at the top of the main window, photos ranked "B" would be next, etc.) You can still use that A, B, C, D, ranking system in Photoshop CS if you like. To rank a photo, Control-click (PC: right-click) on the thumbnail and choose Rank from the pop-up list (as shown here). This brings up the Rank Files dialog (shown at center), and you type in your ranking scheme. To actually see the rankings, you have to go under the File Browser's View menu and choose Show Rank. (Note: The Rank info appears right below the file name, and you can click to the right of the word "Rank" and type your rank directly in that field.)

Besides the A, B, C, D ranking, other popular ranking schemes are 1, 2, 3 (with 1 being best, 2 being second best, etc.) or using the words "Keeper" and "Loser," so photos ranked Keepers would alphabetically appear before photos ranked Losers. My personal favorite is the "Aerosmith/Backstreet Boys" ranking system, which puts photos ranked with Aerosmith first, and the Backstreet Boys last (which really goes without saying. In fact, even if you don't sort alphabetically, I'll bet Photoshop refuses to ever put the Backstreet Boys in front of Aerosmith in any situation. Yes, Photoshop is *that* cool of a program).

Continued

Telling Photoshop what to sort by:

If you used the manual ranking system (also try the Bon Jovi/Captain & Tennille scheme), you need to tell the File Browser to sort your thumbnails by rank (by default, it doesn't do so). You do this by going under the File Browser's Sort menu and choosing Rank (as shown here). Then, your photos will be ranked alphabetically. As you can see from the Sort menu, you can still sort photos in a number of different ways. But there's still one more weird thing about ranking....

You have to refresh:

You'd expect that if you were to rank a file as "A," it would jump to the top of the list, right? Nope. That would be way too easy. Once you rank your images, they stay right in the same order they were (which gives you the impression that ranking is just about useless) until you refresh the Browser. This "refreshing" merely tells the Browser to update itself. What's weird is that when you *flag* a file, it immediately updates, but when you *rank* a file, it doesn't—you have to refresh to see the results. You can refresh by clicking on the right-facing triangle next to the Folders palette (as shown here), and choosing Refresh (it's the only choice in the menu) or by pressing F5 on your keyboard (which is faster and easier). You can also choose Rank again from the Sort menu and that causes a refresh.

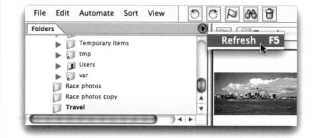

© BRAND X PICTURES

Batch ranking:

Now that you've learned how to rank a single file, what happens if you need to rank 30 or 40 images with the same rank? Well, my friend, you are about to learn the closely guarded, super-secret, hidden-deep-within-CIA-files technique of batch ranking. Things will never be the same. With batch ranking, you're able to select multiple images that you want to share the same rank and assign that rank to all of them at once. Here's a step-by-step.

Step One:

Hold the Command key (PC: Control key) and click on all the photos you want to share the same rank (they will appear highlighted, as shown here).

Step Two:

Control-click (PC: right-click) on any selected thumbnail, and from the pop-up menu that appears, choose Rank. In the Rank Files dialog (shown here) type the letter "A."

Step Three:

Press F5 on your keyboard (the shortcut for Refresh), and all the selected thumbnails are reordered according to their new "A" ranking (as shown here).

TIP: Clear ranking

If you want to clear the ranking on a file, click on it, then go to the File Browser's Edit menu and choose Clear Ranking. To batch clear, Command-click (PC: Control-click) on all the thumbnails you want to clear, then do the same thing.

Deleting Files from Within the File Browser

If a file is so vile that it doesn't even deserve a rank, you may want to delete it altogether just to cut down on clutter (and save drive space). There are a number of different ways to delete files—all of them simple.

Deleting photos:

If you burned a CD when you first inserted your memory card (and I know you did, because now you know how important it is to keep your digital negatives safely stored), then you can safely delete any photo you don't want. You can do this as easily as clicking on the offending thumbnail, then pressing Delete (PC: Backspace). You'll get a warning dialog (shown here) telling you that if you continue this madness (by clicking Yes), Photoshop will actually move this file from the folder where it resides, and put it into the Trash (or Recycling Bin) until you choose to Empty the Trash.

Another way to delete a file is to click on it and then click on the Trash icon up in the File Browser's Toolbar (circled in red here).

And of course, there is (as always) the slow way—go under the File Browser's File menu and choose Delete.

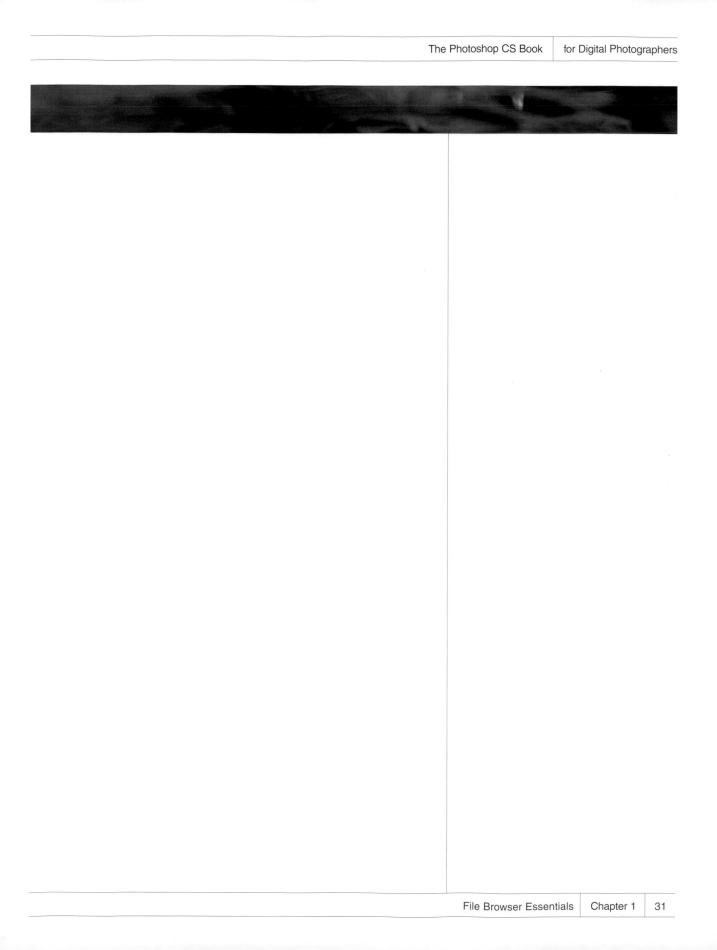

Photographer | Todd Morrison

Chapter 1 was called "Start Me Up," so I thought here in Chapter 2, I'd follow up with "Under My Thumb," which at first sounds like just another hollow Rolling Stones reference, but the true

Under My Thumb
advanced file browser techniques

brilliance of the title is that the File Browser displays thumbnails, which makes the name "Under My Thumb" almost too perfect. And it would be, if it weren't for the reality that I named this chapter for what is actually under my thumb at this very moment—the Spacebar on my laptop's keyboard. That Spacebar is effectively (and literally), under my thumb. Now, how does all this relate to you? Well, the fact that my thumb is on the Spacebar is actually quite important to this chapter. For example, I'll take my thumb off the Spacebar for just a moment to demonstrate its importance.

Thereits'offandsuddenlytheimportanceoftheSpa cebarcomesintofocus.Okay,I'llgobacktoputtingtheS pacebarundermythumb. See how much better that is? Imagine if I wrote the whole chapter like that? This whole thumb/Spacebar paradigm is starting to jell now, isn't it? I know what you're thinking. Isn't a Spacebar that place on Tatooine where Luke and Obi-Wan went looking for a ship to give them safe passage to Alderaan? No, that's not a Spacebar, that's a Cantina. I gotta tell ya, I have serious concerns about you reading a chapter on advanced File Browser techniques if you can't even tell the difference between a Spacebar and the Mos Eisley Cantina on Tatooine. But don't worry, I'm going to make this so easy you'll be editing metadata like Grand Moff Tarkin (or at least Keith Richards) in no time.

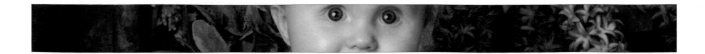

Getting and Editing a Photo's Metadata

Photoshop's File Browser gives you direct access to information that is embedded into your photo by the digital camera itself, plus access to the info embedded by Photoshop once you open the file. This information is lumped together under the heading "Metadata." Here, we briefly look at the available metadata, but more importantly, we look at how to edit that metadata to embed our own custom info.

The Metadata palette:

The bottom-left palette in the File Browser window displays the currently selected photo's metadata. The two areas of the metadata that you'll probably care about most are File Properties (the information Photoshop adds to your photo, like the file size, when it was last edited in Photoshop, its physical dimensions, etc.), and secondly the Camera Data, commonly known as "EXIF data" (EXIF stands for Exchangeable Image File data, and rather than spelling it out, most people pronounce it "EX-IF"). This EXIF data is the info that's automatically embedded into your photo by your digital camera. It includes the make and model of the camera that shot the image, the exposure, shutter speed, f-stop, if your flash fired when the photo was taken, the focal length of your lens, and a couple dozen more background details, many of which are incredibly boring, even to people with big giant über-brains. If you used the built-in Camera Raw plug-in to open a Raw digital camera image, the Camera Raw settings are saved into the metadata as well. In short, if there's something you want to know about your photo, metadata is a good place to start your search.

The File Properties metadata is the info Photoshop embeds into your photo.

The Camera Data (EXIF) is the info embedded into your photo by your digital camera.

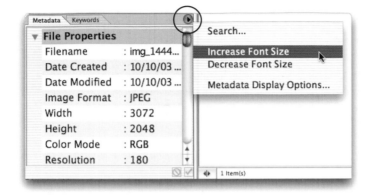

Seeing all that tiny type:

Because there's so much metadata included in each photo, Adobe had to make the font point size pretty darn small. That's not a problem if you're 14 years old, but if you're in your mid-twenties (like me), it can actually seem too small, and then you get angry and start writing letters, circulating petitions, calling emergency meetings of the condo association board, etc. Luckily, in Photoshop CS you don't have to endure tiny metadata type, because you can increase the font size. Just click on the Metadata's pop-down menu and choose Increase Font Size. If it's still not big enough, choose it again. And again. And again, until your neighbors can read it through your window.

Accessing the metadata outside the File Browser:

If you're not working in the File Browser but you want to view the metadata for the currently open image, you can—just go under the File menu and choose File Info. When the dialog appears, in the list of Info in its left panel, click on Camera Data 1 to display the most common EXIF data. Click on Camera Data 2 to display the stuff used only by high-level digital camera geeks and certain government officials. These two readouts are displayed in a nice, easily digestible format; but if you crave the full EXIF data dump, click on the word Advanced in the list on the left, then click on the right-facing triangle to the left of the words "EXIF Properties" to reveal it all.

Continued

Editing your metadata:

There's a special section of the metadata called IPTC (named for the International Press Telecommunications Council) where you can actually embed your own custom metadata information (like your copyright info). To find the IPTC metadata, go to the Metadata palette and scroll down until you see IPTC, then click on its right-facing triangle to reveal its list of info (as shown here). The little pencil icons in the first column indicate which fields can be edited (in other words, which can accept your custom metadata). To enter your own info, click once in the field you want to edit, directly after the colon in the center of the column. The editable fields will then appear (as shown upper right). By default, only four fields are visible: Description, Keywords, Author, and Copyright (and if you look at the upper right capture, you can edit only Description, Author, and Copyright). Although you see only four fields by default, you can edit which fields are displayed by going under the File Browser's mini-menu, under Edit, and choosing Metadata Display Options. This activates the dialog shown here, and when you click on the right-facing triangle for IPTC, you see the full list of available IPTC fields. Only the fields with check marks by them will be visible, so to make a hidden field visible, just click in the first column beside that field. When your personal choices have been made, just click OK and the newly marked fields are now made visible in the Metadata palette.

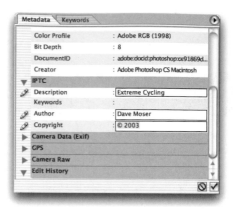

© DAVE MOSER

Changing metadata for multiple photos at the same time:

If you want to apply your copyright info (or any other IPTC metadata) to a number of different photos, it could really take some serious time, but luckily there's a way to apply the same metadata to a number of different images at once. Just go to the File Browser, click on the first photo you want to apply the metadata to, then hold the Command key (PC: Control key), and click on all the other photos you want to apply that same metadata to (just to keep things simple, we'll assume you're wanting to add your copyright info to a group of different photos). Now go to the Metadata palette, scroll down to IPTC, and click beside the Copyright field. When you do this, a warning dialog that's similar to the one shown here (okay, exactly like the one shown here), appears warning you that you've selected to edit the metadata of multiple files (which in this case, is what you want to do). Click the Yes button, then type in your data. When you're done, press Enter and your custom metadata (your copyright info in this case) will be written to all your selected files. Pretty sweet, eh?

Batch Renaming Your Files

The File Browser has a feature that automatically renames an entire folder (or disc) full of images, so your digital-camera photo names are no longer of the cryptic "DSC_01181.JPG," "DSC_01182.JPG," and "DSC_01183.JPG" variety, but are names that will be more recognizable (which you choose), such as "Anderson Portraits 1," "Anderson Portraits 2," "Anderson Portraits 3," etc.—and best of all, the whole process is automated. Here's a step-by-step.

Step One:

First, you have to tell the Browser which photos you want to batch rename. If it's just a certain number of images within your main window, you can hold the Command key (PC: Control key) and click on only the photos you want to rename. But a more likely scenario is that you'll want to rename all the photos open in your Browser, so go under the Browser's mini-menu, under Edit, and choose Select All (as shown here), or press Command-A (PC: Control-A). Once you choose Select All, all the photos in your main window become highlighted.

Step Two:

After you select all the photos that you want to rename, go under the Browser's mini-menu again, under Automate, and choose Batch Rename (as shown here).

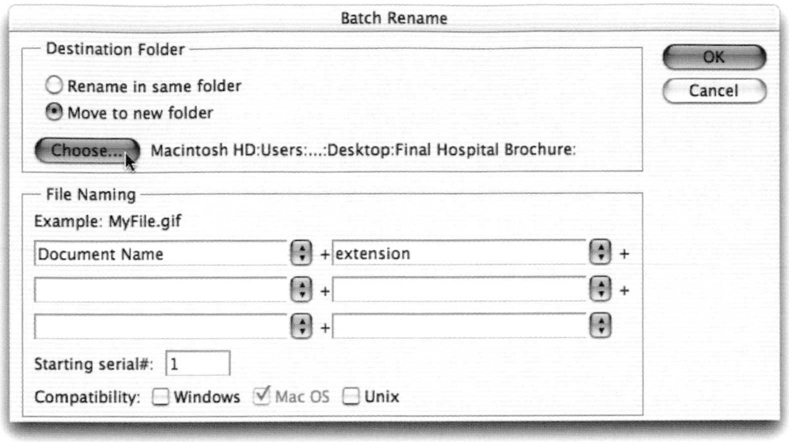

Step Three:

When the Batch Rename dialog appears, you first need to choose a destination for these renamed photos. Your choices are limited to either renaming the photos in the same folder where they reside (if you're working off a CD of saved originals, this really isn't a choice—you'll have to choose "Move to new folder"). If you choose Move to new folder, you need to click the Choose button (as shown), and in the resulting dialog, navigate to the folder you want your photos moved into after they're renamed.

One limitation of batch renaming is that it either renames your originals or moves them to a new folder. I wish there was an option where Photoshop would make copies (leaving the originals untouched) and rename only the copies; but at this point, there's not.

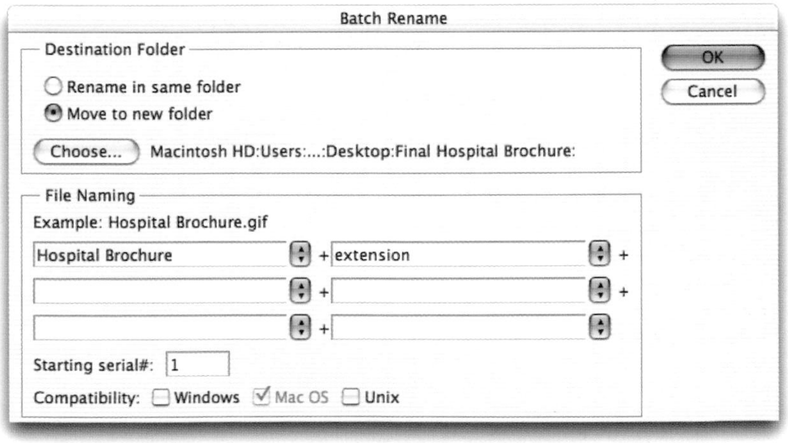

Step Four:

Under the File Naming section of the dialog, the first field on the top left is where you type in the name you've chosen (in the example shown here, I'm renaming the files "Hospital Brochure"). Just click your cursor in this field, and type in your desired name. Don't click OK just yet.

Continued

Step Five:

The next field to the right is where you tell Photoshop the numbering scheme you'd like to use following the name you assigned (after all, you can't have more than one file in the same folder named "Hospital Brochure." Instead, you'd need them to be named "Hospital Brochure2," "Hospital Brochure3," etc.). To use Photoshop's built-in auto-numbering, click-and-hold on the pop-up arrow to the immediate right of the field, and the pop-up menu shown here appears. Here, you can choose to number your photos with a 1- to 4-digit serial number, letters, or by date. In our example, we choose "1 Digit Serial Number" to have Photoshop automatically add a sequential number after the name. There's also a field near the bottom of the dialog (circled here in red) where you choose the number to begin your series.

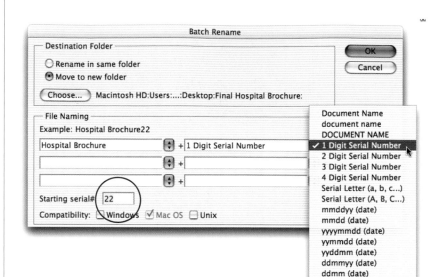

Step Six:

You can choose to add a file extension (either in caps by choosing "EXTENSION" or in all lowercase by choosing "extension"). If your files are JPEG files, Photoshop automatically adds the .jpg extension to every saved file. There are three other naming fields, just in case you're really anal about naming your files.

NOTE: Directly below the File Naming section header is a live example of what your file name will look like. Don't let it throw you that it always shows your file extension as .gif, even though your file is a JPEG—it's just using .gif to let you know that you chose to add an extension.

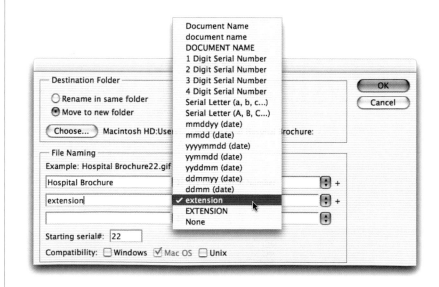

Step Seven:

When you click OK, Photoshop does its thing and your main window becomes empty (that makes sense because you moved the images to a new folder, and the main window is displaying the current folder, which is now empty). So, you need to go to the Folders palette and navigate your way to the folder where you moved all your hospital brochure shots (I named my new folder "Final Hospital Brochure"). Once you navigate to that folder (as shown here) not only will your photos be there, but they'll also be sporting their descriptive new names.

Step Eight:

Batch renaming doesn't just change the preview thumbnails' names—it goes further and applies this name change to the actual photos. To check it out, leave Photoshop and go to the folder on your hard drive where these photos are stored, open it up, and you'll see the new file names have been assigned there.

Setting up Custom File Browser Layouts

The File Browser in Photoshop CS takes advantage of nested palettes, which means you can set up a custom layout that fits your working style. Better yet, these different arrangements of the File Browser can be made into custom workspaces, so you can have different layouts for different editing tasks that are all just one click away. Here's how to set up your own custom layouts.

Step One:

We'll start with a standard setup for your File Browser (as shown here): palettes on the left and main window on the right (pretty much the default layout) so you can return to this setup anytime.

Step Two:

Go under the Window menu, under Workspace, and choose Save Workspace (as shown here).

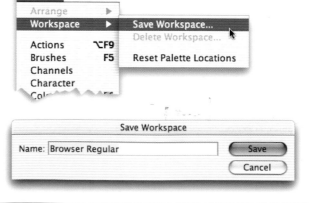

Step Three:

When the Save Workspace dialog appears, give it a name like "Browser Regular" or "FB Standard" and click OK.

Step Four:
Click directly on the Preview tab (right on the word Preview) and drag that palette down to where the Metadata and Keywords palettes are. A black highlight appears around those palettes when you're right over them. When you see that, you can release the mouse button and your Preview palette becomes nested with the Metadata and Keywords palettes (as shown here). You can see a large gray gap in the center of your Palettes area where your Preview palette used to be.

Step Five:
Click on the horizontal divider bar that appears directly above the Metadata, Keywords, and Preview palettes and drag straight upward, covering the gray gap (where the Preview palette used to be). Keep dragging until you reach the bottom divider bar just below the Folder palette. Doing this expands your Preview palette for viewing vertical photos (portrait orientation) at a much larger size (as shown here). Also, since your preview is much larger, you may be able to lower your thumbnail view size down to Medium. The example here shows the larger vertical Preview palette, with Medium-sized thumbnails in the main window. In the next step, you create another workspace with this arrangement: larger horizontal Preview palette, smaller thumbnails.

Continued

Step Six:

Save this workspace by going under the Window menu, under Workspace, and choosing Save Workspace. When the Save Workspace dialog appears (shown here) name it "Browser Tall Preview" and click Save to add this workspace to your Workspace list. Now, let's set up a custom workspace for viewing landscape-orientated photos.

Step Seven:

This time, click on the Metadata tab, and drag it up to nest it with the Folders palette. Do the same with the Keywords and Preview palettes, so all four palettes are nested at the top of the Browser (as shown here). Click on the divider bar below the palettes and drag it down to the bottom of the Browser. Next, grab the vertical divider bar and drag it to the right until a landscape-orientated photo fills the preview area, leaving just a thin column of thumbnails in the main window on the far right. Now tell me...is this a sweet layout for the Browser or what? With a preview this size, even portrait-orientated photos look huge.

Step Eight:

Save this workspace by going under the Window menu, under Workspace, and choosing Save Workspace. When the Save Workspace dialog appears (shown here) name it "Browser Wide Preview" and click Save to add this workspace to your Workspace list.

Step Nine:

Here's a layout you might try if you're using large custom thumbnail sizes and you don't need to see the Preview palette at all. This is ideal for when you're assigning keywords and searching and sorting—you can make the Keywords palette visible up top, but then drag the vertical divider bar to the left far enough to where you can view two large custom thumbnails at once in the main window (as shown here). Save this workspace as "Browser Lg. Thumbs" or "Browser Keywords Layout."

Step Ten:

You've done it—you now have four different layouts that you can choose from by going under the Window menu, under Workspace, and choosing them from the bottom of the menu (as shown here).

NOTE: Saving a workspace doesn't only save the File Browser layout, it also saves all your palette locations, so you'll want to consider that when saving your layouts. Some people like to hit the Tab key, which hides all Photoshop's palettes, including the Toolbox, so there's no onscreen clutter when saving a File Browser workspace. That way, it's just the File Browser onscreen—nothing else. Then, when they're done, they choose a standard workspace with all palettes and the Toolbox visible. The cool thing is that you can create whatever you want.

Not Getting "Burned" When You Burn CDs

Here's where I reveal the bad news: the secret "dark side" of the File Browser that winds up burning a lot of users who don't really understand what the Browser is doing. First the secret, and then we'll look at how to deal with it.

The scenario I'm about to describe has happened to untold thousands of nice people like yourself: You go into the Browser, you rotate some of the photos, you rename certain ones, you delete others, you rank, you sort, and basically get everything just the way you want it. Then you burn your newly edited thumbnails to a CD.

A couple of weeks go by and you pop that CD in, open it in your Browser, and all your changes (names, rotation, deleted files, etc.) are GONE! It's as if you just pulled the images in from your camera—you lost all your changes! Has this already happened to you? Perhaps to someone you know, a loved one, or other disinterested party? It doesn't have to be this way. You can avoid all the heartache and personal trauma by doing one simple thing.

Here's the deal: The changes you make in the Browser window itself are actually stored within a memory cache, kind of an invisible text file that tells Photoshop "this file is rotated, that one has been deleted, this one is now named 'Frank's party,' etc." As long as your images stay in the same folder they were created in, Photoshop will be able to read that cache file, and when you open that file months

You've sorted, renamed, rotated, and ranked the files the way you want them.

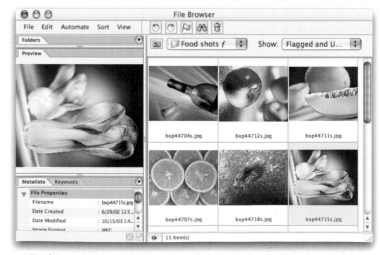

You burn that folder to CD, then some weeks later you open the CD again, and all the naming, rotation, sorting, and ranking are gone—you're back where you started.

Keep those three cache files with your photos to keep all your Browser edits intact.

later, it remembers all the changes you made. However, if you burn those images to CD, or put them on a different hard drive, on a network, or even rename the folder—that breaks the link to the cache, and you lose all the changes.

Luckily, there's a way around this. Before you move these images into a new folder, onto a CD, to a different hard drive, etc., you need to export the cache. This cache file is where Photoshop keeps track of which files are rotated, what their new names are, how they're sorted, etc. Exporting the cache creates three files that will now appear within the same folder as your edited photos.

To export this cache, go to the Browser's mini-menu, under File, and choose Export Cache (as shown above). When you do this, a dialog pops up to let you know the cache has been exported (shown here). Because these three files are now visible (as shown below), you can copy them right along with all your photos onto another drive, another folder, a CD, etc., and by doing that, you're sending along your list of edits made in Photoshop's Browser. That way, when you (or your Italian confidential secretary) open those images in Photoshop's Browser at a later date, all the changes you made will be intact.

IMPORTANT NOTE: If you export your cache, and then update these images in your Browser, you have to export your cache again—it doesn't update automatically.

Photographer | David Cuerdon

If a chapter on cropping and resizing doesn't sound exciting, really, what does? It's sad, but a good portion of our lives is spent doing just that—cropping and resizing. Why is that? It's because nothing, and

Cream of the Crop
cropping and resizing

I mean nothing, is ever the right size. Think about it. If everything were already the right size, there'd be no opportunity to "super-size it." You'd go to McDonald's, order a Value Meal, and instead of hearing, "Would you care to super-size your order?" there would just be a long, uncomfortable pause. And frankly, I'm uncomfortable enough at the McDonald's drive-thru, what with all the cropping and resizing I'm constantly doing. Anyway, although having a chapter on cropping and resizing isn't the kind of thing that sells books (though I hear books on crop circles do fairly well), both are important and necessary, especially if you ever plan on cropping or resizing things in Photoshop. Actually, you'll be happy to learn that there's more than just cropping and resizing in this chapter. That's right—I super-sized this chapter with other cool techniques that honestly are probably a bit too cool to wind up in a chapter called "Cropping and Resizing," but it's the only place they'd fit. But don't let the extra techniques throw you; if this chapter seems too long to you, flip to the end of the chapter and rip out a few pages, and you have effectively cropped the chapter down to size. (And by ripping the pages out yourself, you have transformed what was originally a mere *book* into an *"interactive experience,"* which thereby enhances the value of the book, making you feel like a pretty darn smart shopper.) See, it almost makes you want to read it now, doesn't it?

Custom Sizes for Photographers

Photoshop's dialog for creating new documents has a pop-up menu with a list of Preset Sizes. You're probably thinking, "Hey, there's a 4 x 6, 5 x 7, and 8 x 10—I'm set." The problem is there's no way to switch the orientation of these presets (so a 4 x 6 will always be a 4" wide by 6" tall portrait-oriented document). That's why creating your own custom new document sizes is so important. Here's how.

Step One:

Go under the File menu and choose New. When the New dialog box appears, click on the Preset pop-up menu to reveal the list of preset sizes. The preset sizes for photographers are the set just below the preset for Tabloid, and they include 2 x 3, 4 x 6, 5 x 7, and 8 x 10. The only problem with these is that their orientation is set to portrait and their resolution is set to 300 by default. So, if you want a landscape preset, at less than 300 ppi, you need to create and save your own.

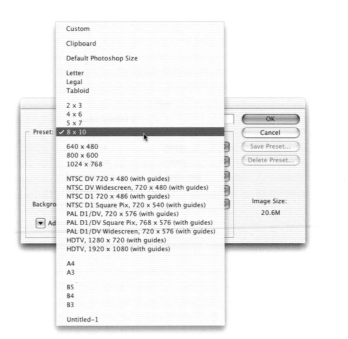

Step Two:

For example, let's say that you want a 5 x 7 set to landscape (that's 7" wide by 5" tall). First, enter 7 inches in the Width field (as shown here), 5 inches in the Height field, and your desired Color Mode and resolution (I input 212 ppi, which is enough for me to have my image printed on a high-end printing press). Once your settings are in place, click the Save Preset button (as shown).

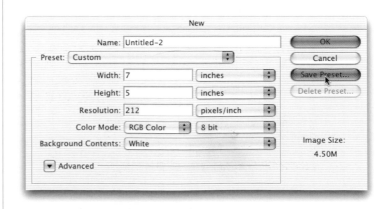

New Document Preset

Preset Name: 7 in X 5 in

OK

Cancel

Include In Saved Settings:
- ☑ Resolution ☑ Content
- ☑ Mode ☑ Profile
- ☑ Bit Depth ☑ Pixel Aspect Ratio

⚠ Values not included in the saved preset will default to their last used value.

Custom

Clipboard

✓ 7 in X 5 in

Default Photoshop Size

Letter
Legal
Tabloid

2 x 3
4 x 6
5 x 7
8 x 10

640 x 480
800 x 600
1024 x 768

NTSC DV 720 x 480 (with guides)
NTSC DV Widescreen, 720 x 480 (with guides)
NTSC D1 720 x 486 (with guides)
NTSC D1 Square Pix, 720 x 540 (with guides)
PAL D1/DV, 720 x 576 (with guides)
PAL D1/DV Square Pix, 768 x 576 (with guides)
PAL D1/DV Widescreen, 720 x 576 (with guides)
HDTV, 1280 x 720 (with guides)
HDTV, 1920 x 1080 (with guides)

A4
A3

B5
B4
B3

Untitled-1

Preset: [   ]   OK
                          Cancel
                          Save Preset...
                          Delete Preset...

Backgro   Image Size:
                 4.50M

New

Name: Untitled-2   OK

Preset: 7 in X 5 in   Cancel

Width: 7   inches   Save Preset...

Adobe Photoshop   Delete Preset...

Are you sure you want to delete 7 in X 5 in? This action cannot be undone.

No   Yes

Background   Image Size:
              4.50M

▼ Advanced

Step Three:

This brings up the New Document Preset dialog box. You can toggle on/off which parameters you want saved, but I use the default setting of including everything (better safe than sorry, I guess).

Step Four:

Click OK and your new custom preset appears in the pop-up list of Presets (as shown here). You only have to go through this once, as Photoshop CS remembers your custom settings, and they will appear in this Preset menu from now on.

Step Five:

If you decide you want to delete a preset, it's simple—just open the New dialog, choose the preset you want to delete from the Preset pop-up menu, then click on the Delete Preset button (as shown here). A warning dialog appears asking you to confirm the delete. Click Yes, and it's gone!

Cropping Photos

After you sort your images in the Browser, one of the first editing tasks you'll probably undertake is cropping a photo. There are a number of different ways to crop a photo in Photoshop. We'll start with the basic garden variety, and then we'll look at some ways to make the task faster and easier.

Step One:
Press the letter "c" to get the Crop tool (you could always select it directly from the Toolbox, but I only recommend doing so if you're charging by the hour).

Step Two:
Click within your photo and drag out a cropping border (as shown here). The area to be cropped away appears dimmed (shaded). You don't have to worry about getting your crop border right when you first drag it out, because you can edit the border by dragging the points that appear in each corner and at the centers of all four sides.

TIP: If you don't like seeing your photo with the cropped-away areas appearing shaded (as in the previous step), you can toggle this shading feature off/on by pressing the Slash key on your keyboard. When you press the Slash key, the border remains in place but the shading is turned off (as shown here).

Step Three:
While you have the crop border in place, you can rotate the entire border by moving your cursor outside the border (note the cursor's position in the lower-right corner of the image shown here), and when you do, the cursor changes into a double-headed arrow. Just click-and-drag and the cropping border rotates in the direction that you drag (this is a great way to save time if you have a crooked image, because it lets you crop and rotate at the same time).

Continued

Step Four:

After you have the cropping border where you want it, just press the Return key (PC: Enter key) to crop (the final cropped photo is shown at right).

Before crop. *After crop.*

TIP: Changing your mind

If you've dragged out a cropping border and then decide you don't want to crop the image, there are three ways to cancel your crop:

(1) Press the Escape (esc) key on your keyboard, and the crop is canceled and the photo remains untouched.

(2) Look up in the Options bar and you'll see the International symbol for "No way" (as shown here). Click the circle with the diagonal line through it to cancel your crop, or…

(3) In the Toolbox, click on another tool. This brings up a warning dialog asking if you want to crop the image. To cancel, don't press Cancel; press Don't Crop.

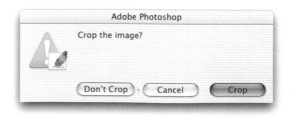

If you're outputting photos for clients, chances are they're going to want them in standard sizes so they can easily find frames to fit their photos. If that's the case, you'll find this technique handy, because it lets you crop any image to a predetermined size (like 5 x 7, 8 x 10, and so on).

Cropping to a Specific Size

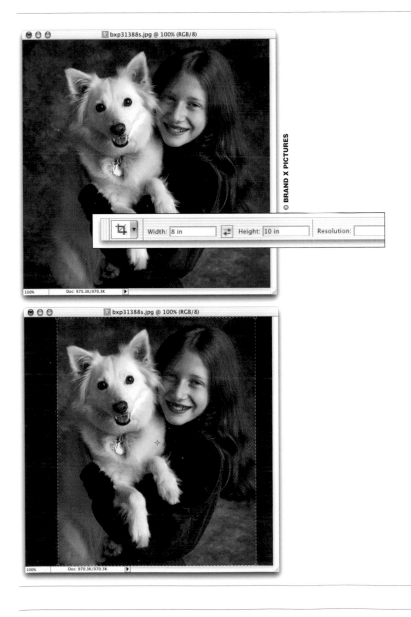

Step One:
The portrait shown here measures 10.806″ x 10.819″ and we want to crop it to be a perfect 8″ x 10″. First, get the Crop tool, and up in the Options bar on the left, you'll see fields for Width and Height. Enter the size you want for Width, followed by the unit of measurement you want to use (for example, use "in" for inches, "px" for pixels, "cm" for centimeters, "mm" for millimeters, etc.). Next, press the Tab key to jump over to the Height field and enter your desired height, again followed by the unit of measurement (as shown in the inset at left).

Step Two:
After you enter these figures in the Options Bar, click within your photo with the Crop tool and drag out a cropping border. You notice that as you drag, the border is constrained to a vertical shape and no side points are visible—only corner points. Whatever size you make your border, the area within that border becomes an 8″ x 10″ photo. In the example shown at left, I dragged the border so it almost touched the top and bottom, to get as much of the subject as possible.

Continued

Step Three:

After your cropping border is onscreen, you can reposition it by moving your cursor inside the border, where your cursor changes to a Move arrow. You can now drag the border into place, or use the Arrow keys on your keyboard for more precise control. When it looks right to you, press Return (PC: Enter) to finalize your crop, and the area inside your cropping border becomes 8″ x 10″. (I made the Rulers visible so you could see that the image measures exactly 8″ x 10″.)

TIP: After you enter a Width and Height in the Options bar, those dimensions remains there. To clear the fields, just choose the Crop tool, and up in the Options bar, click on the Clear button (shown upper right). This clears the Width and Height fields (as shown lower right), and now you can use the Crop tool for freeform cropping (you can drag it in any direction—it's no longer constrained to a vertical 8 x 10).

COOLER TIP: If you already have one photo that is the exact size and resolution you'd like, you can use it to enter the crop dimensions for you. First, open the photo you'd like to resize, and then open your "ideal-size-and-resolution" photo. Get the Crop tool, and then go up in the Options bar and click on the Front Image button (as shown bottom right). Photoshop automatically inputs that photo's Width, Height, and Resolution in the Crop tool's fields. All you have to do is crop, and the other image now shares the exact same specs.

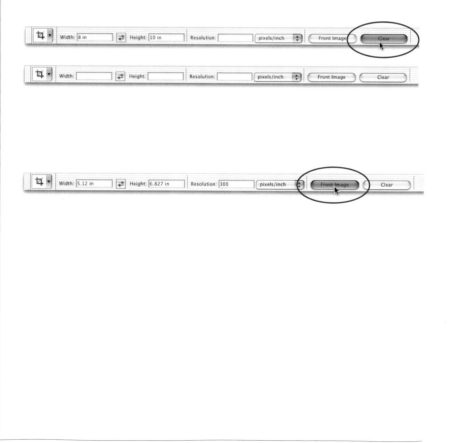

I know, we just learned how to use the Crop tool and now we're jumping into an advanced technique: creating your own custom tools. The reason is, it fits with what we're already doing. Although it's more of an advanced technique, it's not complicated. In fact, once you set it up, it will save you time and money. What we're going to do is create what are called Tool Presets. These Tool Presets are a series of tools (in this case, Crop tools) with all our option settings already in place. So we'll create a 5 x 7, an 8 x 10, a 6 x 4, or whatever Crop tool we want. Then, when we want to crop to 5 x 7, all we have to do is grab the 5 x 7 Crop tool. Here's how.

Creating Your Own Custom Crop Tools

Step One:
Press the letter "c" to switch to the Crop tool, and then go under the Window menu and choose Tool Presets to bring up the Tool Presets palette (shown here). By default, five Crop Tool Presets are already there, all at 300 ppi. That's great if you need these sizes, at 300 ppi; but if you don't, you might as well drag these Tool Presets onto the Trash icon at the bottom of the palette, 'cause if you don't need 'em, they just get in the way. (Also, make sure that Current Tool Only is checked at the bottom of the palette so you see only the Crop tool presets, and not the Presets for every tool.)

Step Two:
Go up to the Options bar and enter the dimensions for the first tool you want to create (in this example, we create a Crop tool that crops to a wallet size area). In the Width field, type 2. Press the Tab key to jump to the Height field and type 2.5 (as shown here). Note: If you have your Rulers set to inches under the Units sections in Photoshop's Units & Rulers Preferences, when you press the Tab key, Photoshop automatically inserts "in" after your numbers, indicating inches.

Continued

Step Three:

Go to the floating Tool Presets palette (the one you opened in Step One) and click the New Tool Preset button at the bottom of the palette (it looks like the New Layer button in the Layers palette). This brings up the New Tool Preset dialog where you can name your new preset. Name it "Crop to Wallet Size" and click OK.

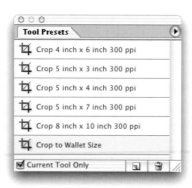

Step Four:

This new tool is added to the Tool Presets dialog (as shown here).

Step Five:

Continue this process of typing in new cropping dimensions in the Crop tool's Options bar until you've created a set of custom Crop tools for the crop sizes you personally use the most. Make sure you make the names descriptive (add Portrait or Landscape, for example, where necessary).

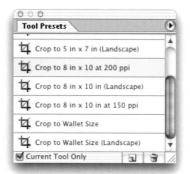

TIP: If you need to change the name of a preset after you create it, just double-click directly on the name to highlight it, and then type in the new name.

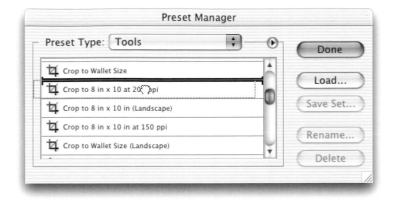

Step Six:

After you create Tool Presets for all the custom Crop tools you'll need, chances are they won't be in the order you want them (it just works out that way). To reorder the tools the way you'd like them to appear, go under the Edit menu and choose Preset Manager. When the dialog appears, choose Tools from the Preset Type pop-up menu, and scroll until you see the Crop tools you created. To reorder your tools, just click-and-drag them to where you want.

Step Seven:

After your tools are in your preferred order, you can close the Tool Presets palette because you don't actually need it to choose your tools. That's because there's an easier way: When you choose the Crop tool in the Toolbox, you can access your custom Crop tool presets from the Options bar. Just click on the first icon from the left (as shown at left). A pop-down library of tools appears and you can choose the one you want from there. As soon as you click on one, you see the Options bar change to reflect the proper measurements, and now you can drag out the cropping marquee and it will be fixed to the exact dimensions you chose for that tool. Imagine how much time and effort this is going to save (really, close your eyes and imagine. Mmmmmm, Tool Presets. Yummy).

Cropping Without the Crop Tool

Sometimes, it's quicker to crop your photo using some of Photoshop's other tools and features than it is to reach for the Crop tool every time you need a simple crop.

Step One:

This is the method I probably use the most for cropping images of all kinds (primarily, when I'm not trying to make a perfect 5 x 7, 8 x 10, and so on. I'm basically just "eyeing" it). Start by pressing "m" to get the Rectangular Marquee tool. (I use this tool so much that I usually don't have to switch to it—maybe that's why I use this method all the time.) Drag out a selection around the area you want to keep (leaving all the other areas to be cropped away outside the selection), as shown.

Step Two:

Go under the Image menu and choose Crop (as shown here).

Step Three:
When you choose Crop, the image is immediately cropped (as shown). There are no crop handles and no dialogs—bang. It just gets cropped, down and dirty, and that's why I like it.

TIP: One instance of where you'll use the Crop command from the Image menu is when you're creating collages. When you drag photos from other documents onto your main document and position them within your collage, the parts of the image that extend beyond the document borders are actually still there. So to keep our file size manageable, we choose All from the Select menu (as shown) or press Command-A (PC: Control-A), and then we choose Crop from the Image menu. This deletes all the excess layer data that extends beyond the image border and brings our file size back in line.

Automated Close Cropping

Here's another handy method of cropping that doesn't use the Crop tool, and best of all, Photoshop does most of the work. It's used for situations where you want blank areas surrounding your image to be cropped away—perfect for product shots, tight cropping of Web graphics, or whenever you want your photo cropped as tightly as possible.

Step One:
Open the image you want to be "close cropped." In the example shown here, we have a product shot surrounded by white space.

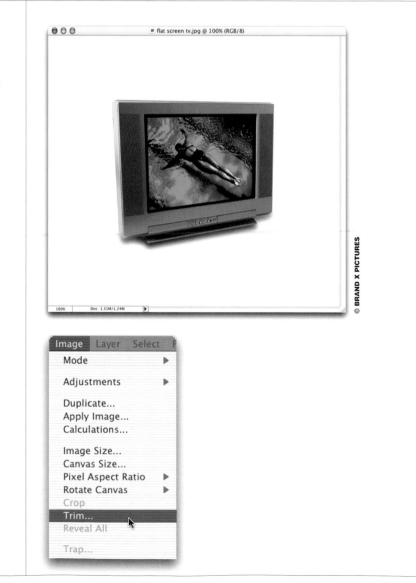

Step Two:
Go under the Image menu and choose Trim.

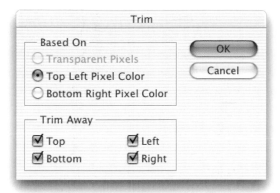

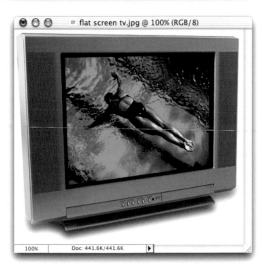

Step Three:

When the Trim dialog box appears, you can choose where you want the trimming (cropping) to occur (from the Top, Bottom, Left, or Right). By default, it trims away blank areas from all sides. This is also where you tell Photoshop which color to trim away. In this case, the area to be trimmed away is white, so using the default "Top Left Pixel Color" works just fine. In fact, 99% of the time, I don't change a single setting.

Step Four:

When you click OK, the photo will be close cropped (trimmed) down to the smallest possible size without deleting any non-white pixels (as shown here).

TIP: Clipping off unwanted areas

If you'd like to take 1" (or more) off your entire image, the easiest way might be to shrink the photo's canvas size. To do this, go under the Image menu and choose Canvas Size. When the Canvas Size dialog appears, click the Relative check box, and then enter -1 in both the Width and Height fields (as shown). When you click OK, you get a dialog warning you that this new canvas size will clip off part of your image, but that's okay; that's what we want. Click Proceed, and your image's width and height is cropped in by 1".

Using the Crop Tool to Add More Canvas Area

I know the heading at left doesn't make much sense—using the Crop tool to *add* more canvas area? How can the Crop tool (which is designed to crop photos to a smaller size) actually make the canvas area (white space) around your photo larger? That's what I'm going to show you.

Step One:

Open the image that you want to give additional blank canvas area. Press the letter "d" to set your Background color to its default color of white.

Step Two:

Press Command-minus (PC: Control-minus) to zoom out a bit (so your image doesn't take up your whole screen), and then press the letter "f." This lets you see the gray desktop area that surrounds your image (as shown at right).

Step Three:
Press the letter "c" to switch to the Crop tool, and drag a cropping marquee border out to any random size, as shown here (it doesn't matter how big or little the marquee is at this point).

Step Four:
Grab any one of the side or corner points and drag outside the image area, out into the gray desktop area that surrounds your image (as shown here). The area that your cropping border extends outside the image is the area that will be added as white canvas space, so position it where you want to add the blank canvas space.

Step Five:
Just press the Return key (PC: Enter key) to finalize your crop, and when you do, the area outside of your image becomes white canvas area. In the example shown here, I added some text in the bottom canvas area. The top line is set in ITC Bradley Hand, and the bottom line is set in Trajan (from Adobe).

Straightening Crooked Photos

If you handhold the camera for most of your shots rather than using a tripod, you can be sure that some of your photos are going to come out a bit crooked. Here's a quick way to straighten them accurately in just a few short steps.

Step One:

Open the photo that needs straightening. Choose the Measure tool from Photoshop's Toolbox (it looks like a little ruler, and it's hidden behind the Eyedropper tool, so just click-and-hold for a moment on the Eyedropper tool until the Measure tool appears in the flyout menu).

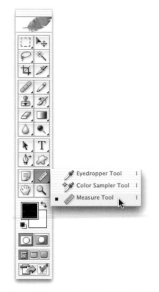

Step Two:

Try to find something in your photo that you think is supposed to be straight (the horizon in this example). Drag the Measure tool horizontally along this straight edge in your photo (as shown), starting from the left and extending right. As soon as you drag the tool, you can see the angle of the line displayed both in the Info palette (which appears automatically) and up in the Options bar, but you can ignore them both because Photoshop is already taking note of the angle and placing that info where you'll need it in the next step.

Step Three:

Go under the Image menu, under Rotate Canvas, and choose Arbitrary, and the Rotate Canvas dialog appears. Photoshop has already put the proper angle of rotation you need to straighten the image (based on your measurement), and it even sets the button for whether the image should be rotated clockwise or counterclockwise.

Step Four:

All you have to do now is click OK, and your photo will be perfectly straightened (check out the horizon line in the photo shown here—straight as an arrow).

Step Five:

After the image is straightened, you might have to re-crop it to remove the extra white canvas space showing around the corners of your photo.

TIP: When you use the Measure tool, the line it lays down stays put right over your photo until you rotate the image. If you want to clear the last measurement and remove the line it drew in your image, press the Clear button that appears up in the Options bar.

Automated Cropping and Straightening

Since nearly everybody (digital or not) has a shoebox full of old vintage family photos up in the attic, I wanted to include a tutorial on the new Crop and Straighten Photos automation. Its name is a bit misleading, because it does much more—it lets you scan multiple photos at one time (on your flatbed scanner), then it looks at each photo, straightens it, and then copies each into its own separate window (saving you the trouble).

Step One:

Place as many photos as will fit at one time on the scanning bed of your flatbed desktop scanner and scan them in. They'll all appear in one large document (as shown here). As you can see, these photos were crooked when placed on the scanning bed, so naturally they appear crooked in the Photoshop document.

© BRAND X PICTURES

Step Two:

Go under the File menu, under Automate, and choose Crop and Straighten Photos (as shown here).

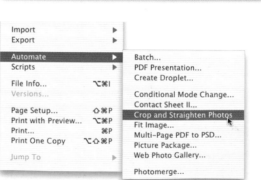

© KALEBRA KELBY

Step Three:

No dialog box appears. Instead, Photoshop looks for straight edges in your photos, straightens the photos, and copies each into its own separate window (as shown here).

TIP: If you've scanned a number of photos, and decide you only want certain ones to be cropped and placed into their own separate documents, just put a selection around those photos, then hold the Option key (PC: Alt key) before you choose Crop and Straighten Photos.

Step Four:

This automation also works on single images (like the one shown here, which is crooked. Since it was taken with a digital camera, you're probably wondering how it got so crooked. I rotated it. Don't tell anybody).

Step Five:

When you choose Crop and Straighten Photos now, it crops and straightens this one photo, but it still duplicates the image into a separate document. Hey, it's not perfect. Speaking of not perfect, it seems to work best when the photos you scan as a group have similar tonal qualities. The more varied the color of the photos is, the harder time it seems to have straightening the images.

Resizing and How to Reach Those Hidden Free Transform Handles

What happens if you drag a large photo onto a smaller photo in Photoshop? (This happens all the time, especially if you're collaging or combining two or more photos.) You have to resize the photo using Free Transform, right? Right. But here's the catch: When you bring up Free Transform, at least two, or more likely all four, of the handles you need to resize the image are out of reach. You see the center point (as shown in the photo in Step Four), but not the handles you need to reach to resize. Here's how to get around that hurdle quickly and easily.

Step One:

For the purposes of this example, open a new document in Photoshop's default size of 7″ x 5″.

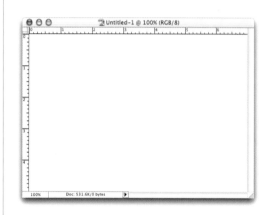

Step Two:

Open a photo that's larger than your 7″ x 5″ document (in other words, open most any photo from your digital camera because it'll be larger than that, or download this one from the book's Web site). The photo shown here is 13.264″ by 8.792″.

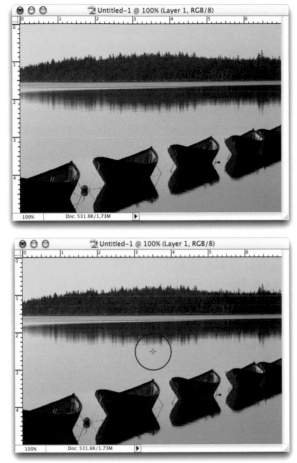

Step Three:

Press "v" to get the Move tool and drag this photo on top of your 7" x 5" document (the photo that you drag appears on its own layer automatically). As you can see, since the photo you dragged in was larger than the document you dragged it into, it extends off the sides and top quite a bit. So, to make it fit comfortably in this new document, you need to scale the photo down quite a bit.

Step Four:

Press Command-T (PC: Control-T) to bring up Free Transform. Here's where the problem begins—you need to grab the Free Transform corner points to scale the photo down, but you can't even see the Free Transform handles in this image (you see the center point, but there's no way to reach the corner handles to scale the image down to size).

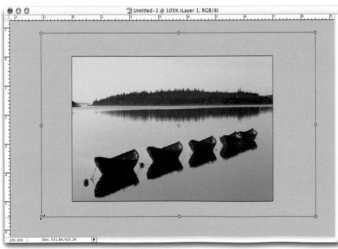

Step Five:

Here's the trick: Once you have Free Transform in place (and can't see the handles) just press Command-0 (PC: Control-0) and Photoshop automatically resizes your document window, and your image, so you can reach all the handles (as shown here), no matter how far outside your image area they once were. Two things: (1) This trick only works once you have Free Transform applied, and (2) it's Command-0 (PC: Control-0)— that's the number zero, not the letter "O".

Resizing Digital-Camera Photos

If you're used to resizing scans, you'll find that resizing images from digital cameras is a bit different, primarily because scanners create high-resolution scans (usually 300 ppi or more), but the default setting for digital cameras usually produces an image that is large in physical dimensions, but lower in ppi (usually 72 ppi). The trick is to decrease the size of your digital-camera image (and increase its resolution) without losing any of its quality. Here's the trick.

Step One:

Open the digital-camera image that you want to resize. Press Command-R (PC: Control-R) to make Photoshop's rulers visible. As you can see from the rulers, the photo is just a little more than 23.5″ wide by just over 18.347″ high.

© KALEBRA KELBY

Step Two:

Go under the Image menu and choose Image Size to bring up the Image Size dialog shown at right. Under the Document Size section, the Resolution setting is 72 pixels/inch (ppi). A resolution of 72 ppi is considered "low resolution" and is ideal for photos that will only be viewed onscreen (such as Web graphics, slideshows, and so on), but is too low to get high-quality results from a color inkjet printer, color laser printer, or for use on a printing press.

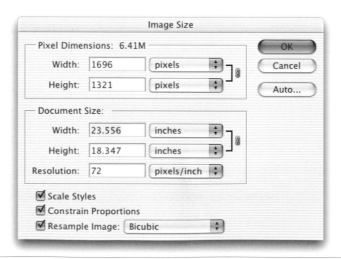

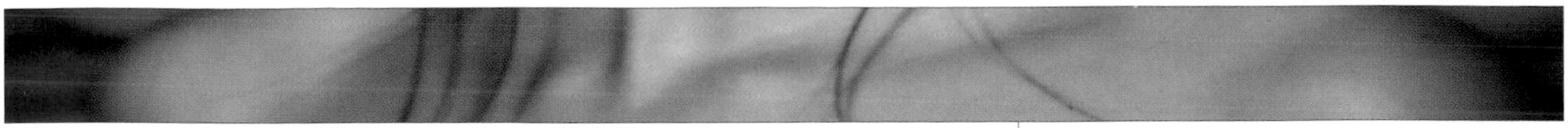

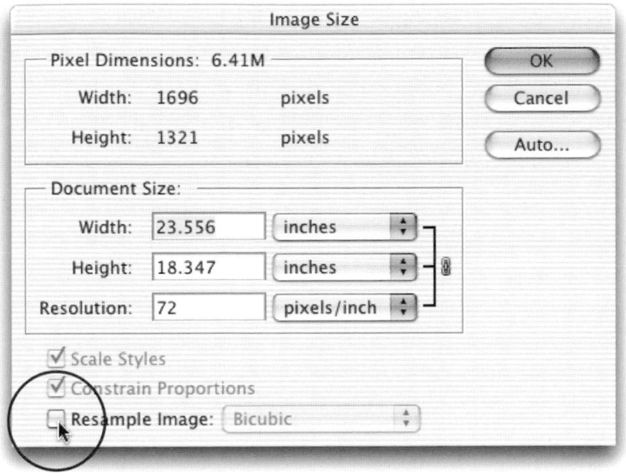

Step Three:

If we plan to output this photo to any printing device, it's pretty clear that we'll need to increase the resolution to get good results. I wish we could just type in the resolution we'd like it to be in the Resolution field (such as 200 or 300 ppi), but unfortunately, this "resampling" makes our low-resolution photo appear soft (blurry) and pixelated. That's why we need to turn the Resample Image check box off (it's on by default). That way, when we type in a resolution setting that we need, Photoshop automatically adjusts the Width and Height of the image down in the exact same proportion. As your Width and Height come down (with Resample Image turned off), your resolution goes up. Best of all, there's absolutely no loss of quality. Pretty cool!

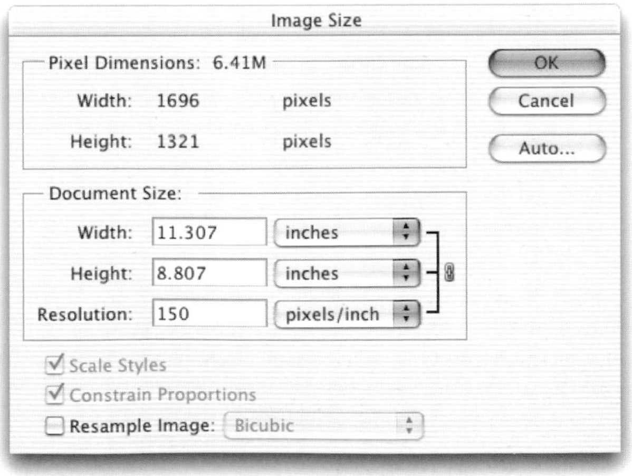

Step Four:

Here, I've turned off Resample Image and I typed 150 in the Resolution field for output to a color inkjet printer. (I know, you probably think you need a lot more resolution, but you usually don't.) At a resolution of only 150 ppi, I can actually print a photo that is 11.307″ wide by almost 9″ high.

Continued

Step Five:

Here's the Image Size dialog for our source photo, and this time, I've increased the Resolution setting to 212 ppi for output to a printing press. (Again, you don't need nearly as much resolution as you'd think.) As you can see, the Width of my image is no longer 23.556"—it's now just 8". The Height is no longer 18.347"—now it's 6.231".

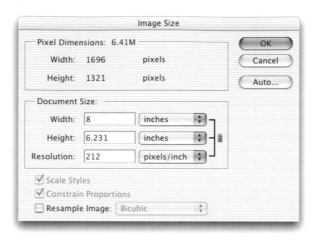

Step Six:

When you click OK, you won't see the image window change at all—it appears at the exact same size onscreen. But now, look at the rulers. You can see that it's now 8" wide by 6.231" high. Resizing using this technique does *three* big things: (1) It gets your physical dimensions down to size (the photo now fits on an 8 x 10 sheet); (2) it increases the resolution enough so you can output this image on a printing press; and (3) you haven't softened, blurred, or pixelated the image in any way—the quality remains the same—all because you turned off Resample Image.

NOTE: Do not turn off Resample Image for images that you scan on a scanner—they start as high-resolution images in the first place. *Turning Resample Image off is only for photos taken with a digital camera.*

Generally speaking, shrinking the physical dimensions of a photo does not create a quality problem—you can make an 8 x 10 into a 4 x 5 with little visible loss of quality. Increasing the size of an image is where you run into problems (the photo often gets visibly blurry, softer, and even pixelated). However, digital photography guru (and *Photoshop User* columnist) Jim DiVitale showed me a trick he swears by that lets you increase your digital-camera images up to full poster size with hardly any loss of quality visible to the naked eye, and I tell ya, it'll make a believer out of you.

The Cool Trick for Turning Small Photos into Poster-Sized Prints

ADVANCED TECHNIQUES
FOR PROS ONLY!

Step One:

Open the digital-camera image you want to increase to poster size. The image shown here was taken with a 3.2-megapixel Nikon digital camera. It's physically 4.727″ wide by 4.787″ high, at 300 ppi.

© KALEBRA KELBY

Step Two:

Go under the Image menu and choose Image Size. When the Image Size dialog appears, make sure Resample Image is turned on, and change the Resample Image Interpolation Method to Bicubic Smoother. Switch the unit of measurement pop-up menus in the dialog from Inches to Percent (as shown) and type in 110, which increases your image by 10%. Believe it or not, when you increase in 10% increments, for some reasons it doesn't seem to soften or blur the image. It's freaky, I know, but to believe it, you just have to try it yourself.

Continued

Step Three:

To get this image up to poster size, it's going to take quite a few passes with this "increase-by-10%" technique, so I recommend creating your own custom Action to do it for you at the press of one key. Here's how: Go under the Window menu and choose Actions. When the palette appears, click the Create New Action button at the bottom of the palette. When the New Action dialog appears, name your action "Upsize 110%," and then choose a Function Key (F-key) that you want to assign this Action to (I chose F11). Then, click the Record button and repeat Step Two. After you've increased to 110%, click the square Stop button at the bottom of the Actions palette to complete your recording process. Now, every time you press the F11 Function Key (or the F-key you actually assign) on your keyboard, your current image will be increased by 10%.

Step Four:

Here's the final image, increased from approximately 4.75″ x 4.75″ to approximately 20″ x 20″, and even onscreen, the loss of quality is almost negligible, yet the image is the size of a standard, full-sized poster. I had to run the Action 15 times to get up to that size, but because I wrote an Action, it took only a fraction of the time (and trouble). Thanks to Jimmy D for sharing this amazing, yet deceptively simple technique with us. Jim rocks!

Photographer | Todd Morrison

Okay, did you catch that reference to the band The Fixx in the title? You did? Great. That means that you're at least in your mid-thirties to early forties. (I myself am only in my mid- to early twenties, but

The Big Fixx
digital-camera image problems

I listen to oldies stations just to keep in touch with baby boomers and other people who at one time or another tried to break-dance.) Well, the Fixx had a big hit in the early '80s (around the time I was born) called "One Thing Leads to Another," and that's a totally appropriate title for this chapter because one thing (using a digital camera) leads to another (having to deal with things like digital noise, color aliasing, and other nasties that pop up when you finally kick the film habit and go totally digital). Admittedly, some of the problems we bring upon ourselves (like leaving the lens cap on; or forgetting to bring our camera to the shoot, where the shoot is, who hired us, or what day it is; or we immersed our flash in a tub of Jell-O®, you know—the standard stuff). And other things are problems caused by the hardware itself (the slave won't fire when it's submerged in Jell-O®, you got some Camembert on the lens, etc.). Whatever the problem, and regardless of whose fault it is, problems happen, and you need to fix them in Photoshop. Some of the fixes are easy, like running the "Remove Camembert" filter, and then changing the Blend Mode to Fromage. Others will have you jumping through some major Photoshop hoops, but fear not, the problems you'll most likely run into are all covered here in a step-by-step format that will have you wiping cold congealed water off your flash unit faster than you can say, "How can Scott possibly be in his mid-twenties?"

Compensating for "Too Much Flash"

Don't ya hate it when you open a photo and realize that either (a) the flash fired when it shouldn't have; (b) you were too close to the subject to use the flash and they're totally "blown out"; or (c) you're simply not qualified to use a flash at all, and your flash unit should be forcibly taken from you, even if that means ripping it from the camera body? Here's a quick fix to get your photo back from the "flash graveyard" while keeping your reputation, and camera parts, intact.

Step One:
Open the photo that is suffering from "flashaphobia." In the example shown here, the flash, mounted on the camera body, washed out the entire subject (although the background behind him looks okay).

Step Two:
Make a copy of the photo layer by dragging it to the New Layer icon at the bottom of the Layers palette. Then, change the layer Blend Mode of this duplicate layer from Normal to Multiply (as shown here). This Blend Mode has a "multiplier" effect, and brings back a lot of the original foreground detail the flash "blew out." However, darkening the entire photo made the background (which was properly exposed) a bit too dark.

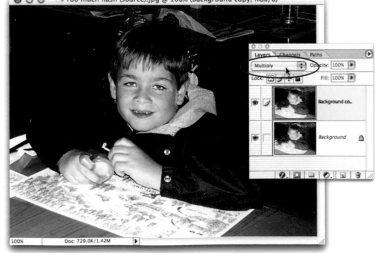

Step Three:
Hold the Option key (PC: Alt key) and click the Layer Mask icon at the bottom of the Layers palette (as shown here). This adds a black Layer Mask, which completely hides the Multiply Blend Mode layer from view (you've masked that layer away, so to speak).

Step Four:
Press the letter "d" to switch your Foreground color to white, choose a soft-edged brush, and start painting over the foreground area in the photo (the subject, the desk, the papers he's resting on, etc.), As you paint, you'll be revealing the darker "Multiply" layer and removing the effect of the flash being too close.

Step Five:
Continue painting over the foreground area, but avoid the background, because the flash wasn't too harsh there. When you're done, the amount of flash is now properly balanced.

NOTE: If you make a mistake and accidentally darken the background, you can switch your Foreground color to black, paint over those areas, and they'll return to how they originally looked. That's the beauty of using a Layer Mask.

Dealing with Digital Noise

If you shoot in low-light situations, you're bound to encounter digital noise. Is there anything worse than these large red, green, and blue dots that appear all over your photo? Okay, besides that "crazy music" those teenagers play, like Limp Bizkit or…well…Limp Bizkit, is there anything worse? This digital noise (often called "blue channel noise," "high ISO noise," "color aliasing," or just "those annoying red, green, and blue dots") can be reduced. Here's how.

Step One:
Open a photo that contains visible digital noise (in this case, it's a shot taken in low light, and those "red, green, and blue" dots appear throughout the photo).

Step Two:
Go under the Image menu, under Mode, and choose Lab Color. Switching to Lab Color is a non-destructive mode change, and won't damage your RGB photo in any way—you can switch back and forth between RGB and Lab Color any time. You won't see any visible difference in your image onscreen, but if you look in the title bar for your document, you see "Lab" in parentheses to let you know you're in Lab Color mode.

Step Three:
When you're in RGB mode, your image is made up of three channels: a Red, a Green, and a Blue channel. When these channels are combined, they create a full-color photo. When you convert to Lab Color, Photoshop composes your photo differently—although it looks the same, it's now made up of a Lightness channel (the luminosity of the photo, where the detail is held) and two color channels, named "a" and "b." Go to the Channels palette and you'll see these channels. Click on the "a" channel

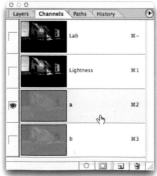

(as shown).

Step Four:

Now that you're affecting only the "a" channel (which consists of color data), go under the Filter menu, under Blur, and choose Gaussian Blur. When the Gaussian Blur dialog appears (shown here), increase the Radius (amount of blur) until you see the dots pretty much disappear, and then click OK. In this case, I increased the Radius to 6.2 pixels.

Step Five:

Now, in the Channels palette, click on the "b" channel (as shown). Press Command-F (PC: Control-F) to apply the Gaussian Blur filter to this "b" channel with the exact same setting we used on the "a" channel. Because you're using the re-apply shortcut, you won't see the Gaussian Blur dialog box—it just automatically applies the filter for you.

Step Six:

Go back under the Image menu, under Mode, and choose RGB to return to RGB mode. You'll notice that the spots are much less pronounced because they no longer appear in red, green, and blue. You blurred the color channels, and by doing so, you eliminated those colors that are distracting to the eye. The effect appears much more muted, and in some cases (depending on the photo), will nearly disappear.

Removing Color Aliasing

Here's another quick trick Jim DiVitale and Kevin Ames use for reducing the color aliasing (digital noise) that often appears in digital photos shot in low-light situations.

Step One:

Open a photo that has visible color aliasing (look at the wall behind the subjects, it's covered with little red, green, and blue dots). Go under the Filter menu, under Blur, and choose Gaussian Blur. Drag the Radius slider all the way to the left, then start dragging to the right until the color aliasing is blurred enough that you can't see it. Click OK to apply the blur.

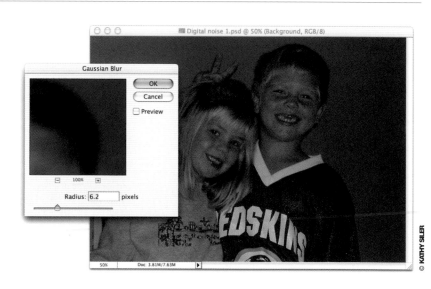

Step Two:

Go under the Edit menu and choose Fade Gaussian Blur. When the Fade dialog appears, change the Fade Mode to Color (as shown) and the color aliasing disappears (look at the wall area now). It's quick, it's easy, and it works. It's also an ideal candidate for becoming an Action, so you can remove color aliasing with just one click.

There's a natural tendency for some photographers to react to their immediate surroundings, rather than what they see through the lens. For example, if you're shooting an indoor concert, there are often hundreds of lights illuminating the stage. However, some photographers think it's one light short—their flash, because where they're sitting, it's dark. When you look at your photos later, you see that your flash lit everyone in front of you (which wasn't the way it really looked—the crowd is usually in the dark), which ruins an otherwise great shot. Here's a quick fix to make it look as if your flash never fired at all.

Fixing Photos Where You Wish You Hadn't Used Your Flash

Step One:
Open a photo where shooting with the flash has ruined part of the image (like the image shown here taken during the PhotoshopWorld opening keynote, where the back ten rows are lit by the flash, when they should be dark. Just the stage lit by the stage lighting should appear out of the darkness).

Step Two:
Press the letter "m" to get the Rectangular Marquee tool, and draw a selection over the area where the flash affected the shot. In the image shown here, the selection encompasses a number of rows in the back of the theater.

Continued

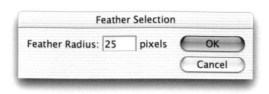

Step Three:

In the next step, we're going to adjust the tonal range of this selected area, but we don't want that adjustment to appear obvious. We'll need to soften the edges of our selection quite a bit so our adjustment blends in smoothly with the rest of the photo. To do this, go under the Select menu and choose Feather. When the Feather Selection dialog appears, enter 25 pixels to soften the selection edge. (By the way, 25 pixels is just my guess for how much this particular selection might need. The rule of thumb is the higher the resolution of the image, the more feathering you'll need, so don't be afraid to use more than 25 if your edge is visible when you finish.)

Step Four:

It will help you make a better adjustment if you hide the selection border (we call it "the marching ants") from view. Note: We don't want to deselect—we want our selection to remain intact but we don't want to see the annoying border, so press Command-H (PC: Control-H) to hide the selection border. Now, press Command-L (PC: Control-L) to bring up the Levels dialog. At the bottom of the dialog, drag the right Output Levels slider to the left to darken your selected area. Because you've hidden the selection border, it should be very easy to match the surroundings of your photo by just dragging this slider to your left.

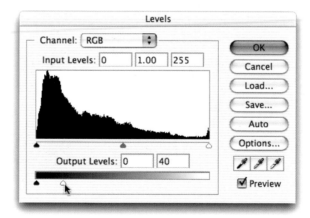

Step Five:

When the photo looks about right, click OK to apply your Levels adjustment. Then, press Command-H (PC: Control-H) to make your selection visible again. (This trips up a lot of people who, since they don't see the selection anymore, forget it's there, and then nothing reacts as it should from that point on.) Last, press Command-D (PC: Control-D) to deselect. The original and "flash-free" photos are shown below.

Before: The flash is obvious and falls quite short of reaching the stage.

After: The effect of the flash is hidden, saving the shot!

Fixing Underexposed Photos

ADVANCED TECHNIQUES
FOR PROS ONLY!

This is a tonal correction for people who don't like making tonal corrections (over 60 million Americans suffer from the paralyzing fear of MTC [Making Tonal Corrections]). Since this technique requires no knowledge of Levels or Curves, it's very popular, and even though it's incredibly simple to perform, it does a pretty incredible job of fixing underexposed photos.

Step One:

Open an underexposed photo. The photo shown here was taken with a point-and-shoot digital camera, inside a 1953 DeHaviland Seaplane without a flash. It could've used either a fill flash or a better exposure setting, and that's why it's so dark.

Step Two:

Press Command-J (PC: Control-J) to duplicate your Background layer (this duplicate will be named Layer 1 by default). On this new layer, change the Blend Mode in the Layers palette from Normal to Screen to lighten the entire photo.

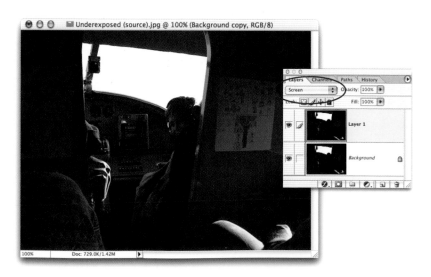

Step Three:
If the photo still isn't properly exposed, just press Command-J (PC: Control-J) and duplicate this Screen layer until the exposure looks about right (this may take a few layers, but don't be shy about it— keep copying layers until it looks right).

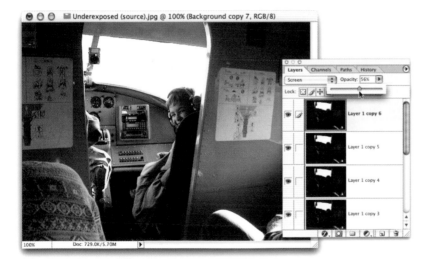

Step Four:
There's a good chance that, at some point ,your photo will still look a bit underexposed, so you'll duplicate the layer again, but now it looks overexposed. What you need is "half a layer." Half as much lightening. Here's what to do: Lower the Opacity of your top layer to "dial in" the perfect amount of light, giving you something between the full intensity of the layer (at 100%) and no layer at all (at 0%). For half the intensity, try 50% (did I really even have to say that last line? Didn't think so). Once the photo looks properly exposed, choose Flatten Image from the Layers palette's pop-down menu.

ADVANCED TECHNIQUES
FOR PROS ONLY!

When You Forget to Use Fill Flash

Wouldn't it be great if Photoshop had a "fill flash" brush, so when you forgot to use your fill flash, you could just paint it in? Well, although it's not technically called the fill flash brush, you can create your own brush and get the same effect. Here's how.

Step One:
Open a photo where the subject or focus of the image appears in shadows. Go under the Image menu, under Adjustments, and choose Levels.

Step Two:
Drag the middle Input Levels slider (the gray one) to the left until your subject looks properly exposed. (Note: Don't worry about how the background looks—it will probably become completely "blown out," but you'll fix that later. For now, just focus on making your subject look right.) If the midtone slider doesn't bring out the subject enough, you may have to increase the highlights as well, so drag the far-right Input Levels slider to the left to increase the highlights. When your subject looks properly exposed, click OK.

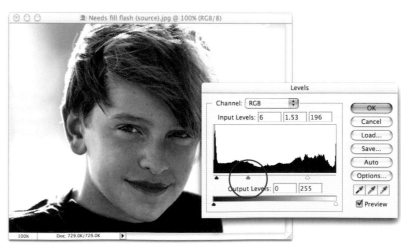

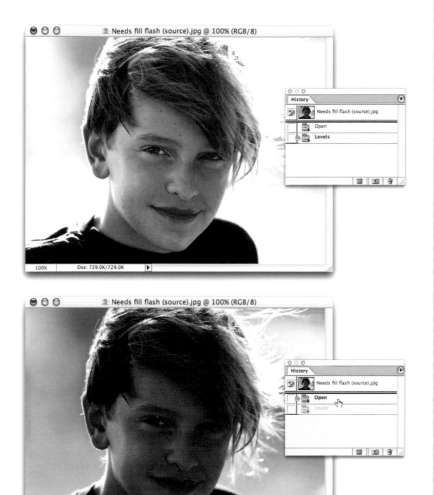

Step Three:

Go under the Window menu and choose History to bring up the History palette. This palette keeps a running "history" of the last 20 adjustments you've made to your photo. In this instance, there should be only two entries (called "History States"). Open should be the first State, followed by Levels, showing that you opened the photo and then made a Levels adjustment.

Step Four:

In the History palette, click on the State named "Open." This returns your photo to how it looked when you originally opened the image (in other words, it looks the way it did before you adjusted the Levels).

Step Five:

In the History palette, click in the first column next to the grayed-out state named "Levels." An icon that looks like Photoshop's History Brush appears in the column, showing that you're going to be painting from what your image looked like after you used Levels.

Continued

Step Six:

Choose the History Brush tool from the Toolbox (as shown here), and choose a soft-edged brush from the Brush Picker in the Options Bar.

Step Seven:

Begin painting with the History Brush over your subject, avoiding the background area entirely. (Here, I'm painting over the left side of the subject's face.) As you paint, you'll notice that you're actually painting in the lightened version of the subject you adjusted earlier with Levels.

Step Eight:

Continue painting with the History Brush until your subject looks as if you used a fill flash. When you're painting, if it appears too intense, just lower the Opacity of the History Brush up in the Options Bar. That way, when you paint, the effect appears less intense. You can see the final repair here, with the background unchanged, but the subject in shadows is "brought out."

Step Nine:
After you finish painting, if it still appears too intense, go to Fade History Brush under the Edit menu. When the Fade dialog box appears, lower the Opacity to decrease the effect. Here, I lowered it to 72%. A before and after is shown.

Before: The backlit subject's face is in the shadows.

After: The face is now lit, and the background stays perfectly exposed.

Opening up Shadow Areas (Digital Fill Flash)

In Photoshop CS, Adobe introduced a slick new way to open up shadow areas (or pull back highlight areas) called—(aptly enough)—Shadow/Highlight. This new lighting correction command can be as simple as moving a slider or you can tweak each little nuance of your photo's shadow and highlight areas by revealing its many options. It's ideal to use in situations where you wish you had used a fill flash (think of it as a highly flexible digital fill flash), and need to bring out detail lost in the shadows, or to reduce your highlights.

Step One:

Open a photo contaning shadow or highlight areas that need adjusting. In this example, the light is coming from the side and slightly behind our subjects, so ideally we'd like to lighten the shadow areas on their faces (in other words, we should have used a fill flash, but hey—that's why they invented Photoshop, right?).

Step Two:

Go under the Image menu, under Adjustments, and choose Shadow/Highlight (as shown here).

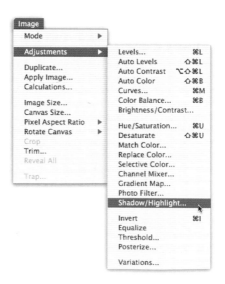

Step Three:

When the Shadow/Highlight dialog appears, by default the shadow areas are lightened by 50% (as shown here). You can increase the amount for additional lightening, or you can decrease the amount if the shadows appear too light. (We're adjusting shadows in this image, but if you were adjusting highlights instead, you'd increase the Highlights Amount to decrease the highlights in the photo.)

Step Four:

When you click OK, your shadow-lighting correction is applied to your photo (as shown here).

Continued

Step Five:

If you want more control than these two sliders offer, click on the Show More Options checkbox at the bottom left-hand corner of the dialog (as shown here). Once you click the check box, you get the "full monty" (as shown in Step Six).

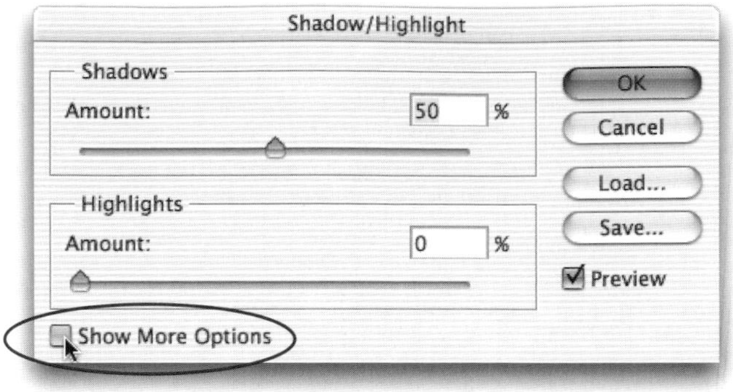

Step Six:

Don't let all these sliders intimidate you because chances are you'll be tweaking either the shadows or the highlights—not both—so you can ignore half the sliders altogether. If you're tweaking shadows, lowering the Tonal Width value lets your correction affect only the darkest shadow areas. Increasing it affects a wider range of shadows. Increase it a bunch, and it starts to affect the midtones as well. It works similarly for the Highlights. The Radius amount determines how many pixels each adjustment affects, so to affect a wider range of pixels, increase the amount. If you increase the shadow detail, the colors may become too saturated. If that's the case, reduce the Color Correction amount (it's basically a color saturation slider that only affects the area you're adjusting). You can also increase or decrease the contrast in the midtones using the Midtone Contrast slider.

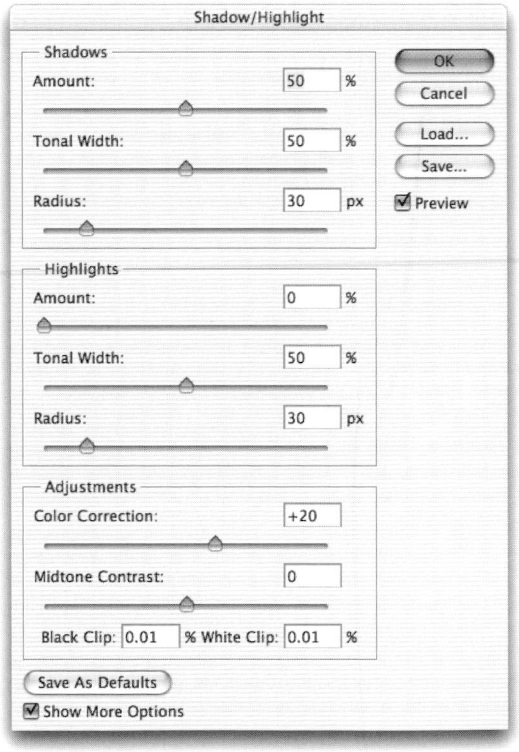

Before opening up the shadows.

After opening up the shadows with Shadow/Highlight.

Instant Red Eye Removal

When I see a digital camera with the flash mounted directly above the lens, I think, "Hey, there's an automated red-eye machine." If you're a pro, you probably don't have to deal with this as much, because your flash probably isn't mounted directly above your lens—you're using bounce flash, holding the flash separately, you've got studio lights, or one of a dozen other techniques. But even when the pros pick up a "point-and-shoot," red eye can find them. Here's the quick "I-just-want-it-gone" technique for getting rid of red eye fast.

Step One:
Open a photo where the subject has red eye. Zoom in on the eyes by dragging a rectangle around them with the Zoom tool (the Magnifying Glass tool).

Step Two:
In Photoshop CS, Adobe has added a tool that makes red-eye removal a no-brainer. It's called the Color Replacement tool. You can find it in the flyout menu of the Healing Brush (as shown here). So switch to the Color Replacement tool and then press the letter "d" to set your Foreground color to black.

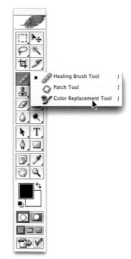

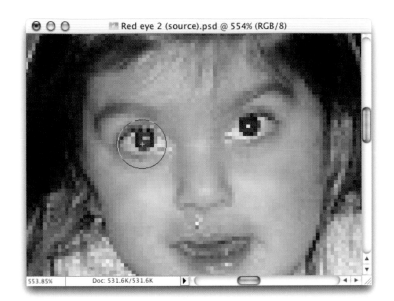

Step Three:

Use the Color Replacement tool and paint directly over the red eye (you can even dab if you'd like). As you paint, the red disappears because the Color Replacement tool's Blend Mode is set to Color in the Options Bar, which desaturates (removes the color from) anywhere you paint.

Step Four:

Paint over all the other eyes in the photo, and you're done—and best of all, the entire process takes just seconds. You almost have to wonder why Adobe didn't call the Color Replacement tool the Red-Eye Removal tool.

Removing Red Eye and Recoloring the Eye

This technique is a little more complicated (not hard; it just has a few more steps), but the result is more professional because you're not just going to remove the red eye (like in the previous "instant red-eye removal" trick) and replace it with the more pleasing "gray eye." Instead, we're going to restore the eye to its original color.

Step One:

Open a photo where the subject has red eye.

Step Two:

Zoom in close on one of the eyes using the Zoom tool (the Magnifying Glass tool). Note: You might not want to do this late at night if you're home alone, because seeing a huge scary eye on your screen can really give you the willies.

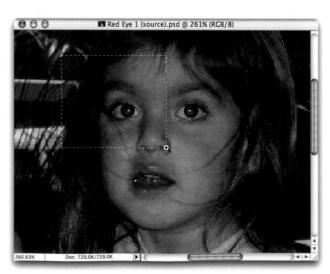

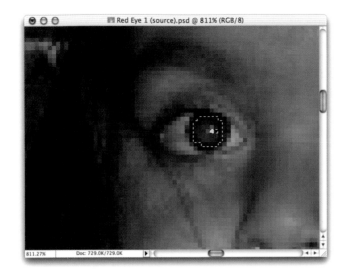

Step Three:

Press the "w" key to switch to the Magic Wand tool, and click within the red area of one of the eyes. One click may select all the red in the eye, but if it doesn't, hold the Shift key and click the Magic Wand again in an area of red that wasn't selected (holding the Shift key lets you add to your current selection). If the Magic Wand selects too much, go up to the Options Bar, lower the Threshold number, and try again. After one eye's red area is selected, scroll over to the other eye, hold the Shift key, and select it the same way so that both red-eye areas are selected.

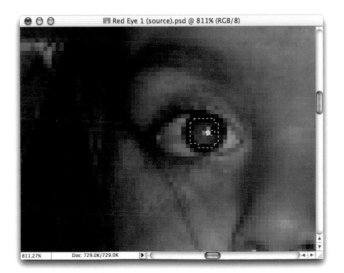

Step Four:

Now, press Shift-Command-U (PC: Shift-Control-U) to desaturate all the color from these selected red areas, leaving the eyes looking pretty gray. It's better than red, but you might want to touch it up a bit, and make it a bit darker, which we'll do in the next step.

Continued

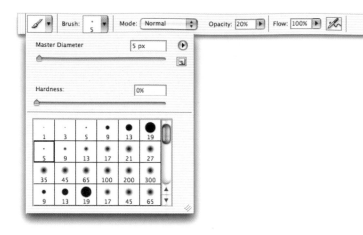

Step Five:

Press the "d" key to set your Foreground color to black. Get the Brush tool and choose a small, soft-edged brush; then, up in the Options Bar, lower the Opacity setting to 20% (and make sure that the Mode is set to Normal).

Step Six:

Zoom out a bit by pressing Command-– (the minus sign) (PC: Control-–) until you can see both eyes onscreen. Paint just a couple of quick strokes over the selected areas of the eye to darken them, but stop before they turn completely black—you just want a good dark gray. You don't have to worry about painting into other areas of the eye, because your selection should still be in place while you're painting.

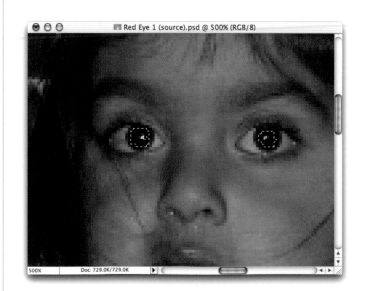

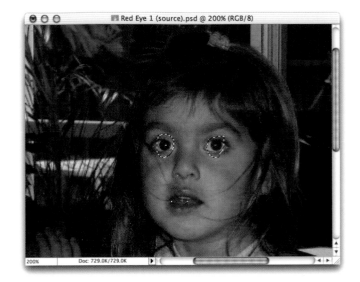

Step Seven:

Once the eyes look dark gray, you can deselect by pressing Command-D (PC: Control-D). Press the "L" key to switch to the Lasso tool, and draw a loose selection around the entire iris of the left eye (as shown). The keyword here is loose—stay well outside the iris itself, and don't try to make a precise selection. Selecting the eyelids, eyelashes, etc. will not create a problem. Hold the Shift key and select the right eye in the same fashion.

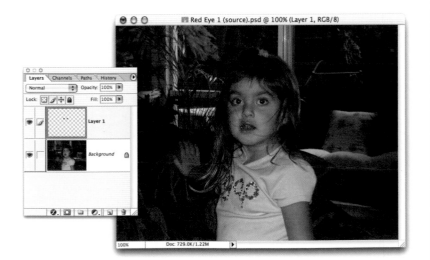

Step Eight:

After you have a loose selection around both irises, press Command-J (PC: Control-J) to put a copy of the eyes up on their own layer above the Background, as Layer 1.

Continued

Step Nine:

While you're on this "eyes" layer, go under the Image menu, under Adjustments, and choose Hue/ Saturation. In the dialog, click on the Colorize check box (in the bottom-right corner). Now you can choose the color you'd like for the eye by moving the Hue slider. In this case, we're going to colorize the iris blue. Don't worry about the color being too intense at this point—we can totally control that later—so if you want blue eyes, choose a deep blue and we'll dial in the exact blue later. Click OK to apply the blue to the irises and the area around them as well. (Don't let it freak you out that other areas right around the iris appear blue. We'll fix that in the next step.)

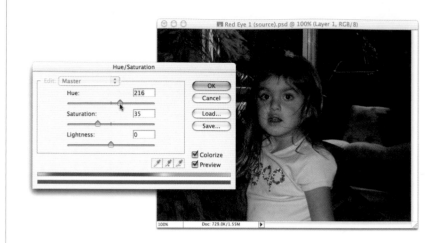

Step Ten:

Press the "e" key to switch to the Eraser tool, make sure that in the Options bar, the Mode is set to Brush, choose a hard-edged brush, and then erase the extra areas around the iris from your loose selection. This sounds much harder than it is—it's actually very easy—just erase everything but the blue iris. Don't forget to erase over the whites of the person's eyes. Remember, the eyes are on their own layer, so you can't accidentally damage any other parts of the photo.

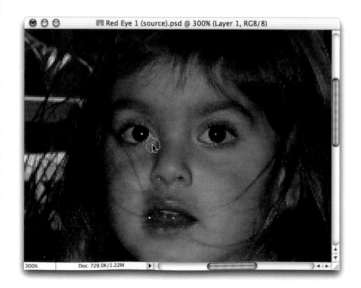

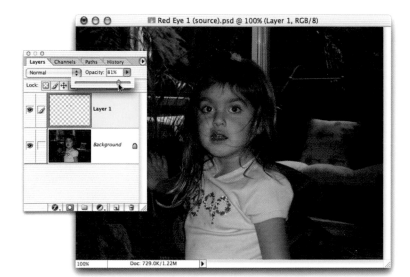

Step Eleven:
If the eye color seems too intense (and chances are, it does), we can lower the intensity in the Layers palette by simply lowering the Opacity slider until the eyes look natural.

Step Twelve:
To finish the red-eye correction and recolor, press Command-E (PC: Control-E) to merge the colored eye layer with the Background layer, completing the repair.

Dodging and Burning Done Right

If you've ever used Photoshop's Dodge and Burn tools, you already know how lame they are. That's why the pros choose this method instead—it gives them a level of control that the Dodge and Burn tools just don't offer, and best of all, it doesn't "bruise the pixels." (That's Photoshop-speak for "it doesn't mess up your original image data while you're editing.")

Step One:

In this tutorial, we're going to dodge areas of this temple to add some highlights, and then we're going to burn in the water and sky a bit to darken some of those areas. Start by opening the photo you want to dodge and burn.

Step Two:

Go to the Layers palette, and from the pop-down menu, choose New Layer. The reason you need to do this (rather than just clicking on the Create New Layer icon) is that you need to access the New Layer dialog box for this technique to work, and you don't get the dialog when you use the Create New Layer icon. If you're a pop-down menu hater or shortcut freak (you know who you are), you can Option-click (PC: Alt-click) the Create New Layer icon instead to bring up the dialog.

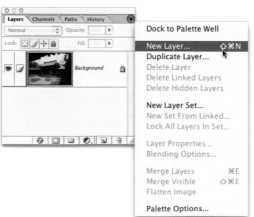

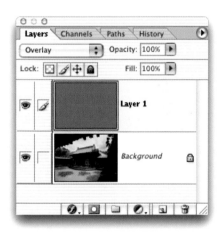

Step Three:
In the New Layer dialog, change the Mode to Overlay; then, right below it, choose "Fill with Overlay-neutral color (50% gray)." This is normally grayed out, but when you switch to Overlay mode, this choice becomes available. Click the check box to make it active, and then click OK.

Step Four:
This creates a new layer, filled with 50% gray, above your Background layer. (When you fill a layer with 50% gray and change the Mode to Overlay, Photoshop ignores the color. You'll see a gray thumbnail in the Layers palette, but the layer appears transparent in your image window.)

Step Five:
Switch to the Brush tool, choose a large soft-edged brush, and then go up to the Options bar and lower the Opacity to approximately 30%.

Continued

Step Six:

Press "d" to set your Foreground color to black. Begin painting over the areas that you want to darken (burn). As you paint, in the Layers palette, you'll see black strokes appear in the thumbnail of your gray transparent layer, and in the image window, you'll see soft darkening (in the example shown here, paint over the water to make it richer).

Step Seven:

If your first stab at burning isn't as intense as you'd like, just release the mouse button, click again, and paint over the same area. Because you're dodging at a low Opacity, the shadows will "build up" as you paint over previous strokes. If the shadows appear too intense, just go to the Layers palette and lower the Opacity setting until they blend in.

Step Eight:

If there are areas you want to lighten (dodge), just press "x" to switch your Foreground color to white and begin painting in the areas that need lightening. In this example, you'll lighten the dark areas inside the temple to bring out some of the detail. You can also lighten any of the red poles, and the area directly above the poles, and even the roof if you like. Okay, ready for another dodging and burning method? Good, 'cause I've got a great one.

Step Nine:

This really isn't Step Nine; it's another way of dodging and burning that I learned from Jim DiVitale, and I have to admit—I'm starting to really dig it. You still do the dodging and burning on a separate layer (no bruising pixels), but you don't have to go through all the New Layer dialog hoops. Just click the New Layer icon, and then change the mode in the Layers palette to Soft Light (as shown at left).

Step Ten:

This is really Step Two of Jim's technique. Now, just set white as your Foreground color, and you can dodge right on this layer using the Brush tool set to 30% Opacity. To burn, just as before—switch to black. The dodging and burning using this Soft Light layer does appear a bit softer and milder than the previous technique, and you should definitely try both to see which one you prefer.

Before Photoshop's magic touches.

After (with the water and sky burned, and the temple dodged).

Repairing Keystoning Without the Crop Tool

Keystoning is often found in photos with buildings or tall objects, where the buildings look as if they're falling away from the viewer (giving the impression that the tops of these buildings are narrower than their bases). The Crop tool has a Perspective function that can fix these distortions, but actually I'm going to recommend that you don't use it, because it doesn't offer a preview of any kind—you're just guessing, so use this technique instead.

Step One:

Open an image that has a keystoning problem (such as the photo shown here, taken with a wide-angle lens, where the building seems to be leaning away from the viewer).

Step Two:

Grab the bottom-right corner of your image window and drag outward to reveal the gray canvas background. Press Command-A (PC: Control-A) to Select All and then press Command-T (PC: Control-T) to bring up the Free Transform function. Grab the center point of the bounding box and drag it straight downward until it touches the bottom-center Free Transform point (as shown here at the cursor location near the bottom of the photo).

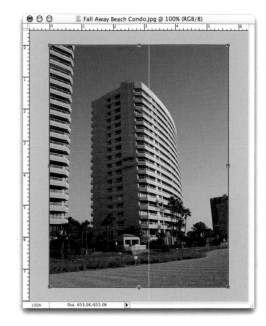

Step Three:

Press Command-R (PC: Control-R) to make Photoshop's rulers visible. Click-and-drag a guide out from the left ruler into your photo (we'll use this straight guide to help us line up our building). In the example shown at left, I lined up the guide with the edge of the bottom balcony on the front (beach side) of the building. Once you add this guide, you can really see how far back the building was leaning, and why a keystoning repair is so necessary.

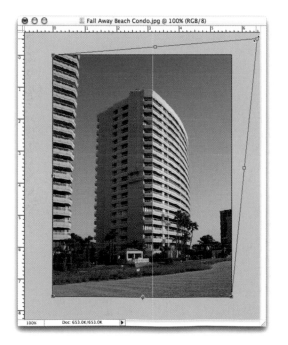

Step Four:

Once your guide is in place, hold the Command key (PC: Control key) and adjust the top-left and right-corner points of the bounding box until the corners of the balconies align with your guide. Making this correction can sometimes make your building look a bit "smushed" and "squatty" (my official technical terms), so you can release the Command/Control key, grab the top-center point, and drag upward to stretch the photo back out and fix the "squattyness" (again, technically speaking).

Continued

Step Five:

When the photo looks right, press Return (PC: Enter) to lock in your transformation. (Note: By repairing this problem with Free Transform, you got to see an onscreen preview of what you were doing, which the Crop tool's Perspective feature doesn't offer.) Now you can drag your guide back to the rulers, and hide the rulers again by pressing Command-R (PC: Control-R). There's still one more thing you'll probably have to do to complete this repair job.

Step Six:

If, after making this adjustment, the building looks "round" and "bloated," you can repair that problem by going under the Filter menu, under Distort, and choosing Pinch. Drag the Amount slider to 0%, and then slowly drag it to the right (increasing the amount of Pinch), while looking at the preview in the filter dialog, until you see the roundness and bloating go away. (In the example shown here, I used 5% for my Amount setting.) When it looks right, click OK to complete your keystoning repair. A before and after are shown on the following page.

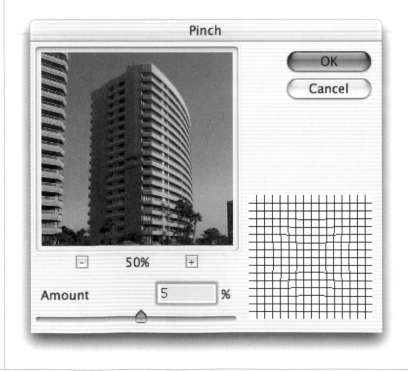

In the original photo, the building appears to be "falling away."

The same photo after repairing the perspective distortion (known as keystoning).

Photographer | David Moser

The subtitle for this chapter is "Color Correction for Photographers," which invites the question "How is color correction for photographers different from color correction for anybody else?" Actually, it's

Color Me Badd
color correction for photographers

quite a bit different, because photographers generally work in RGB or black-and-white. And in reality, digital photographers mostly work in RGB because, although we can manage to build reusable spacecrafts and have GPS satellites orbiting in space so golfers here on earth know how far it is from their golf cart to the green, for some reason creating a color inkjet printer that prints a decent black-and-white print is still apparently beyond our grasp. Don't get me started. Anyway, this chapter isn't about black-and-white, and now that I think about it, I'm sorry I brought it up in the first place. So forget I ever mentioned it, and let's talk about color correction. Why do we even need color correction? Honestly, it's a technology thing. Even with traditional film cameras, every photo needs some sort of color tweaking (either during processing or afterward in Photoshop) because if it didn't need some correction, we'd have about 30-something pages in this book that would be blank, and that would make my publisher pretty hopping mad (and if you haven't seen him hop, let me tell you, it's not pretty). So, for the sake of sheer page count, let's all be glad that we don't live in a perfect world where every photo comes out perfect and 6-megapixel cameras are only 200 bucks and come with free 1-GB memory cards.

Before You Color Correct Anything, Do This First!

Before we correct even a single photo, there are two quick little preferences we need to change in Photoshop to give us better, more accurate corrections. Although it's just two simple changes, don't underestimate their impact—this is critically important stuff.

Step One:

The first thing you need to change is the RGB color space. Photoshop's default color space (sRGB IEC61966-2.1) is arguably the worst possible color space for professional photographers. This color space is designed for use by Web designers, and it mimics an "el cheapo" PC monitor from four or five years ago. Honestly, I wouldn't even recommend this space for Web designers today, and it's fairly ghastly for photographers, especially if their photos will wind up in print (brochures, ads, flyers, catalogs, etc.).

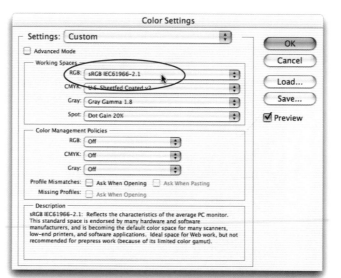

Step Two:

Press Shift-Command-K (PC: Shift-Control-K) to bring up the Color Settings dialog (shown in Step One, with sRGB IEC61966-2.1 as the default RGB Working Space). In the Working Spaces section, from the RGB pop-up menu, choose Adobe RGB (1998) as shown at right. This is probably the most popular RGB setting for photographers because it reproduces such a wide gamut of colors, and it's ideal if your photos will wind up in print. Click OK and this is your new default color work space. Yippee!

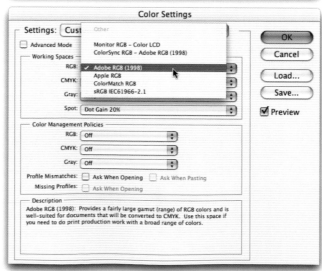

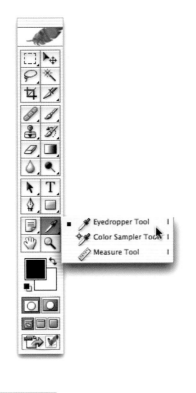

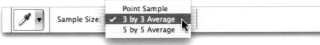

Step Three:

Now we're moving to a completely different area. In the Toolbox, click on the Eyedropper Tool. You'll be using the Eyedropper to read color values from your photo. The default Sample Size setting for this tool (Point Sample) is fine for using the Eyedropper to steal a color from within a photo and then making it your Foreground color. However, Point Sample doesn't work well when you're trying to read values in a particular area (like flesh tones), because it gives you the reading from just one individual pixel, rather than a reading of the area under your cursor.

Step Four:

For example, flesh tone is actually composed of dozens of different colored pixels (just zoom way in and you'll see what I mean). If you're color correcting, you want a reading that is representative of the area under your Eyedropper, not just one of the pixels within that area, which could hurt your correction decision-making. That's why you'll go up in the Options Bar, under Sample Size, and choose 3 by 3 Average from the pop-up menu. This changes the Eyedropper to give you a 3-by-3-pixel average of the area you're reading. Once you complete the changes on these two pages, it's safe to go ahead with the rest of this chapter and start correcting your photos.

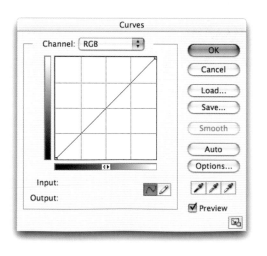

Color Correcting Digital-Camera Images

As far as digital technology has come, there's still one thing that digital cameras won't do: give you perfect color every time. In fact, if they gave us perfect color 50% of the time, that would be incredible; but unfortunately, every digital camera (and every scanner that captures traditional photos) sneaks in some kind of color cast in your image. Generally, it's a red cast, but depending on the camera, it could be blue. Either way, you can be pretty sure that there's a cast. (Figure it this way: If there wasn't, the term "color correction" wouldn't be used.) Here's how to get your color in line.

Step One:

Open the digital-camera photo you want to color correct. (The photo shown here doesn't look too bad, but as we go through the correction process, you'll see that, like most photos, it really needed a correction.)

Step Two:

Go under the Image menu, under Adjustments, and choose Curves. Curves is the hands-down choice of professionals for correcting color because it gives you a greater level of control than other tools, such as Levels (which we use for correcting black-and-white photos). The dialog may look intimidating at first, but the technique you're going to learn here requires no previous knowledge of Curves, and it's so easy, you'll be correcting photos using Curves immediately.

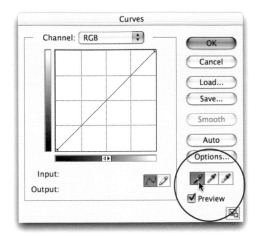

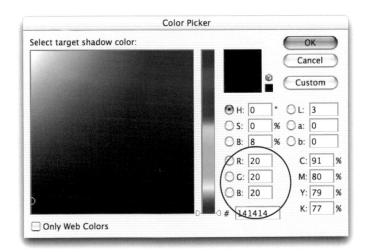

Step Three:

First, we need to set some preferences in the Curves dialog so we'll get the results we're after when we start correcting. We'll start by setting a target color for our shadow areas. To set this preference, in the Curves dialog, double-click on the black Eyedropper tool (it's on the lower right-hand side of the dialog, the first Eyedropper from the left). A Color Picker appears asking you to "Select Target Shadow Color." This is where we'll enter values that, when applied, help remove any color casts your camera introduced in the shadow areas of your photo.

Step Four:

We're going to enter values in the R, G, and B (red, green, and blue) fields of this dialog (the blue field is highlighted here):

For "R," enter 20.
For "G," enter 20.
For "B," enter 20.

Click OK. Because these figures are evenly balanced (neutral), they help ensure that your shadow area won't have too much of one color (which is exactly what causes a color cast—too much of one color). Additionally, using the numbers we're giving you in this chapter help your photos maintain enough shadow and highlight detail if you decide to output them on a printing press (for a brochure, magazine cover, print ad, etc.).

Continued

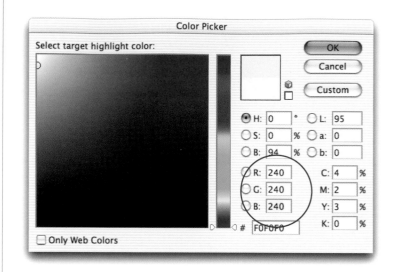

Step Five:

Now, we'll set a preference to make our highlight areas neutral. Double-click on the highlight Eyedropper (the third of the three Eyedroppers in the Curves dialog). The Color Picker appears asking you to "Select Target Highlight Color." Click in the "R" field, and then enter these values:

For "R," enter 240.
For "G," enter 240.
For "B," enter 240.

TIP: To move from field to field, just press the Tab key.

Then, click OK to set those values as your highlight target.

Step Six:

Now, set your midtone preference. You know the drill: Double-click on the midtone Eyedropper (the middle of the three Eyedroppers) so you can "Select the Target Midtone Color." Enter these values in the RGB fields:

For "R," enter 128.
For "G," enter 128.
For "B," enter 128.

Then, click OK to set those values as your midtone target.

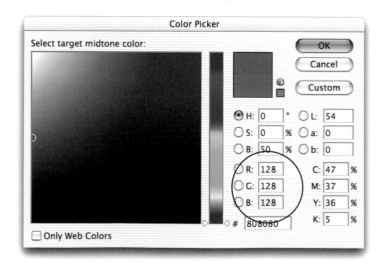

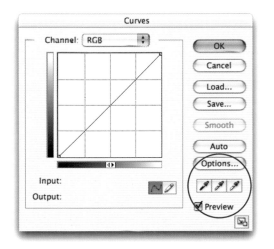

Step Seven:

Okay, you've entered your preferences (target colors) in the Curves dialog. After you make your adjustments and finally click OK in the Curves dialog (don't do this yet), you'll get an alert dialog asking you if you want to "Save the new target colors as defaults." Click Yes, and from that point on, you won't have to enter these values each time you correct a photo, because they'll already be entered for you—they're now the default settings.

Step Eight:

Now that we've entered all these values, you're going to use these Eyedropper tools that reside in the Curves dialog to do most of your correction work. Your job is to determine where the shadow, midtone, and highlight areas are, and click the correct Eyedropper in the right place (you'll learn how to do that in just a moment). So remember, your job: Find the shadow, midtone, and highlight areas, and click the correct Eyedropper in the right spot. Sounds easy, right? It is.

You start by setting the shadows first, so you'll need to find an area in your photo that's supposed to be black. If you can't find something that's supposed to be the color black, it gets a bit trickier—in the absence of something black, you have to determine which area in the image is the darkest. If you're not sure where the darkest part of the photo is, you can use the following trick to have Photoshop tell you exactly where it is.

Continued

Step Nine:

If you still have the Curves dialog open, click OK to exit it for now. Go to the Layers palette and click on the half white/half black circle icon to bring up the Adjustment Layer pop-up menu (it's the fourth icon from the left at the bottom of the palette). Choose Threshold from this pop-up menu (as shown).

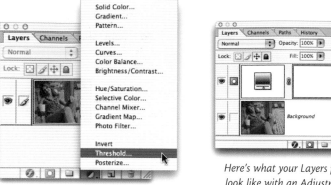

Here's what your Layers palette will look like with an Adjustment layer.

Step Ten:

When the Threshold dialog appears, drag the Threshold Level slider under the histogram all the way to the left. Your photo turns completely white. Slowly drag the Threshold slider back to the right, and as you do, you'll start to see some of your photo reappear. The first area that appears is the darkest part of your image. That's it—that's Photoshop telling you exactly where the darkest part of the image is. Click OK to close the Threshold dialog. This adds a special layer to your Layers palette (shown in Step Nine on the far right).

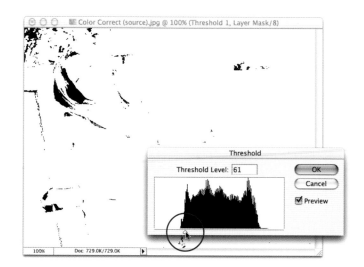

Step Eleven:

Now that you know where your shadow area is, you can mark it. Click-and-hold on the Eyedropper tool in the Toolbox, and from the flyout menu that appears, choose the Color Sampler Tool (as shown). Click this Color Sampler once on the area that is darkest; a target cursor appears, marking that spot. When you do this, the Info palette automatically appears onscreen. You don't need this palette right now, so you can close it. Now to find a white area in your image.

Step Twelve:

You can use the same Threshold technique to find the highlight areas. Go to the Layers palette and double-click on the Threshold Adjustment Layer to bring up the Threshold dialog, but this time, drag the slider all the way to the right. Slowly drag the Threshold slider back toward the left, and as you do, the first area that appears in white is the lightest part of your image. Click OK, then take the Color Sampler tool and click once on the brightest area to mark it as your highlight point.

Step Thirteen:

You're now done with your Threshold Adjustment layer, so you can go to the Layers palette and drag that layer onto the Trash icon to delete it. When you do this, your photo will look normal again, but now there are two target markers visible on your photo, one in her hair and one on the coffee cup (as shown here). Next, press Command-M (PC: Control-M) to bring up the Curves dialog.

Step Fourteen:

First, select the shadow Eyedropper (the one half filled with black) from the bottom right of the Curves dialog. Move your cursor outside the Curves dialog into your photo and click once directly on the center of the #1 target (as shown here). When you click on the #1 target, the shadow areas will be corrected. (Basically, you just reassigned the shadow areas to your new neutral shadow color.) If you click on the #1 target and your photo

Continued

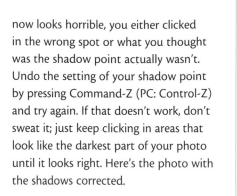

now looks horrible, you either clicked in the wrong spot or what you thought was the shadow point actually wasn't. Undo the setting of your shadow point by pressing Command-Z (PC: Control-Z) and try again. If that doesn't work, don't sweat it; just keep clicking in areas that look like the darkest part of your photo until it looks right. Here's the photo with the shadows corrected.

Step Fifteen:

While still in the Curves dialog, switch to the highlight Eyedropper (the one filled with white). Move your cursor over your photo and click once directly on the center of the #2 target to assign that as your highlight (you'll be clicking right on the coffee cup, as shown). This corrects the highlight colors.

Step Sixteen:

Now that the shadows and highlights are set, you need to correct the midtones in the photo. Click the midtone Eyedropper (the middle of the three, half filled with gray) in an area within the photo that looks medium gray (in the photo shown here, you'll click the midtone Eyedropper in the faded wood table above her left shoulder, as shown). Doing this corrects the midtones, and depending on the photo, this can either be a subtle or dramatic difference, but you'll never know until you try. Unfortunately, not every image contains an area that is gray, so you won't always be able to correct the midtones.

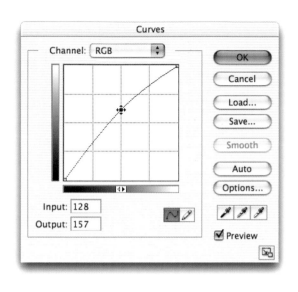

Step Seventeen:

There's one more important adjustment to make before you click OK in the Curves dialog and apply your correction. In the Curves grid, click on the center of the curve and drag it upward a bit to brighten the midtones of the image (as shown at left). This is a visual adjustment, so it's up to you to determine how much to adjust, but it should be subtle—just enough to brighten the midtones a bit and bring out the midtone detail. When it looks right to you, click OK to apply your correction to the highlights, midtones, and shadows, removing any color casts and brightening the overall contrast.

Step Eighteen:

You can now remove the two Color Sampler targets on your photo by going up to the Options bar and clicking the Clear button (as shown). The final before/after photo is shown here.

Before color correction.

After color correction.

Continued

CMYK correction settings

The values I gave you at the beginning of this correction technique were for photos that would be reproduced in RGB mode (i.e., your final output would be to a photo-quality color inkjet printer, a color laser printer, a dye-sub printer, etc.). However, if you're color correcting your photos for final output to a printing press (for a brochure, catalog, print ad, magazine, etc.), you need to use an entirely different set of values for your highlights, midtones, and shadows. Also, these numbers are entered into the CMYK fields, rather than the RGB fields. At right are a set of values that are very common for prepress correction, because they enable significant details to be reproduced on press.

TIP: In Photoshop CS, Adobe added scrubby sliders. I know what you're thinking: "What the heck are 'scrubby sliders'?" If you've ever used Adobe After Effects (and who hasn't), then you know that scrubby sliders can change the values in a numeric entry field without having to type any numbers. Placed over a field's label, the cursor changes into a hand with arrows pointing to either side. All you have to do is click-and-drag to change the field's value. Dragging to the left decreases the current value and dragging to the right increases it. Hold down the Shift key and the numbers will change in larger increments. Try it when you're entering the CMYK values mentioned above and you'll see what I mean. Don't stop there. It works in just about every dialog or palette where there's a numeric field.

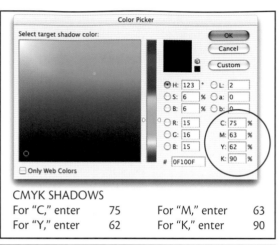

CMYK SHADOWS

For "C," enter	75	For "M," enter	63
For "Y," enter	62	For "K," enter	90

CMYK MIDTONES

For "C," enter	50	For "M," enter	40
For "Y," enter	40	For "K," enter	10

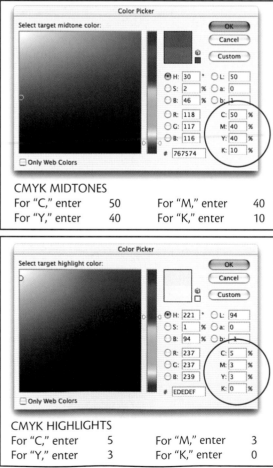

CMYK HIGHLIGHTS

For "C," enter	5	For "M," enter	3
For "Y," enter	3	For "K," enter	0

This is a wonderful timesaving trick for quickly correcting an entire group of photos that have similar lighting. It's ideal for studio shots, where the lighting conditions are controlled, but works equally well for outdoor shots, or really any situation where the lighting for your group of shots is fairly consistent. Once you try this, you'll use it again and again and again.

Drag-and-Drop Instant Color Correction

FOR PROS ONLY! *ADVANCED TECHNIQUES*

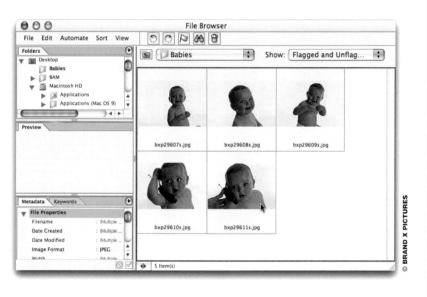

© BRAND X PICTURES

Step One:
First, here's a tip within a tip: If you're opening a group of photos in the File Browser, you don't have to open them one by one. Just hold the Command key (PC: Control key) and click on all the photos you want to open. (If all your photos are consecutive, hold the Shift key and click on the first and last photo in the list to select them all, as shown here.) Then, double-click on any of your selected photos and Photoshop opens all the selected ones. So now that you know that tip, go ahead and open at least four or five images, just to get you started.

Step Two:
At the bottom of the Layers palette, there's a pop-up menu for adding Adjustment layers. Click on it and choose Curves. There are a number of advantages of having this correction applied as a layer, as you'll soon see, but the main advantage is that you can edit or delete this tonal adjustment at any time while you're working, plus you can save this adjustment with your file as a layer.

Continued

Step Three:

When you choose this Adjustment layer, the regular Curves dialog appears, just like always. Go ahead and make your corrections, just as you did in the previous tutorial (setting highlights, midtones, shadows, etc.), and when your correction looks good, click OK.

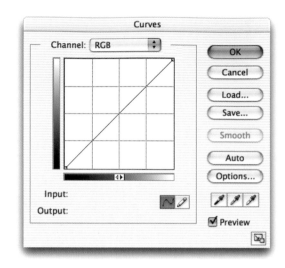

Step Four:

In the Layers palette, you'll see that a new Adjustment layer was created, and if you expand the width of your Layers palette (click-and-drag on the very bottom-right corner of the palette), you can actually read the word "Curves," as shown at right.

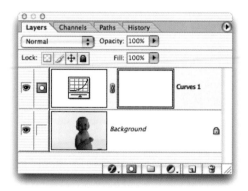

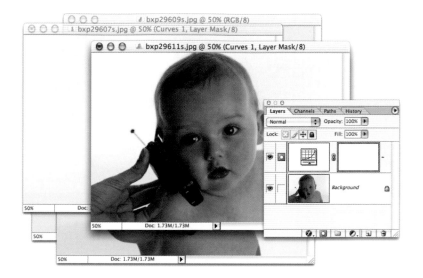

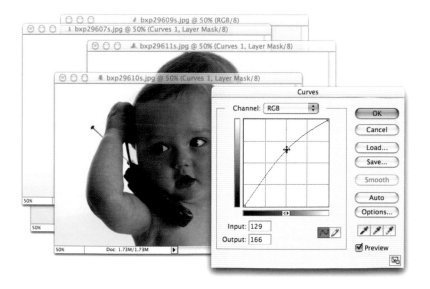

Step Five:

Because you applied this correction as an Adjustment layer, you can treat this adjustment just like a regular layer, right? Right! Now, Photoshop lets you drag layers between open documents, right? So, go to the Layers palette and simply drag this layer right onto one of your other open photos, and that photo will instantly have the same correction applied to it. This technique works because you're correcting photos that share similar lighting conditions. Need to correct 12 photos? Just drag and drop it 12 times (making it the fastest correction in town!). In the example shown here, I've dragged and dropped that Curves Adjustment layer onto one of the other open photos.

Step Six:

Okay, what if one of the "dragged corrections" doesn't look right? That's the beauty of these Adjustment layers. Just double-click directly on the Adjustment Layer icon for that photo and the Curves dialog reappears with the last settings you applied still in place. You can then adjust this individual photo separately from the rest. Try this "dragging-and-dropping-Adjustment-layers" trick once and you'll use it again and again to save time when correcting a digital roll with similar lighting conditions.

Studio Portrait Correction Made Simple

If you're shooting in a studio, whether you're shooting portraits or products, you can use a technique that makes the color correction process so easy that you'll be able to train laboratory test rats to correct photos for you. In the back of this book, I included a solid black/gray/white card (it's perforated so you can easily tear it out). After you get your studio lighting set the way you want it, and you're ready to start shooting, just put this black/gray/white card into your shot (just once) and take the shot. What does this do for you? You'll see.

Step One:

When you're ready to start shooting and the lighting is set the way you want it, tear out the black/gray/white card from the back of this book and place it within your shot (if you're shooting a portrait, have the subject hold the card for you), and then take the shot. After you've got one shot with the black/gray/white card, you can remove it and continue with the rest of your shoot.

Step Two:

When you open the first photo taken in your studio session, you'll see the black/gray/white card in the photo. By having a card that's pure white, neutral gray, and pure black in your photo, you no longer have to try to determine which area of your photo is supposed to be black (to set the shadows), which area is supposed to be gray (to set the midtones), or which area is supposed to be white (to set the highlights). They're right there in the card.

© BRAND X PICTURES

Step Three:

Press Command-M (PC: Control-M) to bring up the Curves dialog. Click the shadow Eyedropper on the black panel of the card (to set shadows), the middle Eyedropper on the gray (for midtones), and the highlight Eyedropper on the white panel (sets the highlights), and the photo nearly corrects itself. No guessing, no Threshold Adjustment layers, no using the Info palette to determine the darkest areas of the image, because now you know exactly which part of that image should be black and which should be white.

Step Four:

Now that you have the Curve setting for the first image, you can correct the rest of the photos using the exact same curve: Just open the next photo and press Option-Command-M (PC: Alt-Control-M) to apply the exact same curve to this photo that you did to the black/gray/white card photo. Or, you can use the drag-and-drop color correction method I showed on page 127.

If you want to take this process a step further, many professionals use a Macbeth color-swatch chart (from GretagMacbeth; www.gretagmacbeth .com), which also contains midtone shades of gray and a host of other target colors. It's used exactly the same way: Just put the chart into your photo, take one shot, and then when you correct the photo, a solid black, solid white, and midtone gray swatch will be in the photo, just begging to be clicked on.

Correcting Flesh Tones for Photos Going to Press

If the photos you're correcting are destined for a printing press, rather than just a color printer (i.e., they'll appear in a brochure, print ad, catalog, flyer, etc.), you have to compensate for how the inks react with one another on a printing press. Without compensating, you can almost guarantee that all the people in your photos will look slightly sunburned. Here's a technique that lets you correct flesh tone "by the numbers" to get perfect skin tones every time.

Step One:

When it comes to getting proper flesh tones on press, you're going to be concerned mainly with the relationship between the magenta and the yellow in the flesh tone areas. Your goal is to have at least 3% to 5% more yellow in your flesh tone area than magenta. The amount of yellow and magenta can be displayed in the Info palette, so start by going under the Window menu and choosing Info to bring up the Info palette (shown here). Then, convert your image to CMYK mode by going under the Image menu, under Mode, and choosing CMYK Color.

Step Two:

First, you need to see what the current balance of yellow to magenta is, so press Command-M (PC: Control-M) to open Curves. Next, move your cursor outside the Curves dialog and into your photo over an area that contains flesh tones (we'll call this our sample area). While your cursor is there, look in your Info palette at the relationship of the magenta and the yellow.

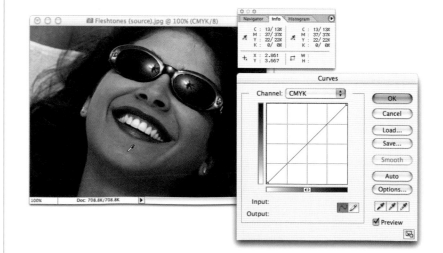

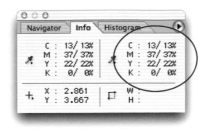

Step Three:

In the Info palette, look at the CMYK readout (on the right side of the palette). If the magenta reading is higher than the yellow reading (as shown here), you have to adjust the balance of the magenta and the yellow. In the example shown here, the magenta reads 37% and the yellow is only 22%, so there's 15% more magenta, and that means instant sunburn; you have to adjust this balance to get perfect flesh tones.

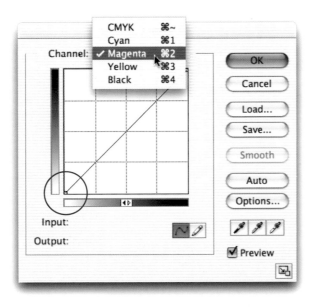

Step Four:

You might be tempted to just lower the amount of magenta, but to keep our adjustment from appearing too drastic, we'll do a balanced adjustment: Lower the magenta some, and then increase the yellow enough until we hit our goal of 3% to 5% more yellow. First, start by lowering the amount of magenta. In the Curves dialog, choose Magenta from the Channel pop-up menu (as shown here). To find out exactly where the magenta in your flesh-tone area resides on the Curve, hold Shift-Command (PC: Shift-Control) and click once in the sample flesh tone area. This adds a point to the magenta channel Curve right where the magenta in the flesh tone is located. (And because you added the Shift key, it also added a point to your yellow Curve, which you'll see in a moment.)

Continued

Step Five:

In the Output field at the bottom of the Curves dialog, type in an amount that's 7% or 8% lower than the value shown. (Remember, the magenta reading was 15% more than the yellow, so you're going to reduce that difference by half.)

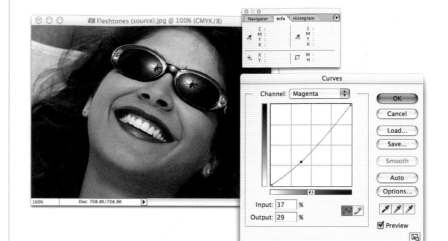

Step Six:

After you lower the magenta, switch to the Yellow channel by choosing it from the Channel pop-up menu at the top of the Curves dialog. You should already see a point on the Curve. This is where the yellow resides in the sample flesh-tone area that you clicked on in Step Four. In the Output field at the bottom of the Curves dialog, type in a figure that's at least 3% higher than the number that you typed in the Output field for the magenta Curve in Step Five. (The Info palette provides a before/after reading, with the before on the left, and the reading after your adjustment on the right, so you can check your numbers in your sample area after you adjust the Curve.) In our example, I lowered the magenta from 37% to 29%, and raised the yellow from 22% to 32%. This gives at least 3% more yellow than magenta in the flesh tones.

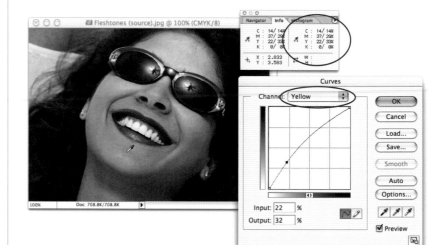

Before sending your corrected image to press, it will look a little yellow on screen.

After it is printed, the flesh tones will look correct.

Adjusting RGB Flesh Tones

So what do you do if you've used Curves to properly set the highlights, midtones, and shadows, but the flesh tones in your photo still look too red? You can't use the "getting-proper-flesh-tones-for-a-printing-press" trick, because that's only for CMYK images going to press. Instead, try this quick trick for getting your flesh tones in line by removing the excess red.

Step One:

Open a photo that you've corrected using the Curves technique shown earlier. If the whole image appears too red, skip this step and go on to Step Three. However, if it's just the flesh-tone areas that appear too red, get the Lasso tool and make a selection around all the flesh- tone areas in your photo. (Hold the Shift key to add other flesh-tone areas to the selection, such as arms, hands, legs, etc.)

Step Two:

Go under the Select menu and choose Feather. Enter a Feather Radius of 3 pixels, and then click OK. By adding this feather, you soften the edges of your selection; this keeps you from having a hard visible edge show up where you made your adjustment.

TIP: Once you make a selection of the flesh- tone areas, you might find it easier if you hide the selection border from view (that makes it easier to see what you're correcting) by pressing Command-H (PC: Control-H).

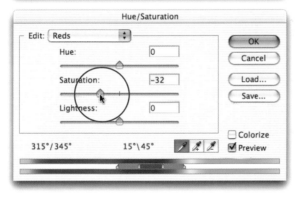

Step Three:

Go under the Image menu, under Adjustments, and choose Hue/Saturation. When the dialog appears, click and hold on the Edit pop-up menu and choose Reds (as shown here) so you're just adjusting the reds in your photo (or in your selected areas if you put a selection around just the flesh tones).

Step Four:

The rest is easy—you're simply going to reduce the amount of saturation so the flesh tones appear more natural. Drag the Saturation slider to the left (as shown) to reduce the amount of red. You'll be able to see the effect of removing the red as you lower the Saturation slider.

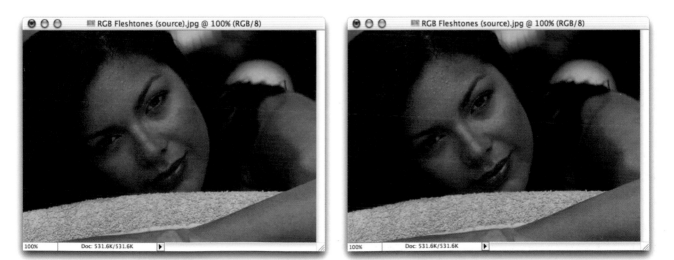

Before adjusting the RGB flesh tones.

After reducing the red in flesh tones.

Making the Tone of One Photo Match Another

If you've ever tired to make the flesh-tones, or overall tone, of one photo match another photo, it takes somewhat of a color-correction miracle. Actually, I should say it "took" somewhat of a minor miracle, because in Photoshop CS, it's a total no-brainer. You just tell Photoshop which color to match and it does it. Pretty brilliantly I might add. Here's how.

Step One:
Open the photo that you want to repair. In this case, the photo has a very warm yellowish glow, and it looks like it may have been taken at the beach sometime close to sunset.

Step Two:
Now find and open a photo that has a skin tone (or overall tone) that you like. This is the photo whose tone you're trying to match (the photo shown here appears to be taken inside a room or studio that is well lit with natural light).

Step Three:

Go back to the image you want to repair (the yellowish couple). Then, go under the Image menu, under Adjustments, and choose Match Color. (Note: If you look under Adjustments and don't find Match Color, you don't have Photoshop CS. That's going to make things tough).

Step Four:

At the bottom of the Match Color dialog, choose the Source photo that has the tone you want to match (in this case, choose the kids shot indoors with lots of natural light). As long as Preview is turned on, you'll see the effect instantly. If the match makes the photo too dark (or too light) you can use the Luminance slider to adjust the overall brightness without affecting the color. Also, you may need to decrease the saturation level of the colors after making this change, in which case, you can drag the Color Intensity slider to the left. If the overall effect is too intense, drag the Fade slider to the right to lessen it.

Step Five:

When you click OK, the tones from the source image (natural light) are applied to your sunset image to create the match shown here. Compare this with the original warm image shown in Step One and you can see what a dramatic effect Match Color can have—the overall tone in the photo in Step Two and this photo now match. Now admit it—is this thing slick or what?

Getting Better Automated Color Correction

Photoshop has had two automated color-correction tools for some time now: Auto Levels and Auto Contrast. They're both pretty lame. And back in Photoshop 7, Adobe introduced Auto Color, which is much better than either Auto Levels or Auto Contrast; but here, we show you how to tweak Auto Color to get even better results, all with just one click.

Step One:
Open a photo that needs correcting, but you don't feel warrants taking your time for a full, manual color correction using Curves.

Step Two:
Go under the Image menu, under Adjustments, and choose Auto Color to apply an auto correction to your photo. When you apply Auto Color, it just does its thing. It doesn't ask you to input numbers or make decisions—basically, it's a one-trick pony that tries to neutralize the highlight, midtone, and shadow areas of your photo. In some cases, it does a pretty darn decent job, in others, well…let's just say it falls a bit short. But in this tutorial, you learn how to super-charge Auto Color to get dramatically better results, and transform it from a "toy" into a real color-correction tool.

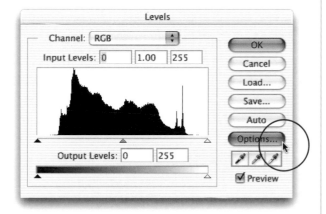

Step Three:

After you apply Auto Color, one way you can tweak its effect on your photo is by going under the Edit menu and choosing Fade Auto Color. (Note: This is only available *immediately* after you apply Auto Color.) When the Fade dialog box appears (as shown), drag the Opacity slider to the left to reduce the effect of the Auto Color. Move the slider until the photo looks good to you. You can also change the Blend Mode (from the Mode pop-up menu) to further adjust your photo (Multiply makes it darker, Screen makes it lighter, etc.). When you click OK in the Fade dialog, your Fade is applied.

Step Four:

So now you know the "Apply-Auto-Color-and-Fade" technique, which is fine, but there's something better: tweaking Auto Color's options before you apply it. Believe it or not, there are hidden options for how Auto Color works. (They're not really hidden, they're just put someplace you'd probably never look.) To get to these Auto Color options, press Command-L (PC: Control-L) to bring up the Levels dialog. On the right side of the dialog, you see a button named Auto. That's not it. Instead, click on the button just below it, named Options. This is where Adobe hid the Auto Color options (along with other options, as you'll soon see).

Continued

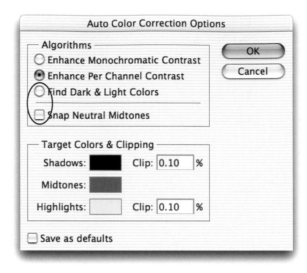

Step Five:

At the top of this dialog, under the Algorithms section, you can determine what happens when you click the Auto button within the Levels or Curves dialogs. If you click the top-most choice, "Enhance Monochromatic Contrast," clicking the Auto button now applies the somewhat lame Auto Levels auto correction. If you choose "Enhance Per Channel Contrast," clicking the Auto button applies the equally lame Auto Contrast auto correction. What you want instead is to choose both "Find Dark & Light Colors" (sets your highlight and shadow points), and "Snap Neutral Midtones" (which sets your midtones). With these settings, Auto Color (the most powerful of the auto-correction tools) is now applied if you click the Auto button in either Levels or Curves.

Step Six:

In the Target Colors & Clipping section, you can click on each Target Color Swatch (Shadows, Midtones, Highlights) and enter the RGB values you'd prefer Auto Color to use, rather than the defaults, which are…well, a bit yucky! I use the same settings that we entered in our manual Curves correction (Shadows: R=20, G=20, B=20; Midtones: R=128, G=128, B=128; and Highlights: R=240, G=240, B=240).

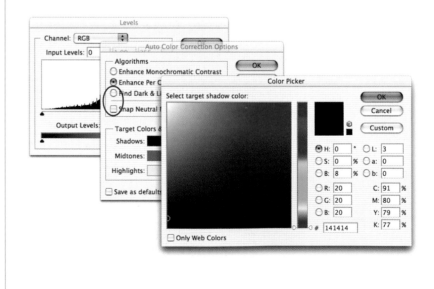

Auto Color Correction Options

Algorithms
- ○ Enhance Monochromatic Contrast
- ○ Enhance Per Channel Contrast
- ● Find Dark & Light Colors

☑ Snap Neutral Midtones

Target Colors & Clipping

Shadows: ⬛ Clip: 0.10 %

Midtones: ⬛

Highlights: ⬜ Clip: 0.10 %

☑ Save as defaults

OK
Cancel

Step Seven:

Weirdly enough, changing these option settings works only once. If you reopen these options later, you'll find that they have all reverted to the original default settings. To keep that from happening, click the Save as Defaults check box at the bottom-left side of the dialog.

Step Eight:

When you click OK to close the options dialog and save the settings, you've done three very important things:
(1) You've majorly tweaked Auto Color's settings to give you better results every time you use it.
(2) You've assigned Auto Color as the default auto correction when you click the Auto button in the Curves dialog.
(3) You've turned Auto Color into a useful tool that you'll use way more than you'd think.

Before color correction.

After tweaking the Auto Color command.

Color Correcting One Problem Area Fast!

This particular technique really comes in handy when shooting outdoor scenes, because it lets you enhance the color in one particular area of the photo (like the sky or water) while leaving the rest of it untouched. Real-estate photographers often use this trick when shooting home exteriors to make it look like the sky was bright and sunny when they took the shot (even though the weather doesn't always cooperate). Here, you use the technique to make the grayish sky look blue, and make the water reflect that nice blue sky.

Step One:

Open an image containing an area of color that you would like to enhance. In this example, we want to make the sky blue (rather than gray) and have the water reflect that nice blue color.

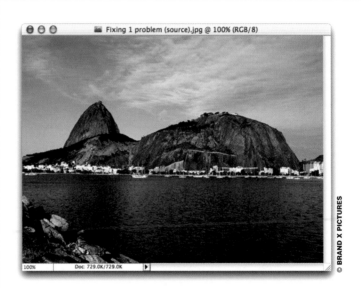

© BRAND X PICTURES

Step Two:

Go to the Layers palette and choose Color Balance from the Adjustment Layer pop-up menu (as shown) at the bottom of the Layers palette (it's the half black/half white circle icon, fourth from the left). A new layer named Color Balance will be added to your Layers palette, but the name will probably be cut off by default. If you want to see the layer's name, you have to widen your Layers palette.

Step Three:

When you choose Color Balance, the Color Balance dialog appears (shown here). Drag the top slider left toward Cyan to add some bright blue into your sky, and then drag the bottom slider right toward Blue until the sky looks as blue as you'd like it. When the sky looks nice and blue, click OK.

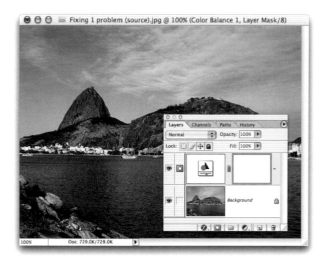

Step Four:

When you do this, the entire photo (mountains and all) will have a heavy blue cast to it (as shown here).

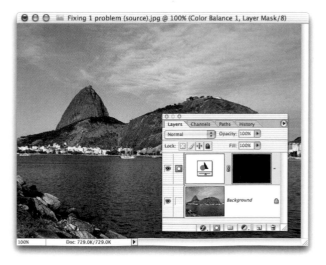

Step Five:

Press the "x" key to set your Foreground color to black. Then, press Option-Delete (PC: Alt-Backspace) to fill your Adjustment layer's mask with black (as shown here). When you do this, the photo returns to its original look (without the blue cast) because the black mask hides the blue layer from view. Next, reveal parts of the blue layer using the Brush tool.

Continued

Step Six:

Press the letter "x" to make your Foreground color white. Next, switch to the Brush tool in the Toolbox, choose a large, soft-edged brush, and begin painting over the sky (as shown here). As you paint, the blue version of your sky is revealed. If you accidentally paint blue over the mountains, just press the "x" key to make black your Foreground, and then as you paint, the original color reappears.

Step Seven:

Continue painting over the sky (as shown) until the entire sky appears sunny and blue.

Step Eight:

Next, you should probably paint over the ocean as well, since it would be reflecting a much bluer sky than it originally was. However, painting in the dark blue might be too obvious, so go up to the Options bar and lower the Opacity setting of the Brush tool to 60% (as shown) so when you paint, the blue won't be as intense.

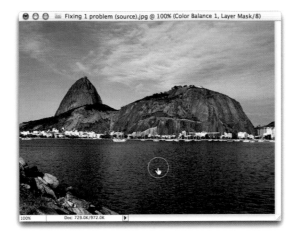

Step Nine:

Paint over the ocean and 60% of the blue Color Balance layer is revealed where you paint. If, after you complete your "bluing," you feel the blue needs to be lighter, change the Layer Blend Mode of this Color Balance Adjustment layer to Screen, and then lower the Opacity a bit. If you feel the blue needs more punch, try Overlay Mode instead. The final correction is shown in the "after" photo (in Normal Mode).

Before, it was just a drab day.

After making the sky and the water more blue.

The Magic of Editing in 16-Bit

ADVANCED
FOR PROS
ONLY!
TECHNIQUES

Because professionals are so concerned with maintaining the absolute highest quality, many now opt to shoot their high-end digital photos in "Raw" mode, so they can do their color correction in 16-bit mode (called "high-bit" editing). Although the file size of these Raw photos is nearly doubled, the advantage is that you can make many tonal corrections without the loss of quality normally associated with editing standard 8-bit images. Plus, since Photoshop CS now offers wider support for 16-bit editing (including using layers, adding type, shapes, etc.), it will probably become more popular than ever.

Before editing in 8-bit mode:

To give you an example of how image quality is maintained with 16-bit images, we'll start by looking at the Histogram for a standard 8-bit image. Here's how the image's Histogram palette looks before any editing has taken place. (Note: The new Histogram palette in Photoshop CS is found under the Window menu. It's shown here in its Expanded View, but there's also an option for viewing each individual channel, and you can view those channels in their corresponding colors.)

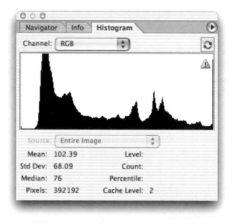

After editing in 8-bit mode:

Here's how the Histogram looks after correcting the highlights, midtones, and shadows in the image using Curves. Notice all the gaps that now appear in the Histogram (those white lines are called combs) indicating a loss in quality. This degradation happens because there are only 256 possible levels (or shades) per channel. When you apply a correction (Levels, Curves, etc.), your image quality and detail degrade because your corrections leave you with less than the 256 possible levels per channel.

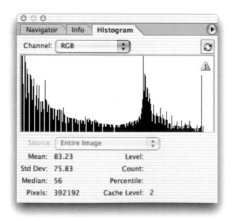

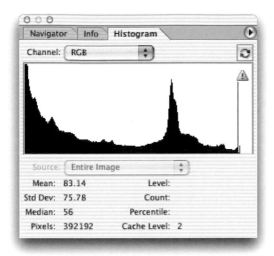

After editing in 16-bit mode:

This capture shows the Histogram for the same photo, with the exact same correction applied; but this time, the correction was done in 16-bit mode, rather than 8-bit. You don't see as many combs (loss of quality) in this histogram because rather than just 256 shades of gray (8-bit mode), 16-bit offers 65,536 possible levels in each channel. With this much information, when you correct a photo, you don't really see image degradation. Basically, you've got levels (shades) to burn. The Histogram shown here proves just that, and that's why so many pros prefer to shoot Raw images and edit in 16-bit.

Converting to 8-bit mode:

Although Photoshop CS lets you use many more features in 16-bit than Photoshop 7 did, to use the majority of Photoshop's filters, you have to convert to 8-bit mode. Downsampling in Photoshop to 8 bits is a no-brainer. Just go under the Image menu, under Mode, and choose 8 Bits/Channel (as shown here). Now you can edit the photo using all of Photoshop's tools and filters.

Shooting in 16-bit:

To get the benefits of editing in 16-bit, you need to shoot Raw 16-bit photos (unfortunately, you don't get the same benefits if you start with a regular 8-bit JPEG and then simply switch to 16-bit mode). Luckily, today, most pro-quality digital cameras enable you to shoot in Raw mode.

Working with Raw Digital-Camera Images

If you take a photo with a traditional film camera and send the film to a lab for processing, they produce an original print from the negative (the negative remains intact). Photoshop CS's Camera Raw plug-in lets you import a Raw photo (the digital negative) from your high-end digital camera. You can decide how it's processed to create your own original, which you can then open and edit in Photoshop CS (while the digital negative remains intact and unchanged). How cool is that? Here's how to start working with Raw images in Photoshop CS (of course, you have to have a digital camera that shoots in Raw format, but you knew that,

But first...

Before we get started, a little history: After Photoshop 7 had been out for almost a year, Adobe introduced a $99 plug-in called Camera Raw that let photographers open Raw images (from high-end digital cameras) directly into Photoshop (without having to convert them into a readable format using a conversion program). In Photoshop CS, the ability to open these Raw photos is built in, and the interface for bringing in those images has been refined and enhanced.

Step One:

You can open a Raw image in one of two ways— from the File Browser (it now displays thumbnails of Raw photos, as shown here, so you can open them by simply double-clicking on their thumbnails in the File Browser). You can also open them using the standard Open command from Photoshop CS's File menu.

© DAVID MOSER

Step Two:
Either way you decide to open it, a Raw image automatically opens in the Camera Raw interface (shown here). The camera, file name, and basic EXIF data appear across the title bar of Camera Raw. A large preview of your Raw photo appears just below that. You can adjust the view size of the image preview either by using the Zoom tool (from the Toolbar on the left), the Select Zoom Level pop-up menu below the preview on the left, or by Control-clicking (PC: right-clicking) within the preview window and choosing a view percentage from the resulting pop-up menu. You can change the rotation of your preview using the rotation buttons below the preview on the right.

Step Three:
Below the preview window are settings that determines the size, resolution, bit-depth, and the color space that your Raw photo will be when imported into Photoshop (keep in mind—you're pro-cessing the original image, so you get all these choices, just like at the lab). The Space pop-up menu should match your current color space, which should be Adobe RGB (1998), as we mentioned earlier in this book. In the Depth pop-up menu, you choose whether the Raw photo will be opened in Photoshop as a regular 8-bit image or a 16-bit image. The Size pop-up menu determines the size (in pixels). The default size shown is the size your camera captured the image. In the Resolution pop-up, you choose the reso-lution desired when the photo is opened in Photoshop.

Continued

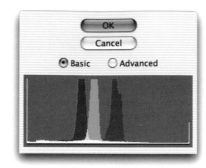

Step Four:

There's also a Histogram that appears to the right of the preview area (as shown). This Histogram simultaneously displays the red, green, and blue channels, and the white represents the image luminance. To see the RGB values in your image, move any tool over the preview area and the values at the point where the tool is located will be displayed just below the preview on the bottom right-hand side (to the immediate left of the rotation buttons).

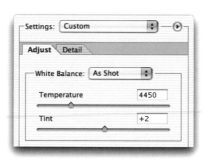

Step Five:

The right column of the Camera Raw interface is where you make processing adjustments that are normally made within the camera, but now you can make them yourself before you import the photo into Photoshop (see, this *is* cool). We'll start at the top of the column (shown here, upper) with the White Balance pop-up menu (we'll cover the Settings pop-up menu in a moment). If you leave it at the default setting (As Shot), the White Balance will remain as it was set in the camera at the time the photo was taken. However, you can choose from a pop-up list of White Balance options that compensate for various lighting conditions (as shown here, lower) and see a live preview of how it affects the Raw image in the preview window.

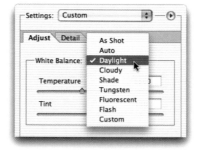

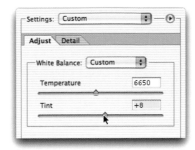

Step Six:

If you don't want to use any of the default settings, you can tweak the White Balance manually by using the Temperature slider to create your own custom color temperature (using the standard Kelvin scale). Dragging to the left cools the tone (making it look bluer), and dragging to the right warms the tone (making it appear more yellow). The Tint slider lets you further fine-tune the White Balance. Dragging to the left introduces more green into the image and dragging to the right introduces more magenta.

Step Seven:

The top five sliders in the next section are for tonal adjustments. The top slider is for Exposure compensation, and it enables you to increase the Exposure by up to four f-stops, and decrease it as much as two f-stops. (Note: Because the values are expressed in increments of f-stops, a +2.50 Exposure value would equal a 2^1/$_2$-stop increase.) If you hold the Option key (PC: Alt key) while making an Exposure adjustment, the preview window reveals any highlights that are being clipped by your changes.

Continued

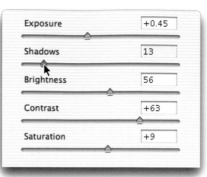

Step Eight:
The Shadows slider lets you push the shadows much in the same way the shadow Input Levels slider in Levels works. To increase the values which will be pushed to black, drag the slider to the right.

Step Nine:
The Brightness, Contrast, and Saturation sliders are somewhat more subtle versions of Photoshop's regular Brightness/Contrast adjustment and the Saturation slider in the Hue/Saturation dialog.

Step Ten:
If you click on the Detail tab (shown here) you're presented with a slider for Sharpness (based on Photoshop's own Unsharp Mask filter). If you don't plan on doing a lot of image editing within Photoshop, you can use this slider to apply sharpening at this stage. The Luminance Smoothing slider helps you remove high ISO noise, as is the Color Noise Reduction slider, which helps deal with color aliasing, and other digital nasties that are introduced by some digital cameras. A setting of 0 turns Color Noise Reduction off.

Step Eleven:
If you click the Advanced button (on the top-right side of the Raw interface) two more tabbed areas appear. The Lens tab lets you correct Chromatic Aberration (which is a fancy name for purplish fringe areas that sometimes appear, especially in consumer-level digital cameras, but it can also appear when using a telephoto lens). Moving the

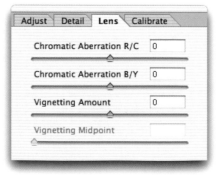

top slider to the right helps remove purplish fringe, and the second slider helps
deal with blue or yellow fringe.

Step Twelve:

The other Advanced tab is Calibrate
(shown here) where you can find what
are essential Hue and Saturation sliders.
You can use these sliders to help deal
with color casts that may have been
introduced within the digital camera
itself. Dragging the Saturation sliders to
the right increases the saturation of each
color (respectively) and dragging them
to the left reduces the saturation of that
color. The Hue sliders move the hue up
or down (for example, in the extreme
bike photo in Step Two, moving the Blue
Hue slider to the right makes the blue
sky appear more purple. Dragging it left
makes the sky more cyan).

Step Thirteen:

Now that you've entered all these settings, you can save them as a preset so
every time you shoot with that camera,
you can quickly pull up the settings that
you commonly use with images from it.
To save your settings, just choose Save
Settings (as shown upper left). This brings
up a dialog where you can give your custom preset a name, and this preset now
appears in the Settings pop-up menu (as
shown lower left). Last, just click OK and
Camera Raw processes the photo according to your specs, and opens the photo in
Photoshop ready to edit, all while leaving
the original Raw image untouched and
preserved as your digital negative.

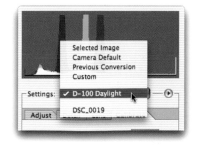

Photographer | Julieanne Kost

One of the problems with people is you can't always get them to stand in front of a white background so you can easily select them, so you can then place them on a different background. It's just not fair. If

The Mask
masking techniques

I were elected president, one of my first priorities would be to sign an executive order requiring all registered voters to carry with them a white seamless roll at all times. Can you imagine how much easier life would be? For example, let's say you're a sports photographer and you're shooting an NFL *Monday Night Football* game with one of those Canon telephoto lenses that are longer than the underground tube for a particle accelerator; and just as the quarterback steps into the pocket to complete a pass, a fullback comes up from behind, quickly unfurls a white, seamless backdrop, and lets you make the shot. Do you know how fast you'd get a job at *Sports Illustrated*? Do you know how long I've waited to use "unfurl" in a sentence and actually use it in the proper context? Well, let's just say at least since I was 12 (three long years ago). In this chapter, you learn how to treat everyone, every object, everything, as though it was shot on a white seamless background.

Extracting People from Their Background

I figured I'd start with probably the most-requested masking task—removing someone from a background while keeping hair detail. We use Extract for this, and even if you've used Extract dozens of times, there's a trick near the end that is so simple, yet so incredibly effective, it will change the way you use Extract forever, or my name isn't Deke McClelland.

Step One:

Open the photo containing a person (or an object) that you want to extract from its background. Go under the Filter menu and choose Extract (it's the first filter from the top).

Step Two:

This brings up the Extract dialog. Get the Edge Highlighter tool (it's the top tool in Extract's Toolbar and looks like a marker) and use it to trace the edges of the object you want to remove (as shown here). As you trace, leave half the marker border on the background and half on the edge of the object you want to extract.

TIP: Use a small brush size when tracing areas that are well defined (like along the shirt), and a very large brush for areas that are less defined, such as flyaway hair. You can change the brush size by holding down the Left Bracket key to make it smaller or the Right Bracket to make it larger.

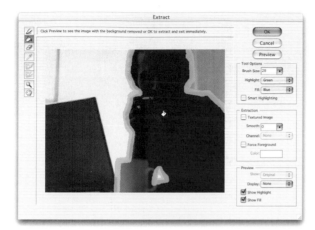

Step Three:

After your Highlighter edge is in place, you now have to tell Photoshop what parts of the photo to retain when extracting. This is pretty simple—you just switch to the Fill tool (it's the second tool from the top in Extract's Toolbar and looks like a paint bucket) and click it once inside the Highlighter edge border you drew earlier (as shown here). This fills the inside of your highlighter border with a light blue tint.

Step Four:

If the blue tint spills out to the rest of your photo when you click the Fill tool, that means your subject isn't completely enclosed by the edge border. If that happens, just press Command-Z (PC: Control-Z) to undo, then take the Edge Highlighter and make certain there are no gaps at the bottom or sides of your border. Now you can click the Preview button to see how your extraction looks (as shown here).

Step Five:

It's time to take a good look at the photo and see if Extract did what you really wanted it to. Namely, did it work on the hair, which is the hard-to-select area? If it worked, click OK because fixing the rest of the photo is a breeze, as you'll see. Even if parts of his clothes are dropping out, or there are dropouts in his face, hands, etc., don't sweat it—as long as the edge of the hair looks good, click OK to perform the extraction.

Continued

Step Six:

Now that the extraction is done, it's "fix-up" time. Here, you can see dropouts (slightly transparent areas) in his hair, a few little spots in his shirt, and a couple little spots in other places. Start by simply duplicating the layer. That's right, just press Command-J (PC: Control-J). The mere act of duplicating the layer fixes about 90% of the dropouts in your photo. It sounds weird, but it works amazingly well, and when you try it, you'll be astounded. Press Command-E (PC: Control-E) to merge these two layers.

Step Seven:

For the rest of the dropouts, just get the History Brush tool (shown here) and simply paint over these areas. The History Brush paints those missing pieces back in because it's really an "undo on a brush" if you just grab it and go. So, if part of your subject drops out, use the History Brush to paint it right back in. You can usually fix the dropouts in about two minutes using this technique.

Step Eight:

Here's a capture taken during the fix-up stage, where I'm painting over dropouts on the handle of the coffee mug. The History Brush is painting the original image back in.

© BRAND X PICTURES

Step Nine:

Next, open the photo that you want to use as a background behind your extracted person. It's best to drag this background photo onto your extracted-person document, because as long as you work in the same document where you extracted, you'll have access to the History Brush for your extracted image. That way, if you see a dropout when you bring in the background, you can return to that layer and quickly touch it up with the History Brush.

Step Ten:

The background appears over your extracted image on its own layer, probably covering your extracted image (as shown here).

Step Eleven:

Go to the Layers palette and drag the layer with your background photo behind the layer with your extracted photo, to put your extracted person in front of the background you just dragged in (as shown here, where the woman in the background photo is covered up by the extracted man). You'll usually have to switch to the Eraser tool to erase any little leftover "junk" outside his hair, along his shirt, etc., but you can usually clean up these leftovers pretty easily once you see them over the background.

Continued

Step Twelve:

In this example, the original photo was wider than the new background, so you're left with a lot of empty space to his left. Press "c" to get the Crop tool, drag a cropping border out around just the background area, then press Return (PC: Enter) to crop the photo down to size (as shown here). Now that the photo is cropped, a new problem is visible—his skin tone looks too warm for the bluish background you've placed him on (and this is something you'll deal with often when combining photos—the tones have to match to look realistic).

Step Thirteen:

To cool down his warm skin tones, make sure the top layer is active in the Layers palette, and then go under the Adjustment Layer pop-up menu at the bottom of the palette and choose Photo Filter (as shown here). These Photo Filters replicate the traditional screw-on lens filters we used to use with film cameras to adjust bad lighting situations.

Step Fourteen:

In the Photo Filter dialog, you can choose a filter from the Filter presets pop-up menu (like the Cooling Filter [82] I chose here), or choose to fill with a solid color. You can also control the density of the effect using the Density slider (I left it set at 25%). Click OK and the warm tones are cooled and your subject's flesh tones and overall tone now better fit the background image you dragged him onto.

The original photo.

The subject extracted, placed onto a different background, and his tone cooled to match the background.

Precise Selections Using the Pen Tool

Of all the selection tools in Photoshop, this is probably the single-most important one, and if you get good at it, it makes your life so much easier, because you'll be spending a lot of time making precise selections and no tool does it better. This tutorial is aimed at photographers who haven't really worked with the pen before, so if you're a pro with the pen, you can skip this, and I won't take any offense. Okay, I might be a little hurt, but I'll get over it. In time.

Step One:

In this example, we're going to put a path around the door, turn the path into a selection, and then drag the door onto a different background. Start by getting the Pen tool from the Toolbox. Click it once at a starting point within your photo (there is no "official" start-ing point, but in this case, you can start by clicking once on the top-left corner of the door, as shown). Remember, just click it once—don't click and drag. (Note: Make sure that the Paths icon is selected up in the Options bar. It's the middle icon of the group of three icons near the left of the bar. Otherwise, you may end up creating a Shape Layer or filled pixels, which you don't want for this technique.)

Step Two:

Move your cursor to the top-right corner of the door, then click once more. A straight path is drawn between the two points.

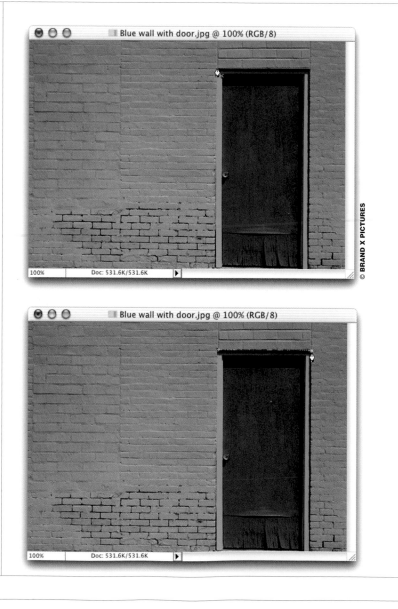

Step Three:

Continue moving the cursor down along the door and clicking on each corner to draw another straight line from the last point. Go down the right side, across the bottom of the door, and back up to the top-left corner where you started. A tiny circle appears on the bottom-right corner of your Pen tool cursor, letting you know you've come "full circle." Click on your starting point to close your path. You should now have a path all the way around the door.

Step Four:

If you need to adjust one of the points to make it fit snugly to the door frame, press Shift-A until you have the Direct Selection tool (the hollow arrow), click on the path to make the points active, and then click on the point you want to move and drag it into place. When your path looks nice and tight against the door frame, press Command-Return (PC: Control-Enter) to turn your Path into a selection (as shown here).

Step Five:

Now, open a different background photo (in this case, it's a red brick wall), then go back to your door image. Press "v" to get the Move tool, click within your selected door, and drag-and-drop it onto the red brick background (as shown here). Okay, that's the basic "point-and-click" straight-line method of using the Pen tool. Now, on to making curves with the Pen tool (where the real power of this tool lies).

Continued

© BRAND X PICTURES

Step Six:

The previous Pen tool project used straight lines, but this project adds curves. (The ability to draw smooth paths around curved objects is the real power of the Pen tool.) Click on a starting point. In the example shown here, I clicked once at the top-left corner of the club's shaft for my starting point, then I moved down to the top of the club head's sleeve and clicked again, and a straight path was drawn between the two points.

Step Seven:

The sleeve (where the shaft inserts into the head of the club) is just a tiny bit larger than the shaft, so click once more, out just a hair from the shaft, then move your cursor to the base of the club head (as shown here) and click to draw a straight line down the sleeve to the base of the club head.

Step Eight:

Now, move your cursor over the top center of the head of the club (as shown), but don't just click—click, hold, and drag, and as you drag, the path begins to curve and two Curve Adjustment handles appear (as shown here). As you drag, you'll be actually dragging out one of these handles. The farther you drag, the more your path curves. It takes a few tries to get the hang of how far to pull, and how the curve reacts to your pulling, but in short order, you get a snug fit fairly easily.

Step Nine:

Move your cursor down to the left end of the club head, and do the "click-hold-and-drag" thing again to create another curve (as shown here). You basically use the two techniques you've just learned to trace the edges of your club with a path. Here's a refresher: (1) Click from point to point to draw straight lines, and (2) click, hold, and drag to draw curves around objects.

Step Ten:

Move your cursor around the top-left side of the club head, click, hold, and drag to create another smooth curve around the club (as shown here).

Step Eleven:

Move your cursor down to where the club meets the ball, click, hold, and drag again. (Are you seeing a pattern here?)

Continued

Step Twelve:

Continue down the bottom of the ball, then click, hold, and drag again (as shown). You're about to learn one of the annoying things about drawing curves with the Pen tool—the curve doesn't always go in the right direction. When you get to the base of the ball, the curve wants to go the opposite direction (that's just the way curves work, and you'll run into this again and again, so you might as well learn how to fix this problem now).

Step Thirteen:

Here's how to fix it: Press Command-Z (PC: Control-Z) to undo the point of curve that went the wrong way. Hold the Option key (PC: Alt key), and then click your previous point. Now click, hold, and drag at the base of the ball just like before, but now when you draw your curve, it will go in the right direction (as shown here).

Step Fourteen:

When you try to change directions, and you click, hold, and drag on the side of the tee, it's going to happen again (as shown here), but at least now you know the fix. Hold the Option key (PC: Alt key), click your previous point, and then you can continue as usual and the curve will now go in the proper direction.

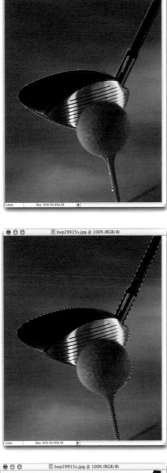

Step Fifteen:

Once you Option-click (PC: Alt-click) on your previous point, you can try the curve again and it will work just fine (as shown). **TIP:** To make your path as smooth as possible, try not to add too many points as you're tracing around your object. If you see an area that doesn't look right (because you didn't put a curve in where it was necessary), just get the Add Anchor Point tool. Move it over the path where you want to add a curve point, and click, hold, and drag to add a curve point along the path.

Step Sixteen:

After your path is complete, you can turn it into a selection by pressing Command-Return (PC: Control-Enter) as shown here. If you want to see just the club/ball/tee and not the background, press Command-J (PC: Control-J) to put the group on its own separate layer. Then, in the Layers palette, click on the Background layer, press Command-A (Control-A) to Select All, and then press Delete (PC: Backspace) to remove the background.

Step Seventeen:

The capture at far left shows the result of deleting the background photo from the Background layer. The only problem is that the bright colors from the original photo still reflect in the club. To get rid of those colors, set your Foreground color to black, get the Brush tool, and choose a hard-edged brush. In the Options bar, change the Blend Mode of the Brush tool to Color, then paint over the face of the club and the ball. As you paint, the color is replaced with grayscale (as shown). The next step starts another important path option (outputting to a printing press).

Continued

Step Eighteen:

If you're going to export this photo into a professional page-layout application (like Adobe InDesign or QuarkXPress) for printing to a printing press and you want only the club/ball/tee visible, and not the background, you have to create a Clipping Path. This tells the page-layout application to clip away (hide) everything outside your path. To create a Clipping Path, start by making the Paths palette visible. When you do, you'll see the path you created (by default, it's named "Work Path.") Double-click on this path, and in the Save Path dialog, give it a name (as shown).

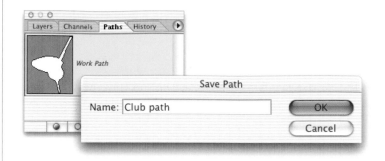

Step Nineteen:

After your path is named, choose Clipping Path from the Paths palette's pop-down menu to bring up the Clipping Path dialog. Make sure your named path is selected from the Path pop-up menu (shown above right). Adobe has fixed it so you can leave the Flatness setting blank and it will work in almost all situations, but if for some reason, you get a PostScript error when outputting to a high-resolution imagesetter, resave the file with a Flatness setting of between 7 and 10 so the paths will be interpreted correctly.

Step Twenty:

Finally, save your file in EPS format (which supports the embedding of Clipping Paths). When you import this EPS file into your page-layout application (shown here in Adobe InDesign), you can position your club/ball/tee image over an existing background and only the club/ball/tee will be visible, with the area around it appearing transparent (rather than white).

Saving Your Intricate Selections

If you've spent 15 or 20 minutes (or even more) putting together an intricate selection, once you deselect it, it's gone. (Well, you might be able to get it back by choosing Reselect from the Select menu, as long as you haven't made any other selections in the meantime, so don't count on it. Ever.) Here's how to save your finely honed selections and bring them back into place anytime you need them.

Step One:
To save a currently active selection, go under the Select menu and choose Save Selection. This brings up the Save Selection dialog (as shown). Just click OK to save your selection.

Step Two:
You can view your saved selection by going to the Channels palette, where your selection is saved as an extra channel named "Alpha 1" (by default). You can turn this channel into a selection anytime by dragging it to the Load Channel as Selection icon at the bottom of the Channels palette (as shown).

Step Three:
Another way to load a saved selection is to choose Load Selection from the bottom of the Select menu. This brings up the Load Selection dialog, where you can choose which channel you want to load from the Channel pop-up menu (handy if you've saved multiple selections). You can use it to either add or subtract a saved selection from a currently active selection.

Loading the Highlights as a Selection

Instant loading of the highlights (the luminosity of a photo) enables you to quickly lighten your photo without disturbing the midtone or shadow areas. Also, loading the highlights makes it very easy to inverse the selection and have just the shadows selected so you can enhance the shadow detail.

Step One:
Open the photo that has highlights you want to correct. In this case, we want to lighten the highlights without disturbing the midtone or shadow areas.

Step Two:
Before we go any further, I want you to see the advantage of this technique versus just changing the layer Mode to Screen (which brightens everything, including the shadows). So just as a quick experiment, press Command-J (PC: Control-J) to duplicate the Background layer, then in the Layers palette, change the Blend Mode of this layer to Screen. Notice how it brightens everything. Just look at the shadow areas in the background—they're brightened, too! Okay, our experiment's done—delete this duplicate layer by dragging it to the Trash icon at the bottom of the Layers palette.

Step Three:

Press Option-Command-~ (PC: Alt-Control-~) (that's the Tilde key, right above the Tab key on your keyboard). This loads the highlights (luminosity) in your photo as a selection (as shown). Now, press Command-J (PC: Control-J) to put the loaded selection on its own layer.

Step Four:

Now that the highlights are separated out onto their own layer, you could use Levels or Curves to lighten them, or you could simply change the Blend Mode from Normal to Screen in the Layers palette, as I've done here. If choosing Screen makes the highlights a little too hot for your taste, you can lower the Opacity of this layer until it looks right to you.

Step Five:

Here's the final image with the highlights lightened using this technique. Compare this with the capture shown in Step Two, where the whole image is lightened, and you'll immediately see the wonderful difference being able to just adjust the highlights makes. This technique works equally well for selecting just the shadows, enabling you to open up the shadows with Levels, Curves, or a change to Screen Mode. Start by loading the selection (as in Step Three) and after the highlights selection is in place, go under the Select menu and choose Inverse to select the shadows.

Photographer | Jeannie Theriault

This should be called "The Kevin Ames Chapter."
Actually, it really should be called the "I Hate Kevin
Ames Chapter" because I already had this entire
chapter written, until I stopped by Kevin's studio in

Head Games
retouching portraits

Atlanta one night to show him the rough draft of the
book. What should have been a 15-minute visit went
on until after midnight, with him showing me some
amazing portrait-retouching tricks for the book. So
I had to go back home and basically rewrite, update,
and tweak the entire chapter. Which I can tell you,
is no fun once you think a chapter is done and
you're about a week from deadline, but the stuff he
showed me was so cool, I literally couldn't sleep that
night because I knew his techniques would take this
chapter to the next level. And even though Kevin
was incredibly gracious to let me share his techniques with my readers (that's the kind of guy Kevin
is), there was no real way I was going to name this
"The Kevin Ames Chapter." That's when it became
clear to me—I would have to kill him. But then, I
remembered Kevin had mentioned that Jim DiVitale
had developed some of the techniques that he had
shown me, so now it was going to be a double
murder. I thought, "Hey, they both live in Atlanta,
how hard could this be?" but the more I thought
about it, what with having to fly back up there and
having to fly on Delta (stuffed in like human cattle),
I figured I'd just give them the credit they deserve
and go on with my life. Thus far, it's worked out okay.

Removing Blemishes

When it comes to removing blemishes, acne, or any other imperfections on the skin, our goal is to maintain as much of the original skin texture as possible. That way, our retouch doesn't look pasty and obvious. Here are three techniques we use that work pretty nicely, and when you have all of these methods in your retouching arsenal, if one doesn't carry out the repair the way you'd hoped, you can try the second or even the third.

TECHNIQUE #1
Step One:
Open a photo containing some skin imperfections you want to remove (in this example, we're going to remove the mole below his lips and to the left).

Step Two:
Choose the Clone Stamp tool in the Toolbox. From the Brush Picker up in the Options bar (click on the Brush thumbnail on the left-hand side), choose a soft-edged brush that's slightly larger than the blemish you want to remove. You can use the Master Diameter slider at the top of the Brush Picker to dial in just the size you need. Once you're working, if you need to quickly adjust the brush size up or down, use the Bracket keys on your keyboard: the Left Bracket key makes your brush smaller; the Right, larger.

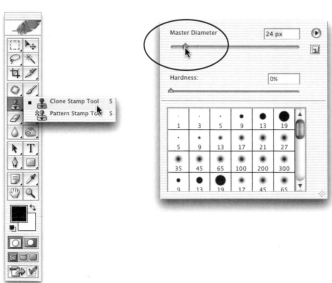

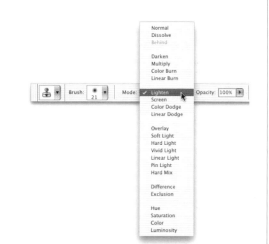

Step Three:

Up in the Options bar, change the Blend Mode of the Clone Stamp tool to Lighten. With its Mode set as Lighten, the Clone Stamp will affect only pixels that are darker than the sampled area. The lighter pixels (the regular flesh tone) will pretty much stay intact, and only the darker pixels (the blemish) will be affected.

Step Four:

Find an area right near the blemish that's pretty clean (no visible spots, blemishes, etc.), hold the Option key (PC: Alt key), and click once. This samples the skin from that area. Try to make sure this sample area is very near the blemish so the skin tones will match. If you move too far away, you risk having your repair appear in a slightly different color, which is a dead giveaway of a repair.

Step Five:

Now, move your cursor directly over the blemish and click just once. Don't paint! Just click. The click will do it—it will remove the blemish instantly (as shown here), while leaving the skin texture intact. But what if the blemish is lighter than the skin, rather than darker? Simply change the Blend Mode to Darken instead of Lighten—it's that easy. On to Technique #2.

Continued

TECHNIQUE #2
Step One:
Switch to the Lasso tool in the Toolbox. Find a clean area (no blemishes, spots, etc.) near the blemish that you want to remove (in this case, it's a mole just below his glasses on the right side. You can see it just above the cursor shown here). In this clean area, use the Lasso tool to make a selection that is slightly larger than the blemish (as shown).

Step Two:
After your selection is in place, go under the Select menu and choose Feather. When the Feather Selection dialog appears, enter 1 pixel as your Feather Radius and click OK. Feathering blurs the edges of our selected area, which helps hide the traces of our retouch. Feathering (softening) the edges of a selection is a very important part of facial retouching, and you'll do this quite a bit, to "hide your tracks," so to speak.

Step Three:
Now that you've softened the edges of the selection, hold Option-Command (PC: Alt-Control), and you'll see your cursor change into two arrowheads—a white one with a black one overlapping it. This tells you that you're about to copy the selected area. Click within your selection and drag this clean skin area over the blemish to completely cover it.

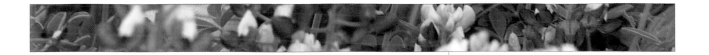

Blemish 2.jpg @ 100% (RGB/8)

100%   Doc: 531.6K/531.6K

Step Four:

When the clean area covers the blemish, release the keys (and the mouse button, of course) to drop this selected area down onto your photo. Now, press Command-D (PC: Control-D) to deselect. The photo at left shows the final results, and as you can see, the blemish is gone. Best of all, because you dragged skin over from a nearby area, the full skin texture is perfectly intact, making your repair nearly impossible to detect.

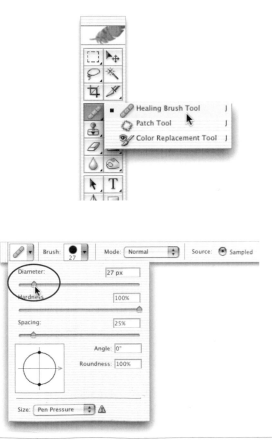

Healing Brush Tool   J
Patch Tool   J
Color Replacement Tool   J

Brush: ● 27   Mode: Normal   Source: ● Sampled

Diameter: 27 px
Hardness: 100%
Spacing: 25%
Angle: 0°
Roundness: 100%
Size: Pen Pressure

TECHNIQUE #3

You can also use the Healing Brush (shown here) to remove blemishes effectively and quickly. (A full tutorial is coming up soon, so I won't put you through the whole thing twice.) Just like the Clone Stamp tool, the key thing to remember when using the Healing Brush for repairing blemishes is to choose a brush size that's just slightly larger than the blemish you're trying to remove. The default for the Healing Brush is hard-edged, and that's fine—it works great that way. However, you have to choose your brush size from the Diameter slider (as shown here). From that point, you can use it much as you would the Clone Stamp (Option-/Alt-clicking in a clean area), but you don't have to choose Lighten from the Options bar—the Healing Brush doesn't need it.

Removing Dark Circles Under Eyes

Here are two different techniques for removing the dark circles that sometimes appear under a person's eyes. Especially after a hard night of drinking. At least, that's what I've been told.

TECHNIQUE #1

Step One:

Open the photo that has the dark circles you want to lessen. Select the Clone Stamp tool in the Toolbox. Then (from the Brush Picker in the Options bar), choose a soft-edged brush that's half as wide as the area you want to repair.

Step Two:

Go up to the Options bar and lower the Opacity of the Clone Stamp tool to 50%. Then, change the Blend Mode to Lighten (so you'll only affect areas that are darker than your sample).

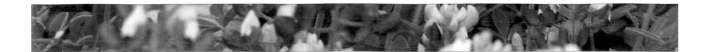

Step Three:

Hold the Option key (PC: Alt key) and click once in an area near the eye that isn't affected by the dark circles. If the cheeks aren't too rosy, you can click there, but more likely, you'll click on (sample) an area just below the dark circles under the eyes (as shown here).

Step Four:

Now, take the Clone Stamp tool and paint over the dark circles to lessen or remove them (the result is shown here). It may take two or more strokes for the dark circles to pretty much disappear, so don't be afraid to go back over the same spot if the first stroke didn't work. The photos below show the original photo (on the left), then the retouched version with both eyes retouched on the right.

Before.

After.

Continued

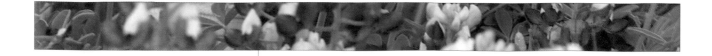

TECHNIQUE #2
Step One:
Go to the Toolbox and choose the Patch tool (click-and-hold on the Healing Brush until the flyout menu appears as, shown here).

Step Two:
With the Patch tool, make sure that it's set to Source in the Options bar and draw a selection around one of the dark circles under the eye (as shown here). The Patch tool operates much like the Lasso tool for drawing selections. Also, like the Lasso tool, once your selection is in place, if you need to add to it, just hold the Shift key and "lasso" in some more area. If you need to subtract from your Patch tool selection, hold the Option key (PC: Alt key) instead.

Step Three:
After your selection is in place, click directly within the selected area and drag it to a part of the face that's clean and doesn't have any edges. By that, I mean you don't want your dragged selection to overlap the edge of any other facial features, such as the nose, lips, eyebrows, edge of the face, and so on. You need a clean, uninterrupted area of skin. In Photoshop CS, you'll see a preview of what your patch will look like—that's why you see two selections in the capture shown here.

Step Four:

After you've found that clean area, release the mouse button and the Patch tool automatically samples it, snaps back to the original selected area, and performs the retouch for you.

Step Five:

Press Command-D (PC: Control-D) to deselect, and you see the dark circle is completely gone (as shown at left). The Healing Brush can also be used to diminish or erase dark circles, but the Patch tool does it so quickly and effortlessly that I greatly prefer it when it comes to dark circles.

Before (dark circles under the eyes).

After removing them with the Patch tool.

Lessening Freckles or Facial Acne

This technique is popular with senior-class portrait photographers who need to lessen or remove large areas of acne, pockmarks, or freckles. This is especially useful when you have a lot of photos to retouch (like a senior-portrait retoucher) and don't have the time to use the methods shown previously, where you deal with each blemish individually.

Step One:
Open the photo that you need to retouch.

Step Two:
Go under the Filter menu, under Blur, and choose Gaussian Blur. When the Gaussian Blur dialog appears, drag the slider all the way to the left, and then drag it slowly to the right until you see the freckles (or acne) blurred away. The photo should look very blurry, but we'll fix that in just a minute, so don't let that throw you off—make sure it's blurry enough that the freckles are no longer visible, and then click OK.

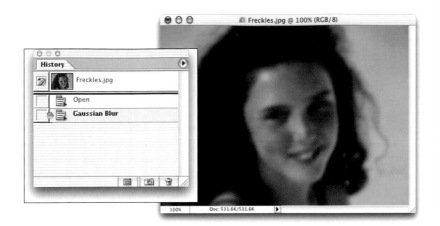

Step Three:
Go under the Window menu and choose History to bring up the History palette. This palette keeps track of the last 20 things you've done in Photoshop. If you look in the list of steps (called "History States"), you should see two States: The first will read "Open" (this is when you opened the document), and the second will read "Gaussian Blur" (this is where you added the blur).

Step Four:
Click on the Open State to return your photo to what it looked like when you originally opened it (as shown here). The History palette also works in conjunction with a tool in the Toolbox called the History Brush. When you paint with it, by default, it paints back to what the photo looked like when you opened it. It's like "Undo on a brush." That can be very handy, but the real power of the History Brush is that you can have it paint from a different state. You'll see what I mean in the next step.

Step Five:
In the History palette, click in the first column next to the State named "Gaussian Blur." If you painted with the History Brush now, it would paint in what the photo looked like after you blurred it (which would do us no good), but we're about to fix that.

Continued

Step Six:

To keep from simply painting in a blurry version of our photo, go up to the Options bar and change the History Brush's Blend Mode to Lighten. Now when you paint, it affects only the pixels that are darker than the blurred state. Ahhh, do you see where this is going? Now, you can take the History Brush and paint over the acne areas, and as you paint, you'll see them diminish quite a bit (as shown below). If they diminish too much, and the person looks "too clean," press Command-Z (PC: Control-Z) to undo your History Brush strokes, then go up to the Options bar and lower the Opacity of the brush to 50% and try again.

Before.

After.

Photoshop 7.0 introduced two new tools that are nothing short of miracle workers when it comes to removing wrinkles, crowsfeet, and other facial signs of aging. We've touched on these tools slightly in previous techniques in this chapter, but here's a closer look at how to use these amazing tools to quickly take 10 or 20 years off a person's appearance.

Removing the Signs of Aging

© BRAND X PICTURES

TECHNIQUE #1: HEALING BRUSH
Step One:
Open the photo of the person whose signs of aging you want to remove.

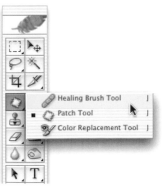

Step Two:
Choose the Healing Brush from the Toolbox (as shown).

Continued

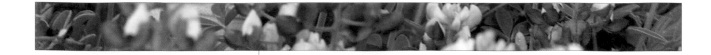

Step Three:
Hold the Option key (PC: Alt key) and click on an area of smooth skin (as shown). This samples the texture of the area you're clicking on and uses it for the repair.

Step Four:
With the Healing Brush, paint a stroke over the wrinkles you want to remove (I painted over the wrinkles just below her eyes). When you first paint your stroke, for a moment, the tones won't match and it'll look like an obvious retouch; but a second later, the Healing Brush does its calculations and presents you with its final "magic" that beautifully blends in the original texture, seamlessly removing the wrinkle. Continue this process of sampling a clean area and painting over a wrinkled area until all the signs of aging are removed. (The "After" capture below shows 30 seconds of retouching with the Healing Brush—a total of about five strokes.)

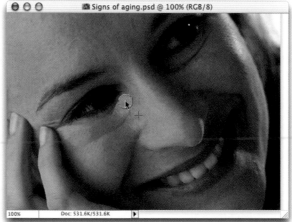

Before (clearly visible wrinkles under both eyes).

After (after removing the wrinkles under the eyes).

© BRAND X PICTURES

TECHNIQUE #2: PATCH TOOL
Step One:
You can achieve similar results using the Patch tool (shown at left), and personally, I prefer this tool over the Healing Brush for most instances, because the Patch tool lets you correct larger areas faster. After you have the Patch tool, make sure that it's set to Source in the Options bar and draw a selection around the wrinkled area (as shown here). It works like the Lasso tool, so if you need to add to your selection, hold the Shift key. To subtract from it, hold Option (PC: Alt).

Step Two:
After your selection is in place, drag it to an area on the person's face that has a clean texture (in Photoshop CS, you see a preview of what your patch will look like—that's why you see two lasso selections in the capture shown here). Make sure your selected area doesn't overlap any other facial features (such as the nose, lips, eyes, edge of the face, etc.), and then release the mouse button. When you do, the selection snaps back to the area that you originally selected.

Step Three:
After your Patch tool selection has snapped back into place, the wrinkles are gone. Press Command-D (PC: Control-D) to deselect and view the amazing job the Patch tool did (as shown here).

Pro Wrinkle Removal

The Healing Brush and Patch tools are pretty amazing for removing wrinkles, but the problem may be that they do just that—they completely remove wrinkles. Depending on the age of the subject you're retouching, the photo may look obviously retouched (in other words, if you're retouching someone in their 70s and you make them look as if they're 20 years old, it's just going to look weird). Here's a simple trick Kevin Ames uses for more realistic healing.

Step One:
Open the photo you want to "heal." Duplicate the Background layer in the Layers palette by pressing Command-J (PC: Control-J). You perform your "healing" on this duplicate layer.

© BRAND X PICTURES

Step Two:
Use the Healing Brush to remove the wrinkled area. As you can see, with every wrinkle removed, this photo looks obviously retouched.

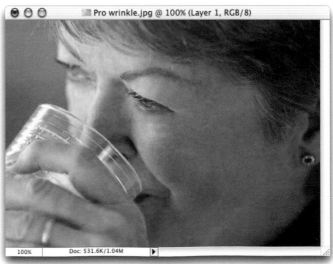

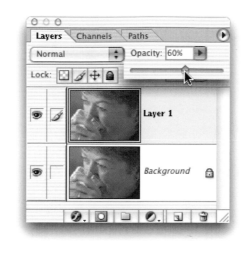

Step Three:
Go to the Layers palette and reduce the Opacity of this layer to bring back some of the original wrinkles. What you're really doing here is letting a small amount of the original photo (on the Background layer, with all its wrinkles still intact) show through. Keep lowering the Opacity until you see the wrinkles so they're visible, but not nearly as prominent. Here's the final retouch with the Opacity of the healed layer lowered to 60% so I'm getting just a little less than half the wrinkles back, and the photo looks much more realistic.

Before.   *After.*

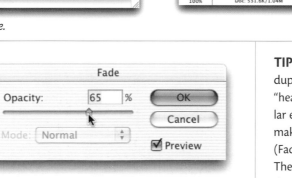

TIP: If you don't want to (or forget to) duplicate your layer before you begin "healing" your photo, you can get a similar effect by immediately using Fade after making a stroke with the Healing Brush (Fade is found under the Edit menu). There, you can lower the Opacity (as shown here) to bring back some of the original wrinkles.

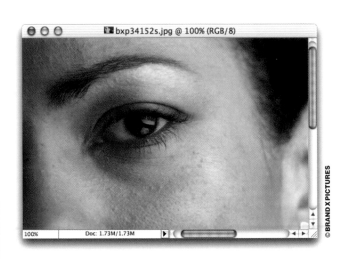

The Secret to Better Healing

We had just wrapped up the Photoshop "Midnight Madness" session at the PhotoshopWorld Conference & Expo, when a woman came up to me and said, "I've got a really neat trick for the Healing Brush if you want to see it." She was right—this trick rocks! As amazing as the Healing Brush is, it sometimes gives you a mottled look, or you can see the texture repeated in your "healing." Well, her trick, which changes the shape of the brush, makes those nasties go away. A big thanks to NAPP member Stephanie Cole for letting me share this wonderful tip with you.

Step One:

Open the photo you want to "heal" with the Healing Brush and zoom in close on the area where the healing will take place (in the example shown here, we're going to remove the little wrinkles under her eyes).

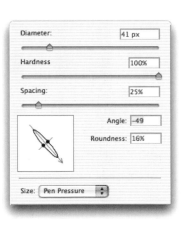

Step Two:

Get the Healing Brush from the Toolbox, then go up to the Options bar and click on the down-facing arrow next to the Brush Thumbnail to bring up the Brush Picker (it's set to a black, round, hard-edged brush by default). Set the Hardness to 100% and the Spacing to 25%, but the real trick comes in shaping the brush. You're going to make a tall thin oval brush by setting the Angle to -49 and the Roundness to just 16% (as shown here).

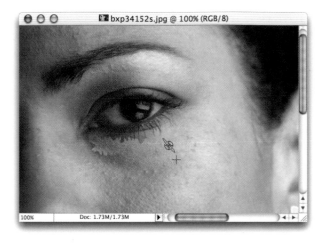

Step Three:

Hold the Option key (PC: Alt key), and click in an area with smooth texture (in the example shown here, you can click just below the wrinkled area, to the right of the bridge of her nose. Then, start painting with the Healing Brush, going from left to right, over the wrinkles. As you paint, the brush creates what looks like a star pattern (as shown here), and it's this pattern that makes the texture look so random and realistic. The captures below show the traditional method (with a round brush) on the left, and Stephanie Cole's tall oval brush technique on the right.

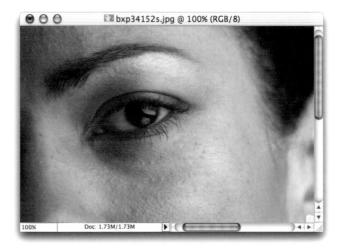

Before: With a round Healing Brush, you can see the texture (notice how two tiny bumps are repeated? Also notice the slight darkening added by the healing).

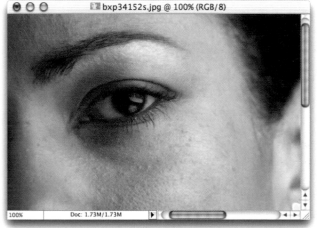

After: Using Stephanie's tall thin brush technique, you don't see the repeated skin texture, nor do you get the darkening under the eye or a mottled look.

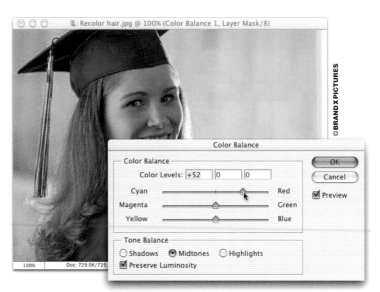

Colorizing Hair

This technique (that I learned from Kevin Ames) gives you maximum control and flexibility while changing or adjusting hair color, and because of the use of Layer Masks and an Adjustment layer, you're not "bruising the pixels." Instead, you're following the enlightened path of "non-destructive retouching."

Step One:

Open the photo you want to retouch. Choose Color Balance from the Adjustment Layer pop-up menu at the bottom of the Layers palette. When the dialog appears, move the sliders toward the color you'd like as the hair color. You can adjust the shadows, midtones, and highlights by selecting each in the Tone Balance section of the Color Balance dialog and then moving the color sliders.

Step Two:

In this case, we want to make the hair redder, so we'll move the top slider toward Red for the shadows, then the midtones, and then the highlights. Now, click OK, and the entire photo will have a heavy red cast over it (as shown).

Step Three:

Press "x" until your Foreground color is black, and press Option-Delete (PC: Alt-Backspace) to fill the Color Balance mask with black. Doing so removes the red tint from the photo.

Step Four:

Get the Brush tool in the Toolbox, choose a soft-edged brush, press "d" to set your Foreground color to white, and begin painting over her hair. As you paint, the red tint you added with Color Balance is painted back in (as shown). Continue painting on the hair until it's fully tinted. You may want to paint a few strokes over her eyebrows as well. Once the hair is fully painted, go to the Layers palette and change the Blend Mode of your Color Balance Adjustment Layer from Normal to Color, and then lower the Opacity until the hair color looks natural (as shown below).

Before.

After.

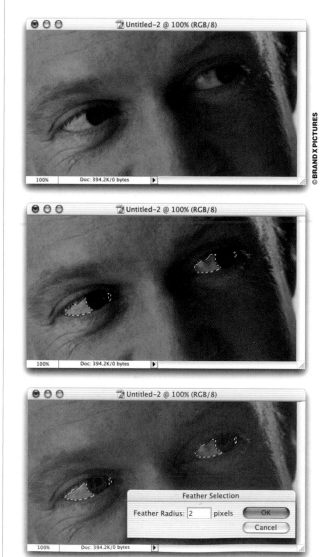

Whitening the Eyes Quick Trick

This is a great little technique for quickly whitening the whites of the eyes, and it has the added benefit of removing any redness in the eye along the way.

Step One:
Open the portrait you want to retouch.

Step Two:
Choose the Lasso tool from the Toolbox and draw a selection around the whites of one of the eyes. Hold the Shift key and draw selections around the whites of the other eye, until all the whites are selected in both eyes.

Step Three:
Go under the Select menu and choose Feather. You need to use Feather to soften the edges of your selection so your retouch isn't obvious. In the Feather Selection dialog, enter 2 pixels and click OK.

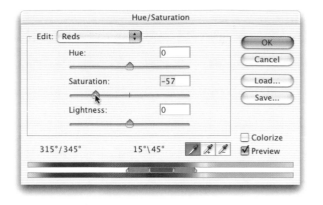

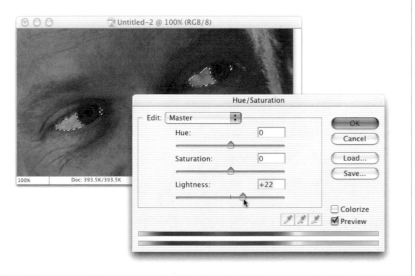

Step Four:
Go under the Image menu, under Adjustments, and choose Hue/Saturation. When the Hue/Saturation dialog appears, choose Reds from the Edit pop-up menu at the top (to edit just the reds in the photo). Now, drag the Saturation slider to the left to lower the amount of saturation in the reds (which removes any bloodshot appearance in the whites of the eyes).

Step Five:
While you're still in the Hue/Saturation dialog, from the Edit menu, switch back to Master. Drag the Lightness slider to the right to increase the lightness of the whites of the eyes (as shown here). Click OK in the Hue/Saturation dialog to apply your adjustments, and then press Command-D (PC: Control-D) to deselect and complete the enhancement. The enhancement appears fairly subtle in the capture shown below, but when you try it yourself at full size, the effect appears much more pronounced.

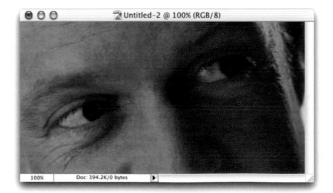

Before.

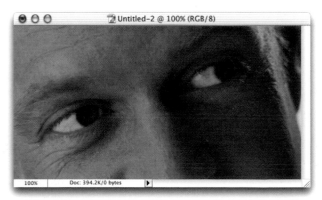

After (bloodshot eyes lessened, and whites brightened).

Whitening Eyes

Here's Kevin Ames's technique for brightening the whites of the eyes, and I have to say, even though it takes a little longer and has a few more steps, it really does a brilliant job, and offers the most realistic whites brightening I've seen.

Step One:

Open the photo with eyes you want to whiten.

© BRAND X PICTURES

Step Two:

Go to the Layers palette and choose Curves from the Adjustment Layer pop-up menu at the bottom of the palette. When the Curves dialog appears, don't make any adjustments—just click OK. When the Curves Adjustment Layer appears in your Layers palette, change the Blend Mode of this Adjustment layer from Normal to Screen.

Step Three:

When you switch to Screen Mode, the entire photo lightens. Press the letter "x" until your Foreground color is black; then, press Option-Delete (PC: Alt-Backspace) to fill the Curves Adjustment Layer mask with black. This removes the lightening effect brought on by changing the Mode to Screen.

Step Four:

Press the letter "d" to switch your Foreground color to white. Then, get the Brush tool, choose a very small, soft-edged brush, and paint over the whites of the eyes and along the bottom of the eyelid. As you paint, it brings back the Screen effect you applied earlier, lightening the areas where you paint.

Step Five:

The eyes will look too white (giving your subject a possessed look), so lower the Opacity of this Curves Adjustment Layer to make the whitening more subtle and natural. Below right, you see the final whitening with the Opacity of the Curves Adjustment layer down to just 35%.

Before.

After.

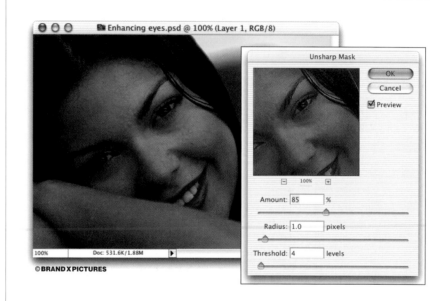

Enhancing and Brightening Eyes

This is another one of those "30-second miracles" for brightening eyes, enhancing the catch lights, and generally drawing attention to the eyes by making them look sharp and crisp (crisp in the "sharp and clean" sense, not crisp in the "I burned my retina while looking at the sun" kind of crisp).

Step One:

Open the photo you want to retouch. Go under the Filter menu, under Sharpen, and choose Unsharp Mask. When the Unsharp Mask dialog appears, enter your settings (if you need some settings, go to the first technique in Chapter 9, "Professional Sharpening Techniques"); then, click OK to sharpen the entire photo.

Step Two:

After you've applied the Unsharp Mask filter, apply it again using the same settings by pressing Command-F (PC: Control-F), and then apply it one more time using the same keyboard shortcut (you'll apply it three times in all). The eyes will probably look nice and crisp at this point, but the rest of the person will be severely oversharpened, and you'll probably see lots of noise and other unpleasant artifacts.

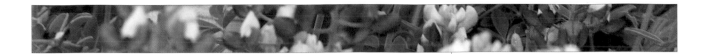

Step Three:
Go under the Window menu and choose History to bring up the History palette. This palette keeps track of your last 20 steps, and you'll see the four steps you've done thus far listed in the palette (an Open step, followed by three Unsharp Mask steps. By the way, these steps are actually called "History States"). Click on the Open State to return your photo to how it looked before you applied the Unsharp Mask filter.

Step Four:
In the History palette, click once in the first column beside the last Unsharp Mask State (as shown here). Now, switch to the History Brush and choose a soft-edged brush about the size of the iris. Click once right over the iris, and it will paint in the crisp, thrice-sharpened eye, leaving the rest of the face untouched. It does this because you clicked in that first column in the History palette. That tells Photoshop "paint from what the photo looked like at this point." Pretty cool!

Before.

After (the eyes sparkle).

Changing Eye Color

Well, Kevin Ames did it to me again. He calls me up, and we're talking about how I have just about finished the update to this book, and he says, "You're going to hate me again." I let him know I hadn't stopped hating him for all the extra work he made me do in the last version of the book, then he says, "No, you're really gonna hate me." Stupidly, I said, "Why?" and he said, "Have you tried the Color Replacement tool for changing eye color?" He's really getting on my nerves.

Step One:
Open the photo that contains an eye color you want to change. In this case, the subject has green eyes and we want to change them to blue (hey, it's not me—that's what the client wants).

Step Two:
Go to the Toolbox and choose the Color Replacement tool (as shown here). (Note: It's hidden behind the Healing Brush.) If you take a good look at the Toolbox icon for this tool (when it's highlighted like the one shown here), it looks as if Adobe had this tool in mind for removing red eye (and it actually works quite well for that I might add, but we're going to do a more respectable job here).

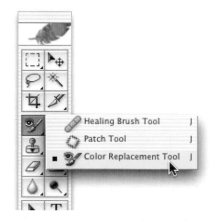

Step Three:
Now, you need to open a source photo, a photo that has the color eye you'd like. Take the Color Replacement tool and move it over the eye in your source photo. Hold the Option key (PC: Alt key) over the eye and click once to sample that eye color.

Step Four:
Now, switch back to the photo where you want to change the eye color, and begin painting over the eye. As you paint, the new color (from the blue eye you sampled earlier) replaces the green eye (as shown in the subject's left eye here).

Step Five:
Here's the final image, with the color changed on both eyes. If you've had any experience with using the Background Eraser tool (which erases regions based on color), you'll feel right at home with this tool, which makes its changes based on color, and you can tweak how the tool "does its thing" using similar options in the Options bar (although the default settings work quite well for most situations).

Enhancing Eyebrows and Eyelashes

After Kevin Ames showed me this technique for enhancing eyebrows and eyelashes, I completely abandoned the method I'd used for years and switched over to this method because it's faster, easier, and more powerful than any technique I've seen yet.

Step One:
Open the photo that you want to enhance.

Step Two:
Get the Lasso tool from the Toolbox and draw a loose selection around the eyebrow. It isn't necessary to make a precise selection; make it loose like the one shown here. Your subject might be turned so that there's only one eyebrow showing; but if there are two (meaning they don't have a uni-brow), after you select one eyebrow, hold the Shift key down and select the other eyebrow (as shown).

Step Three:
After your eyebrow(s) is selected, press Command-J (PC: Control-J) to put the eyebrow(s) on its own separate layer (as shown).

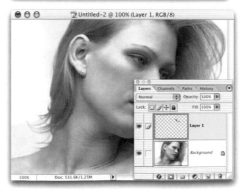

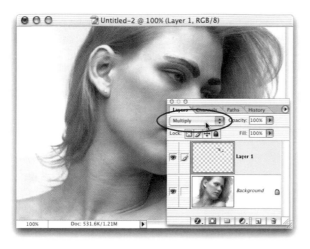

Step Four:
In the Layers palette, switch the Blend Mode of this eyebrow layer from Normal to Multiply, which darkens the entire layer (as shown here).

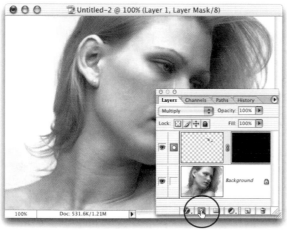

Step Five:
Hold the Option key (PC: Alt key) and click on the Layer Mask icon at the bottom of the Layers palette (as shown). Holding down the Option/Alt key fills the Layer Mask with black, which hides the Multiply effect from view. As you can see, the eyebrow looks normal again. Next, press the letter "d" to make white your Foreground color.

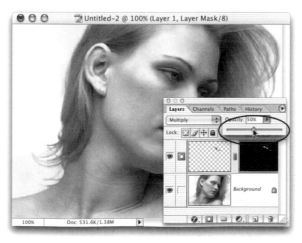

Step Six:
Choose a soft-edged brush that's about the size of the largest part of the eyebrow. Now, paint over the eyebrows, going from right to left. As you paint, hold the Left Bracket key to make your brush smaller as you trace the eyebrow. As you do, it darkens the eyebrow by revealing the Multiply effect. The final effect will probably be too intense, but you can fix that by lowering the Opacity of the Multiply layer in the Layers palette (as shown here).

Continued

Step Seven:

Now on to the eyelashes. In the Layers palette, click on the Background layer. Get the Lasso tool again and draw a loose selection around the eye(s), and make sure your loose selection fully encompasses the eyelashes (as shown here).

Step Eight:

Once the eye and eyelash area is fully selected, press Command-J (PC: Control-J) to copy it up to its own separate layer. Change the Blend Mode of this layer from Normal to Multiply, which darkens the entire layer (as shown).

Step Nine:

Hold the Option key (PC: Alt key) and click on the Layer Mask icon at the bottom of the Layers palette to add a Layer Mask filled with black to this layer. Just like on the eyebrows, doing this hides the Multiply effect (as shown). Make sure your Foreground color is still set to white, and then choose a very small soft-edged brush and paint along the base of the eyelashes to darken that area (as shown). Also paint along the top eyelid, at the base of the eyelashes to make the lashes appear thicker, fuller, longer, and more luxurious. (Incidentally, the reason we put the eyelashes and eyebrows on separate layers, rather than doing them at the same time, is so you can control the Opacity of each part individually.)

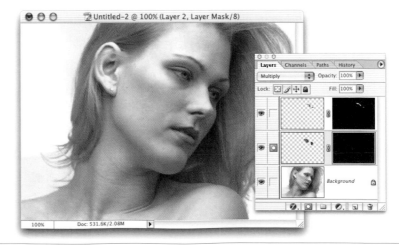

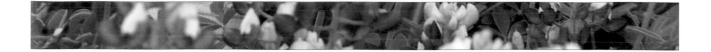

Before.   *After.*

© BRAND X PICTURES

Individual Eyelashes:
Step One:

When it comes to enhancing individual lashes, you can use the same technique: Just zoom in close on the eye and choose a very, very small brush (as shown). Then, start at the base of the eyelash (where it meets the lid) and trace the eyelash, following its contours to darken it. You may have to use a 1- or 2-pixel-sized brush to trace the lashes, but it will be worth it.

Step Two:

When you're done painting over the eyelashes, zoom back out to reveal your final retouch (as shown here). If the effect seems a bit too intense to you, just lower the Opacity of the layer.

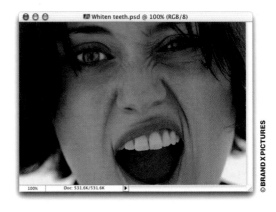

Whitening Teeth

This really should be called "Removing Yellowing, Then Whitening Teeth" because almost everyone has some yellowing, so we remove that first before we move on to the whitening process. This is a simple technique, but the results have a big impact on the overall look of the portrait, and that's why I do this to every single portrait where the subject is smiling.

Step One:
Open the photo you need to retouch.

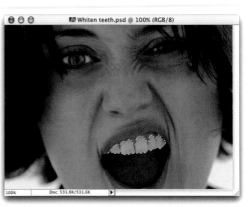

Step Two:
Switch to the Lasso tool, and carefully draw a selection around the teeth, being careful not to select any of the gums (as shown here).

Step Three:
Go under the Select menu and choose Feather. When the Feather Selection dialog appears, enter 1 pixel and click OK to smooth the edges of your selection. That way, you won't see a hard edge along the area you selected after you've whitened the teeth.

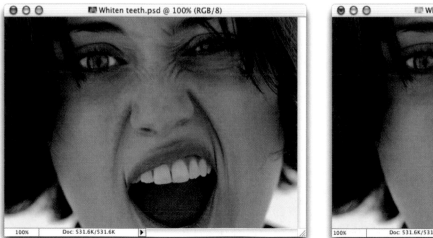

Step Four:
Go under the Image menu, under Adjustments, and choose Hue/Saturation. When the dialog appears, choose Yellows from the Edit pop-up menu at the top. Then, drag the Saturation slider to the left to remove the yellowing from the teeth.

Step Five:
Now that the yellowing is removed, switch the Edit pop-up menu back to Master, and drag the Lightness slider to the right to whiten and brighten the teeth. Be careful not to drag it too far, or the retouch will be obvious. Click OK in the Hue/Saturation dialog, and your enhancements will be applied. Last, press Command-D (PC: Control-D) to deselect and see your finished retouch (shown below).

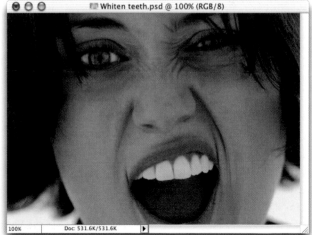

Before.

After.

Removing Hot Spots

If you've ever had to deal with hot spots (shiny areas on your subject's face caused by uneven lighting or the flash reflecting off shiny surfaces, making your subject look as if he or she is sweating), you know they can be pretty tough to correct. That is, unless you know this trick.

Step One:
Open the photo that has hot spots that need to be toned down.

Step Two:
Select the Clone Stamp tool in the Toolbox. Up in the Options bar, change the Blend Mode from Normal to Darken, and lower the Opacity to 50%. By changing the Blend Mode to Darken, we only affect pixels that are lighter than the area we're sampling, and those lighter pixels are the hot spots.

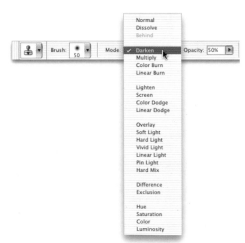

Step Three:

Make sure you have a large, soft-edged brush; then hold the Option key (PC: Alt key) and click once in a clean area of skin (an area with no hot spots) as shown here, on his forehead. This will be your sample area, or reference point, so Photoshop knows to affect only pixels that are lighter than this.

Step Four:

Start gently painting over the hot spot areas with the Clone Stamp tool, and as you do, the hot spots fade away. As you work on different hot spots, you have to resample (Option-/Alt-click) on nearby areas of skin so the skin tone matches. For example, when you work on the hot spots on his nose, sample an area of skin from the bridge of his nose (or even his forehead) where no hot spots exist. Below is the result after about 60 seconds of hot-spot retouching using this technique.

Before.

After.

Glamour Skin Softening

This is another technique I learned from Chicago-based retoucher David Cuerdon. David uses this technique in fashion and glamour photography to give skin a smooth, silky feel.

Step One:

Open the photo that you want to give the glamour skin-softening effect and duplicate the Background layer. The quickest way to duplicate a layer is to press Command-J (PC: Control-J).

Step Two:

Go under the Filter menu, under Blur, and choose Gaussian Blur. When the dialog appears, enter between 3 and 6 pixels of blur (depending on how soft you want the skin), to put a blur over the entire photo.

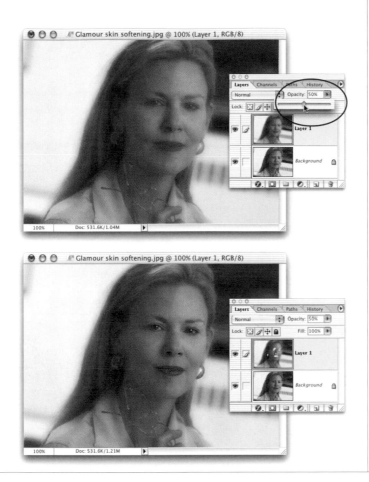

Step Three:

Lower the Opacity of this layer by 50% (as shown here). At this point, the blurring effect is reduced, and now the photo has a soft glow to it. You may want to stop here, with an overall soft, glamorous effect (used often in portraits of senior citizens). However, if this is too much softening for your subject, go on to the next step, which lets you selectively bring back detail in the facial areas that would have detail.

Step Four:

Switch to the Eraser tool, choose a soft-edged brush, and erase over the facial areas that are supposed to have sharp detail (her eyes, eyebrows, lips, and teeth) thereby revealing the original features on the layer beneath your blurry layer. David completes his retouch here, leaving the subject's clothes, hair, background, etc. with the soft glow. I prefer to switch to a larger soft-edge Eraser tool and erase over everything else in the photo (hair, background, etc.) except her skin. The final image is shown below.

Before.

After.

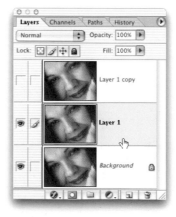

Advanced Skin Softening

This technique that I picked up from Kevin Ames does an amazing job of simulating a Hasselblad Softar #2 filter in that it softens the skin tones, but at the same time, introduces a little bit of soft flare and lowers the contrast of the image. Perfect for fashion photography.

Step One:

Open the photo you want to soften.

Step Two:

Press Command-J (PC: Control-J) twice to create two duplicates of your Background layer in the Layers palette. Then, hide the top copy (Layer 1 copy) by clicking on the Eye icon next to it in the Layers palette, and then click on the middle layer (Layer 1) to make it active (as shown).

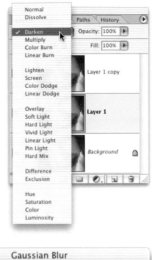

Step Three:
In the Layers palette, switch the Blend Mode of this middle layer from Normal to Darken.

Step Four:
Go under the Filter menu, under Blur, and choose Gaussian Blur. Apply a 40-pixel blur to the photo.

Step Five:
In the Layers palette, hide the middle layer from view, and then click on the top layer (Layer 1 copy). Change the Blend Mode of this top layer to Lighten.

Continued

Step Six:

Now, run a 60-pixel Gaussian Blur on this top layer.

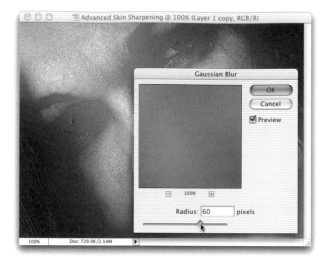

Step Seven:

After you apply the blur, click back on the middle layer (Layer 1) and lower its Opacity to 40% in the Layers palette.

Step Eight:

Hide the Background layer from view, and then create a new layer by clicking on the Create New Layer icon at the bottom of the Layers palette. Click-and-drag this layer to the top of your layer stack (as shown). Then, hold the Option key (PC: Alt key) and choose Merge Visible from the Layers palette's pop-down menu. This creates a flattened version of your document in your new layer.

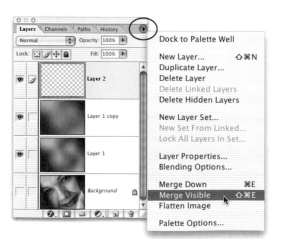

Step Nine:

In the Layers palette, make the Background layer visible again (as shown), but hide the two duplicate layers in the middle (Layer 1 and Layer 1 copy).

Step Ten:

Make sure the top layer in the stack (Layer 2) is the active layer, and then lower the Opacity of this layer to 40%.

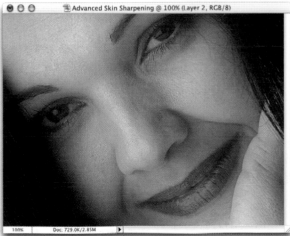

Step Eleven:

Lowering the Opacity of that layer creates the overall softening effect (which is fine if you want an overall effect), but in most cases, you won't want to soften the detail areas (eyes, lips, etc.).

Continued

Step Twelve:

Click on the Layer Mask icon at the bottom of the Layers palette to add a Layer Mask to your blurred layer. Press the letter "x" until your Foreground color is black, get the Brush tool, use a soft-edged brush, and paint over the areas that should have full detail (lips, eyes, eyebrows, eyelashes, hair, clothing—pretty much everything but the skin). The right photo below shows the results of the softening effect. The left photo shows the original (from Step One) without the softening.

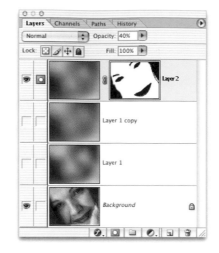

The original photo before applying the skin-softening technique.

The final photo with softened skin.

De-Emphasizing Nostrils

Don't ask me how Kevin Ames came up with this one, but as soon as he showed it to me, I knew I had to include it in the book. It's the easiest, most direct, and most effective way that I've seen of reducing the intensity of nostrils.

Step One:
Open a photo where you want to de-emphasize the subject's nostrils.

© BRAND X PICTURES

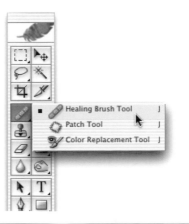

Step Two:
Choose the Healing Brush tool from the Toolbox.

Continued

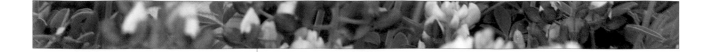

Step Three:

Option-click (PC: Alt-click) the Healing Brush in a clean area of skin on the cheek or general face area (as shown).

Step Four:

Paint with the Healing Brush over one of the nostrils (as shown). As you paint, the bright skin area appears over the nostril.

Step Five:

When you release the mouse button, the texture of the area you sampled appears in the nostril. It appears darker than it did in Step Four (as the Healing Brush does its "thing"), but it will most likely be too light and look a bit milky.

Step Six:

Fade

Opacity: 48 %

Mode: Normal

OK

Cancel

☑ Preview

Go under the Edit menu and choose Fade Healing Brush. When the Fade dialog appears (shown here), lower the Opacity slider until the nostril looks more natural—lighter and less distracting because of your retouch with the Healing Brush. Repeat Steps Three through Six for the second nostril. Below is the final photo with the Healing Brush faded to 32%. The retouch should be somewhat subtle, but compare the captures shown below and you can see how the emphasis is taken off the nostrils by lightening them.

Before.

After.

Transforming a Frown into a Smile

This is a pretty slick technique for taking a photo where the subject was frowning and tweaking it just a bit to add a pleasant smile in its place—which can often save a photo that otherwise would've been ignored.

Step One:

Open the photo that you want to retouch.

Step Two:

Go under the Filter menu and choose Liquify. When the Liquify dialog appears, choose the Zoom tool (it looks like a magnifying glass) from the Liquify Toolbar (found along the left edge of the dialog). Click it once or twice within the preview window to zoom in closer on your subject's face. Then, choose the Warp tool (it's the top tool in Liquify's Toolbar, as shown here).

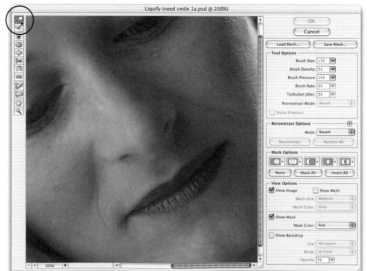

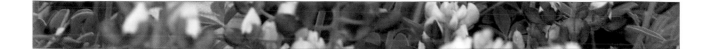

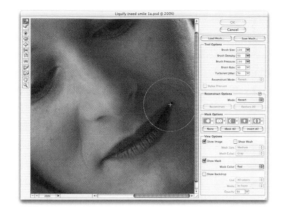

Step Three:
Press the Left/Right Bracket keys on your keyboard to adjust the brush size until it's about the size of the person's cheek. Place the brush near the corner of the mouth (as shown here), click and "tug" slightly up. This tugging of the cheek makes the corner of the mouth turn up, creating a smile.

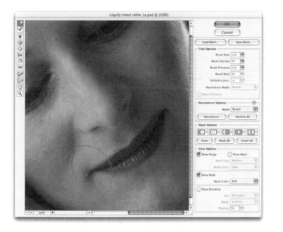

Step Four:
Repeat the "tug" on the opposite side of the mouth, using the already tugged side as a visual guide as to how far to tug. Be careful not to tug too far, or you'll turn your subject into the Joker from *Batman Returns.* Click OK in Liquify to apply the change, and the retouch is applied to your photo (as shown).

Before.

After.

Digital Nose Job

This very simple technique decreases the size of your subject's nose by 15 to 20%. The actual shrinking of the nose part is a breeze and only takes a minute or two—you may spend a little bit of time cloning away the sides of the original nose, but since the new nose winds up on its own layer, it makes this cloning a lot easier. Here's how it's done.

Step One:

Open the photo that you want to retouch. Get the Lasso tool, and draw a loose selection around your subject's nose. Make sure you don't make this selection too close or too precise—you need to capture some flesh-tone area around the nose as well (as shown in Step Two).

Step Two:

To soften the edges of your selection, go under the Select menu and choose Feather. When the Feather Selection dialog appears, for Feather Radius, enter 10 pixels (for high-res, 300-ppi images, enter 22 pixels), and then click OK.

Step Three:

Press Command-J (PC: Control-J) to copy your selected area onto its own layer in the Layers palette.

Step Four:

Press Command-T (PC: Control-T) to bring up the Free Transform bounding box. Hold Shift-Option-Command (PC: Shift-Alt-Control); then, grab the upper-right corner point of the bounding box and drag inward to add a perspective effect to the nose. Doing this gives the person a pug nose, but you fix that in the next step.

Step Five:

To get rid of the "pug-nose" effect, release all the keys, then grab the top-center point (as shown) and drag straight downward to make the nose look natural again, but now it's smaller. When the new size looks about right, press Return (PC: Enter) to lock in your changes. If any of the old nose peeks out from behind the new nose, click on the Background layer and use the Clone Stamp tool to clone away those areas: Sample an area next to the nose, and then paint (clone) right over it. Below, see the difference our 30-second retouch made in the image.

Before.

After.

Okay, if you remember that movie (*Invasion of the Body Snatchers*), you're way older than I am (remember, I'm only 19); therefore, for the rest of this chapter intro, I'll refer to you as either "gramps"

Invasion of the Body Snatchers
body sculpting

or "meemaa" (depending on your gender and what kind of mood I'm in). This chapter is a testament to the fact that people's bodies are simply not perfect, with the possible exception of my own, which I might say is pretty darn fine because of all the healthy food I eat at sundry drive-thru eating establishments that shall remain nameless (Wendy's). Anyway, your goal (my goal, our common goal, etc.) is to make people look as good in photos as they look in real life. This is a constant challenge because many people eat at McDonald's. Luckily, there are a ton of tricks employed by professional retouchers (who use terms like digital plastic surgery, botox in a box, digital liposuction, liquid tummy tucks, noselectomies, stomalectomies, and big ol' nasty feetalectomies) for a person who hasn't seen a sit-up or a stomach crunch since they tested for the President's Council on Physical Fitness and Sports (which for me, was just one year ago, when I was a senior). In this chapter, you learn the pros' secrets for transforming people who basically look like Shrek into people who look like the person who produced *Shrek* (I don't really know who that is, but those Hollywood types always look good, what with their personal trainers and all).

Slimming and Trimming

This is an incredibly popular technique because it consistently works so well, and because just about everyone would like to look about 10–15 pounds thinner. I've never applied this technique to a photo and (a) been caught, or (b) not had the client absolutely love the way they look. The hardest part of this technique may be *not* telling the client you used it.

Step One:

Open the photo of the person that you want to put on a quick diet.

Step Two:

Press Command-A (PC: Control-A) to put a selection around the entire photo. Then, press Command-T (PC: Control-T) to bring up the Free Transform function. The Free Transform handles appear at the corners and sides of your photo. These handles might be a little hard to reach, so I recommend expanding your image window a little bit by dragging its bottom-right corner outward. This makes some of the gray canvas area visible (as shown here), and makes grabbing the Free Transform handles much easier.

Step Three:

Grab the left-center handle and drag it horizontally toward the right to slim the subject. The farther you drag, the slimmer they become. How far is too far (in other words, how far can you drag before people start looking like they've been retouched)? Look up in the Options Bar at the W (width) field for a guide—you're pretty safe to drag inward to around 95% (or even 94%) without getting caught.

Step Four:

For our example, look in the Options bar (shown here) where I scaled her to 94.2%, and she still looks very natural. Press Return (PC: Enter) to lock in your transformation. Doing this transformation leaves you with some excess white canvas area on the left side of the photo; so press "c" to switch to the Crop tool, crop the photo to remove the white, and you're done.

Before.

After.

Removing Love Handles

This is a very handy body-sculpting technique, and you'll probably be surprised at how many times you'll wind up using it. It uses Liquify, which many people first dismissed as a "toy" for giving people "bug-eyes" and "huge lips," but it didn't take long for professional retouchers to see how powerful this tool could really be.

Step One:

Open the photo that has a love handle repair just waiting to happen. (In the photo at right, we're going to remove the small love handle on the right side of the body. I know this is probably the last person in the world that needs a love handle removal, but when you're looking through stock photos, finding a person that doesn't have a perfect physique is nearly impossible.)

Step Two:

Go under the Filter menu and choose Liquify. When the Liquify dialog appears, click on the Zoom tool in the Toolbar on the left-hand side of the dialog. Then, drag out a selection around the area you want to work on to give you a close-up view for greater accuracy.

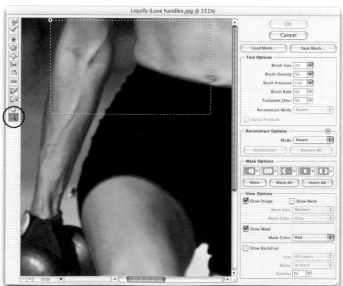

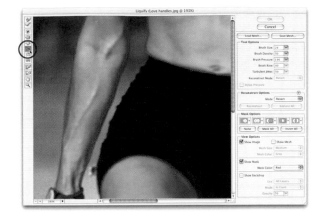

Step Three:
Get the Push Left tool from the Toolbar (as shown here). It was called the Shift Pixels tool in Photoshop 6 and 7, but Adobe realized that you were getting used to the name, so they changed it, just to keep you off balance.

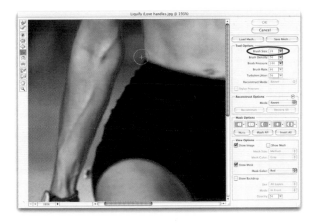

Step Four:
Choose a relatively small brush size (like the one shown here) using the Brush Size field near the top-right of the Liquify dialog. With it, paint a downward stroke starting just above and outside the love handle and continuing downward. The pixels shifts back in toward the body, removing the love handle as you paint. (Note: If you need to remove love handles on the left side of the body, paint upward rather than downward. Why? That's just the way it works.) When you click OK, the love handle repair is complete.

Before.

After.

Fixing Grannies

This is a body-sculpting technique I picked up from (once again) Kevin Ames, and it's great for trimming any excess skin from under the arms (these excess areas are sometimes referred to as "grannies" by mean retouchers).

Step One:

Open the photo that has an arm you want to tuck in, making it look thinner.

© BRAND X PICTURES

Step Two:

Press the letter "p" to get the Pen tool from the Toolbox and click it once at the base of her arm (near her armpit); then, move to her elbow area and click-and-drag to create the second point. As you drag, the path curves. Your goal is to have this part of the path dig a little bit into her skin (as shown), because you're now determining where the arm's edge will soon be.

Step Three:

Draw any points you need to close this path (bringing the path back to the point where you started). Then, press Command-Return (PC: Control-Enter) to turn the path into a selection.

Step Four:

Get the Clone Stamp tool from the Toolbox and Option-click (PC: Alt-click) on a background area near the arm you want to retouch (as shown).

Step Five:

Choose a soft-edged brush, and clone over the edge of the arm that falls within the selected area. Because you isolated the area first, you can't accidentally erase too much of her arm—Photoshop won't let you clone outside the selected area. Also, it's okay to use a soft-edged brush, because whichever brush you use, hard or soft, it will be stopped at the edge of the selected area. Press Command-D (PC: Control-D) to deselect and view the final result.

Before.

After.

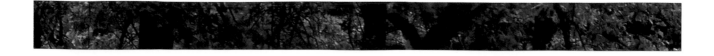

Slimming Thighs and Buttocks

This is a technique I picked up from Helene DeLillo that works great for trimming thighs and buttocks by repositioning parts of the existing areas. It's deceptively simple and amazingly effective.

Step One:

Open the photo that you need to retouch. In this case, we're going to reduce the size of the buttocks and thighs. (Note: The person in this photo doesn't really need a buttocks or thigh reduction, but as I mentioned earlier, you don't find many out-of-shape people in stock photos.)

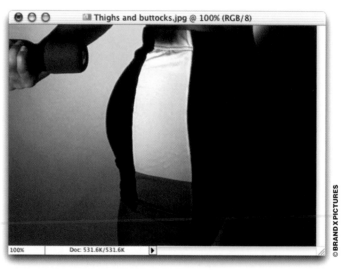

Step Two:

Press the letter "L" to get the Lasso tool from the Toolbox and make a selection loosely around the area you want to retouch. It's important to select some background area (as shown here) because that background will be used to cover over the existing area. The more you need to trim from the person, the more background area you need to select.

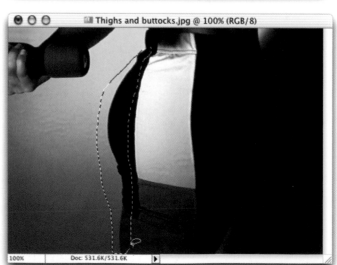

Step Three:
Once you have your selection in place, press Command-J (PC: Control-J) to put the selected area up on its own layer.

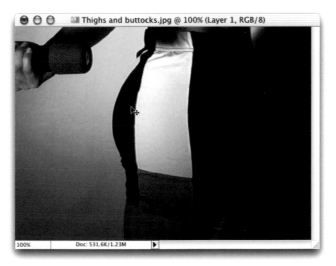

Step Four:
Press "v" to switch to the Move tool, click on the area you had selected (it's on its own separate layer now), and drag inward (right) toward the rest of her body. You're literally moving the edge of her body inward, thereby reducing the width of her thigh and buttocks.

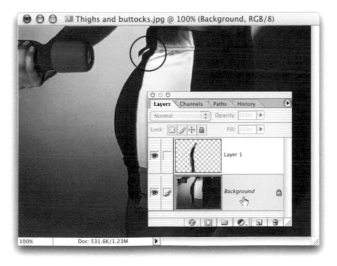

Step Five:
When you do this, you usually have a small chunk of the old body left over that you have to remove from the original Background layer (you can see the small chunk just above her buttocks, as shown here). The first step to fixing this tiny chunk is to go to the Layers palette and click on the Background layer (as shown).

Continued

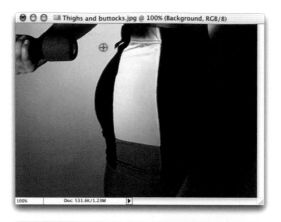

Step Six:

Get the Clone Stamp tool from the Toolbox, choose a small, hard-edged brush, and Option-click (PC: Alt-click) in an area very near where you need to retouch (as shown here, where I sampled from the area just to the left of the tiny chunk at the base of her lower back).

Step Seven:

To complete the retouch, paint (clone) over the little chunk to smooth out this area (a before and after is shown below). The fact that the photo had a relatively simple background made this retouch fairly easy. If you perform this retouch on skin (rather than pants), when you move the selected area in, you may have a visible hard line to deal with. The trick is to lower the Clone Stamp tool's Opacity to 50% in the Options bar, sample just outside the hard line, and then clone over the line to make it blend in with the existing skin.

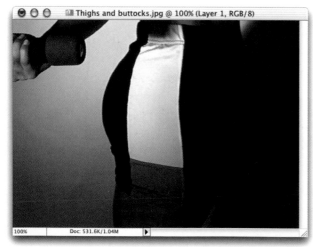

Before.

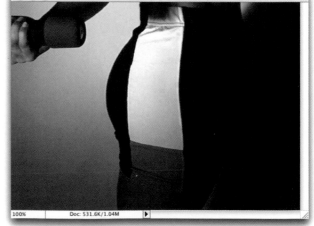

After.

This is a body-sculpting technique that basically has you "slicing off" extra tummy and hip areas, and is especially good at trimming the waist. One of the things that make this technique easy is a little up-front preparation—lassoing off the sections that surround the area where you're retouching so you don't accidentally slice off parts you don't want sliced off (so to speak).

Digital Tummy Tucks

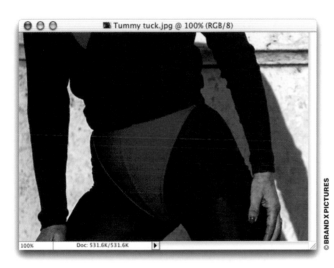

Step One:

Open the photo containing a tummy you want to tuck. In this example, we're going to trim the waist area and while we're there, we'll trim the hips just a bit too.

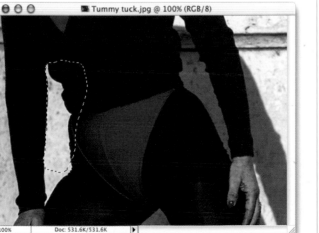

Step Two:

First, to make this retouch easier, start by isolating the area near where you want to retouch. For example, in the capture shown here, you want to trim the waist, but you don't want to accidentally trim her right arm; so get the Lasso tool and draw a selection that covers the area to the right of her arm, and let this selection extend into her body much farther than you're actually going to trim (as shown here).

Continued

Step Three:

Press the letter "s" to get the Clone Stamp tool from the Toolbox, then go up to the Brush Picker (in the Options bar) and choose a hard-edged brush (as shown here). The key here is the hard-edged brush; because her outfit has a hard edge (it's not soft or delicate, like hair), you have to choose a brush that matches the edge you're retouching. If you tried this with a soft-edged brush, it would look blurry on the edges, and be an absolute dead giveaway.

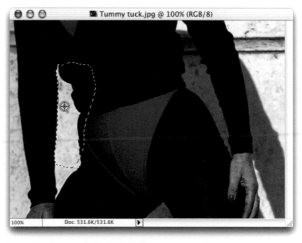

Step Four:

Take the Clone Stamp tool and move it over a background area directly beside the area you want to retouch. Hold the Option key (PC: Alt key) and click once on this background area (as shown) to set this as the source for your cloning (in other words, it's this background area that will be cloned over her waist in the next step).

Step Five:

Now that you've chosen a source area (the background area to the right of her arm), click your cursor within her skin (okay, it's not skin, it's her top) and literally "dig in" to the skin (as shown here) and paint a downward stroke. As you do, the edge of her top is replaced with the cloned source background. You basically just trimmed away those small "rolls" that appear because of the loose fit of her top around the waist.

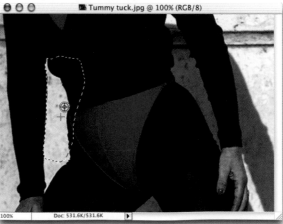

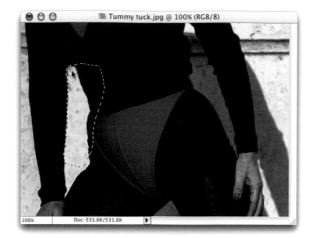

Step Six:

To trim the waist area further, paint an upward stroke (still digging into the skin, right above your last stroke) as shown here. Note the position of the cursor, just under where her arm and waist meet. You'll start just below that, and paint upward, trimming as you go.

Step Seven:

Since we're already trimming the tummy, why not trim the hips a bit as well (while you're in the neighborhood)? You do that by using the same "dig-in-to-the-skin" trick—just start right at the waist (where her pink bottom is) and paint a stroke right down the hips to trim them up (as shown

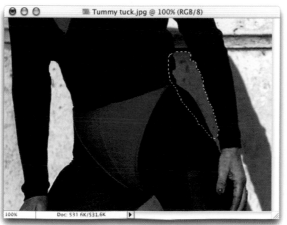

here).

Step Eight:

Now that you've trimmed the right side of the body, let's use the same technique on the left side, starting with the Lasso tool to isolate the area you'll be working on (as shown here).

Continued

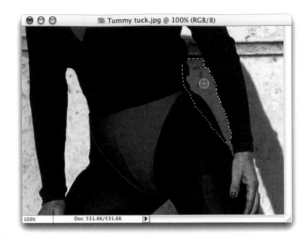

Step Nine:

Once isolated, get the Clone Stamp tool again and Option-click (PC: Alt-click) on the background right next to the area you want to trim to set that area as your cloning source (as shown here).

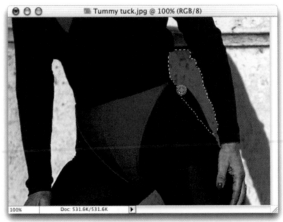

Step Ten:

Now, you'll "dig in" to the edge again, trimming away the tummy and hips. It looks like you'll have to clone a bit higher on this side, so after you do the waist and hips, press Command-D (PC: Control-D) to deselect. Now, you can use your hard-edged Clone Stamp tool to clone the wall above your old selection over the edge of her outfit that appears just below her left arm. The final retouch is shown below.

Before.

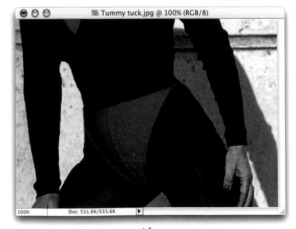

After.

This is where the fun begins. Okay, I don't want to discount all the immeasurable fun you've had up to this point, but now it gets *really* fun. Mondo-crazy fun. This is where we get to play around in

38 Special
photographic special effects

Photoshop and change reality, and then send the client an invoice for our "playtime." Did the model not have the right color blouse on? No sweat, change it in Photoshop. Was it an overcast day when you shot the exterior of your client's house? Just drop in a new sky. Do you want to warm up a cold photo like you did in the old days by screwing on an 81A filter? Now you can do it digitally. Do you want to take your income to the next level? Just take a crisp shot of a $20 bill, retouch it a bit, print out a few hundred sheets on your color laser printer and head for Vegas. (Okay, forget that last one, but you get the idea.) This is where the rubber meets the road, where the nose gets put to the grindstone, where the meat meets the potatoes... . (Where the meat meets the potatoes? Hey, it's late.)

Blurred Lighting Vignette

This technique is very popular with portrait and wedding photographers. It creates a dramatic effect by giving the appearance that a soft light is focused on the subject, while dimming the surrounding area (which helps draw the eye to the subject).

Step One:

Open the photo that you want to vignette. Get the Elliptical Marquee tool from the Toolbox and draw an oval-shaped selection where you'd like the soft light to fall on your subject. Go to the Layers palette and add a new layer by clicking on the Create New Layer icon.

Step Two:

Hold the Option key (PC: Alt key) and click once on the Layer Mask icon at the bottom of the Layers palette. This creates a Layer Mask from the oval, and holding the Option/Alt key automati-cally fills your oval mask with black.

Next, in the Layers palette, click once directly on the regular Layer thumbnail. Press "d" to set your Foreground color to black, then press Option-Delete (PC: Alt-Backspace) to fill the layer with black. Then, lower the Opacity to 65% in the Layers palette and your photo should look like the one shown here—a clear oval over your subject with a dark tint surrounding the oval area.

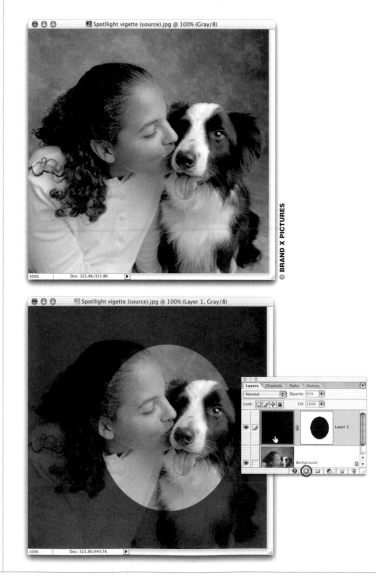

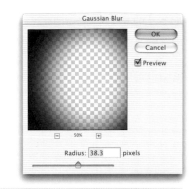

Step Three:
In the Layers palette, click once directly on the Layer Mask thumbnail for your layer (the thumbnail with the black oval in it). Go under the Filter menu, under Blur, and choose Gaussian Blur. When the Gaussian Blur dialog appears, drag the slider all the way to the left, then start dragging it to the right to soften the edges of the oval until it looks like a soft light in your photo.

Step Four:
When you click OK to apply the Gaussian Blur, the effect is complete, and now you have a soft lighting vignette falling on your subject and fading as it moves farther away.

NOTE: If this photo will be printed on a press (in an ad, brochure, and so on), some banding could appear within the vignette when it appears in print. Luckily, you can prevent that banding by going under the Filter menu, under Noise, and choosing Add Noise. When the Add Noise dialog appears, for Amount choose 3%, for Distribution choose Gaussian, and make sure you turn on the Monochromatic check box at the bottom of the dialog. Click OK and a tiny amount of noise will be applied. The noise may be slightly visible onscreen, but disappears when printed at high resolution.

Using Color for Emphasis

This technique is popular in commercial advertising because the client can focus the consumer's attention on their product in an artistic way. There are a number of different way to do this, but this particular method seems to be the fastest, and most forgiving if you make a mistake along the way. In the example here, we're going to focus the attention on the bride's bouquet by leaving it in color and making the rest of the image black-and-white.

Step One:
Open the photo that contains an object you want to emphasize through the use of color. In this case, we're going to draw the viewer's eye to the bouquet.

Step Two:
Go under the Image menu, under Adjustments, and choose Desaturate to remove all color from the photo (as shown here).

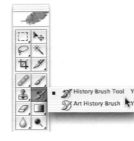

Step Three:
Go to the Toolbox and choose the History Brush (as shown here).

Step Four:
Get a soft-edged brush from the Brush Picker in the Options bar, and begin to paint over the area you want in color (in this case, you paint right over the bouquet, as shown here).

Step Five:
Continue painting over the flowers until the entire bouquet appears in full color. You may have to shrink the size of your brush to set some of the smaller petals, and if that's the case, it helps to zoom in close (use the Zoom tool) so you can really see the edges where you're painting. The final effect is shown here.

Adding Motion Where You Want It

This is a painless way to add motion to a still photo, and because you're using a Layer Mask, you have a lot of flexibility in where the effect is applied, making it easy to remove or edit any excess motion.

Step One:

Open the photo you want to give a motion effect. Duplicate the Background layer in the Layers palette by pressing Command-J (PC: Control-J).

© BRAND X PICTURES

Step Two:

Go under the Filter menu, under Blur, and choose Motion Blur. The Motion Blur dialog presents two settings: Angle lets you choose which direction the blur comes from and Distance determines the amount of blur. In this case, set the Angle to 0° so the blur is horizontal, and increase the Distance slider (amount) until it looks realistic.

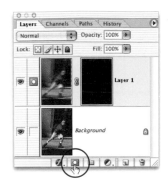

Step Three:
Hold the Option key (PC: Alt key) and click on the Layer Mask icon at the bottom of the Layers palette. Holding the Option/Alt key fills the Layer Mask with black, hiding the Motion Blur effect you applied to this layer.

Step Four:
Get the Brush tool from the Toolbox, and choose a medium-sized, soft-edged brush. Press the letter "x" until your Foreground color is white, then begin painting over the areas you want to have motion (as shown). As you paint, you reveal the Motion Blur that's already applied to the layer.

Step Five:
Complete the effect by painting over all the areas that you want to have motion. If you make a mistake and reveal motion on an area where you don't want it, simply switch your Foreground to black, then paint over the "mistake" area and the blur will be removed.

Focus Vignette Effect

This is another technique for focusing attention. This time, instead of using light (as we did in the first tutorial in this chapter), we're focusing attention by blurring non-critical areas, and leaving the focal point sharp.

Step One:

Open the photo that you want to apply the focus vignette effect. Press Command-J (PC: Control-J) twice to make two duplicates of the Background layer in your Layers palette (as shown below).

Step Two:

Hide the top layer (Layer 1 copy) by clicking on the Eye icon next to it in the far-left column of the Layers palette. Then, click on the middle layer to make it active.

Step Three:

Go under the Filter menu, under Blur, and choose Gaussian Blur. When the dialog appears, increase the Radius to make it "good and blurry." (That's a technical term used by highly technical people, like myself.)

Step Four:

Go to the Layers palette and click on the top layer (Layer 1 copy) to make it active. Get the Elliptical Marquee tool from the Toolbox and draw an oval around the area you want to remain in focus.

Step Five:

To soften the edges of your selection, go under the Select menu and choose Feather. For Feather Radius, enter 50 pixels (or higher if you want a smoother transition) and click OK. Remember, a 5-megapixel photo requires more blur than a 3-megapixel photo to get the same effect. The higher the resolution of the photo, the higher you have to adjust your settings to get the same effect.

Step Six:

Click on the Layer Mask icon (second icon from the left at the bottom of the Layers palette) to activate the effect (much in the same way Parmesan cheese activates pasta).

Adjusting the Color of Individual Objects

This effect is one of the most called upon by art directors working with photographers because of the cardinal rule of working with clients— they were born to change their minds. Now, if the client wishes they had sent a different color shirt for the photo shoot, you don't reshoot, you just retouch.

Step One:

Open the photo that contains an element that needs to be a different color. Select the area you want to recolor using any selection tool you'd like (Lasso tool, Pen tool, Extract—it doesn't matter which you use, but you have to have a pretty accurate selection). In this case, I want to change just the color of the fins—not the straps, so I used the Magic Wand tool to select all the blue areas, leaving the yellow straps unselected. Holding the Shift key and clicking in different areas of blue with the Magic Wand tool adds those areas to your selection.

Step Two:

Choose Hue/Saturation from the Adjustment Layer pop-up menu at the bottom of the Layers palette.

© BRAND X PICTURES

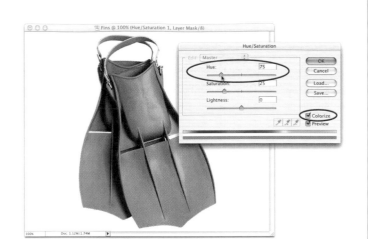

Step Three:

When the dialog appears, click on the Colorize check box at the bottom right of the dialog and then start dragging the Hue slider. As you drag, the color of the selected area changes.

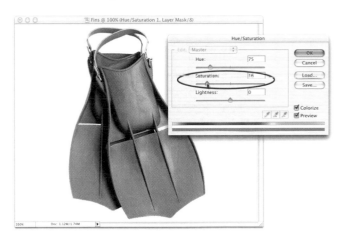

Step Four:

If the color appears too intense after dragging the Hue slider, just drag the Saturation slider (as shown) to the left to decrease the saturation of the color. If you don't like the color at all (and frankly, this green looks kind of pukey), no sweat—just drag the Hue slider to a different shade (in the example shown in the next step, I dragged the Hue slider until I got a nice purple).

Step Five:

Click OK in the Hue/Saturation dialog to complete the color change. (Here, we changed the color and lowered the Saturation.)

Replacing the Sky

This is the absolute #1 request I get from real-estate photographers: how to replace the sky in exterior shots taken for their clients. In the world of selling homes, "every day should be a bright sunny day," and with a little Photoshop magic, it can be.

Step One:

Open the photo that needs a new, brighter, bluer sky.

Step Two:

You have to select the sky, and in the example shown here I used the Magic Wand to select most of it. Then, I chose Similar from the Select menu to select the rest of the sky, but as usual, it also selected part of the house. So I had to hold the Option key (PC: Alt key) and use the Lasso tool to deselect some excess areas on the roof and in the windows. You can use any combination of selection tools you'd like.

Step Three:

Shoot some nice sunny skies (like the one shown here) and keep them handy for projects like this. Open one of these "sunny sky" shots, and then go under the Select menu and choose All to select the entire photo. Then, press Command-C (PC: Control-C) to copy this sky photo into memory.

Step Four:

Switch back to your original photo (the selection should still be in place), go under the Edit menu, and choose Paste Into.

Step Five:

When you choose Paste Into, the sky will be pasted into your selected area on its own layer over the old sky. If the sky seems too bright for the photo, simply lower the Opacity of the new sky layer in the Layers palette to help it blend in better with the rest of the photo.

Replicating Photography Filters

This is a totally digital way to replicate some of the most popular photography filters, such as the 81A and 81B Color Correction filters used by many photographers. These are primarily used to warm photos, especially those taken outdoors where a bright sky radiates to give photos a bluish cast. They're also useful when shooting in shade on a sunny day, or for correcting bluish light from overcast days. Luckily in Photoshop CS, it's simple to replicate both filters.

Step One:
Open the photo that needs the warming effect you'd get by applying an 81A Color Correction filter to your lens.

Step Two:
Choose Photo Filter from the Adjustment Layer pop-up menu at the bottom of the Layers palette (as shown here).

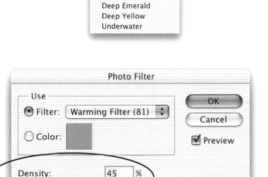

Step Three:
The Photo Filter dialog appears. Click-and-hold on the Filter pop-up menu and a list of filters appears. Since we're trying to warm the filter with an 81A-like effect, choose Warming Filter (81) from the menu (as shown).

Step Four:
Once you select which filter you're going to use, it's time to play with the Density slider to warm the photo. It's been my experience that the 25% default density setting is too subtle, so you'll probably wind up increasing the Density (in this example, increase it to around 45%, as shown).

Step Five:
When you click OK, the entire photo looks warmer (especially the flesh tones). If you like the warming of the flesh tones, but liked the background color or clothing color the way they were, just switch to the Brush tool, choose a soft-edged brush, set black as your Foreground color, and paint over the areas you *don't* want warmed by the filter. As you paint, those areas return to the cool blue (this is why it's so great that Adobe made these Photo Filters Adjustment Layers—they're editable!).

Layer Masking for Collaging

Photoshop collage techniques could easily fill a whole chapter, maybe a whole book; but the technique shown here is probably the most popular—and one of the most powerful—collage techniques used today by professionals. Best of all, it's easy, flexible, and even fun to blend photos seamlessly.

Step One:

Open the photo that you want to use as your base photo (this serves as the background of your collage).

Step Two:

Open the first photo that you want to collage with your background photo.

Step Three:

Press the letter "v" to switch to the Move tool in the Toolbox, and then click-and-drag the photo from this document right onto your background photo. It appears on its own layer.

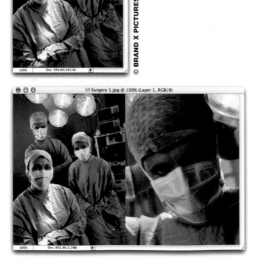

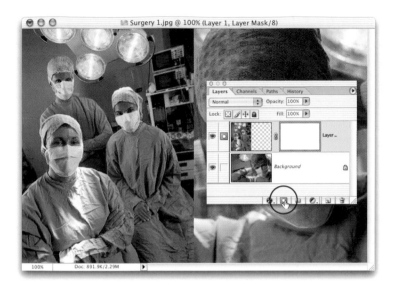

Step Four:
Click on the Layer Mask icon at the bottom of the Layers palette (as shown).

Step Five:
Press the letter "g" to get the Gradient tool from the Toolbox, and then press Return (PC: Enter) to bring up the Gradient Picker (it appears at the location of your cursor within your image area). Choose the Black to White gradient (it's the third gradient in the Picker, as shown).

Step Six:
Click the Gradient tool just inside the right edge of your top photo, then drag to the left. The point where you first click makes the top layer totally transparent, and the point where you stop dragging 100% opacity. Everything else blends in between.

Continued

Step Seven:

When you release the mouse, the top photo blends into the background. As you can see from the capture shown here, the top layer is totally transparent at the center, and the opacity increases toward the left until it becomes solid.

Step Eight:

Open another photo you'd like to blend in with your existing collage. Switch to the Move tool, and click-and-drag this photo onto the top of your collage in progress. Click on the Layer Mask icon at the bottom of the Layers palette to add a Layer Mask to this new layer.

Step Nine:

Click the Gradient tool in the center of your photo, and drag straight downward (as shown here) to blend this new photo in with the other layers.

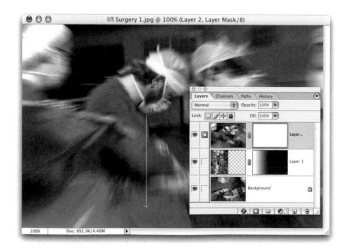

Step Ten:
Dragging downward (rather than side to side) leaves the top of the photo on this layer visible, blending off to transparency at the bottom and revealing the rest of the collage (as shown here).

Step Eleven:
If the image at the top seems too distracting, go to the Layers palette and lower the Opacity of this layer to 50%, to give the effect shown here.

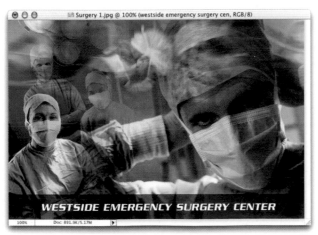

Step Twelve:
To finish the collage, I added a new layer, drew a horizontal rectangular selection across the bottom of the collage, and filled this selection with black. I then went to the Layers palette and lowered the opacity to 60% to make it transparent. Last, I added some type using the font Serpentine (from Adobe) as shown here in the final image.

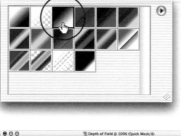

Depth-of-Field Effect

This is a digital way to create the classic in-camera depth-of-field effect, and thanks to Photoshop's Quick Mask, it's easy to pull off. Of course, for this technique to be effective, you have to start with the right photo, one that would benefit from a depth-of-field effect. (Close-up photos of people are ideal, as are product shots, as long as they're not shot straight on or, if they are, they need to have a detailed background behind them.)

Step One:

Open the photo on which you want to apply a depth-of-field effect. Switch to Quick Mask mode by pressing the letter "q."

Step Two:

Press the letter "g" to get the Gradient tool from the Toolbox, and press the Return key (PC: Enter key) to make the Gradient Picker appear within your image area. Double-click on the third gradient in the Picker (the Black to White gradient) to choose it.

Step Three:

Click the Gradient tool on your photo starting in the area you want to remain in focus, and then drag toward the area you want to appear out of focus. In this example, I want the hand on the right to appear in focus, and the hand on the left to appear out of focus, so I start by dragging from the fingers on the right over to the fingers on the left (as shown).

Step Four:
Since you're in Quick Mask Mode, you see a red-to-transparent gradient appear onscreen.

Step Five:
Press the letter "q" again to leave Quick Mask and return to Standard Mode. You see the selection you created in Quick Mask Mode appear within your image area.

NOTE: If the selected area in your image is the opposite of what is shown here, double-click on the Quick Mask icon just below the Color Swatches in the Toolbox to bring up the Quick Mask Options dialog. Under Color Indicates, choose Masked Areas. Click OK to enter Quick Mask Mode and then redraw your gradient.

Step Six:
Go under the Filter menu, under Blur, and choose Lens Blur. When the dialog appears (shown here), move the Radius slider to choose the amount of blur you'd like for the farthest point in your image, then click OK. Although you see a hard selection within your image area, it's actually a smooth blend from full blur to no blur. When you apply this filter, you'll see what I mean because the left side of your photo should be blurred, and progressing to the right, the photo becomes less and less blurry.

Continued

Step Seven:

Go under the Select menu and choose Inverse, which switches the selected area from the blurred area to the in-focus area (as shown here).

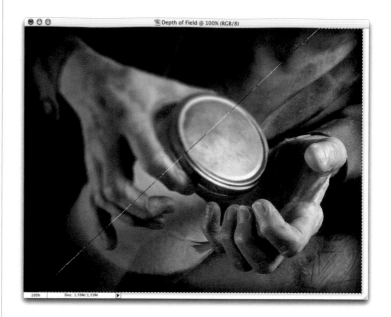

Step Eight:

Now, to exaggerate the effect, apply an Unsharp Mask filter to the area that's supposed to be in focus by going under the Filter menu, under Sharpen, and choosing Unsharp Mask. When the dialog appears, try 85 for Amount, 1 for Radius, and 4 for Threshold, then click OK.

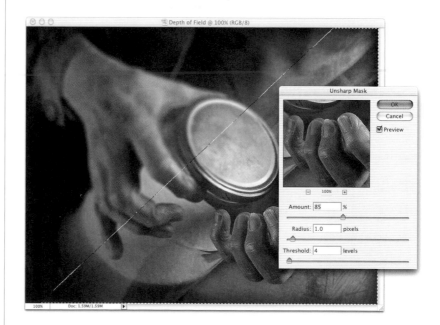

Step Nine:

Deselect by pressing Command-D (PC: Control-D). As you can see, the final effect (bottom right) has the area closest to the lens in sharp focus, and the depth-of-field effect increases for the part that appears farther away.

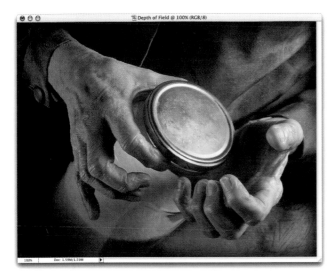

Before.

After.

Stitching Panoramas Together

You don't need a $500 stand-alone application to stitch together simple panoramas because you can do it in Photoshop. You can, however, make the process dramatically easier if you follow these two simple rules before you shoot your pano: (1) Use a tripod. That's not to say you can't shoot panos handheld, but the consistency a tripod brings to panos makes a world of difference when you try to stitch the photos together. And (2), when you shoot each segment, make sure that part of the next segment overlaps at least 15% of your previous segment (you'll see why this is important in the tutorial).

Step One:
Open the first segment of your pano. The photo shown here is the first of three segments that we'll be stitching together.

Step Two:
Next, go under the Image menu and choose Canvas Size. In the capture shown here, you can see the Width of the first segment is 5.014 inches. We're stitching three segments together, so we need to add enough blank canvas to accommodate two more photos of the same size, so make sure the Relative check box is turned on, then enter 14 inches as the Width setting. This extra blank canvas needs to be added to the right of your first segment, so in the Anchor grid (at the bottom of the dialog) click the left center grid square (as shown here).

© BRAND X PICTURES

Step Three:

Click OK and 14″ of white canvas space is added to the right of your photo (if it doesn't look like the capture shown here, press Command-Z [PC: Control-Z] to Undo, then go back and check your Anchor grid setting and make sure you clicked on the *left* center grid square).

Step Four:

Now, open the second segment of your pano. Notice that the rocks on the far right of the first segment also appear in the second segment. That's absolutely necessary because now we have common objects that appear in both photos, and we can use the rocks as a target to line up our panos.

Step Five:

Press the letter "v" to get the Move tool from the Toolbox and click-and-drag your second segment into the first segment's document window. Drag the second segment over until it overlaps the first segment a bit. I've zoomed in here so you can see the two segments overlapping.

Continued

Step Six:

Go to the Layers palette and lower the Opacity of this second segment's layer to 50% (as shown here). This is pretty much the secret of stitching together panos. As long as there's a common element in both photos, you can lower the Opacity of the top layer, and drag it with the Move tool until the two objects line up perfectly together.

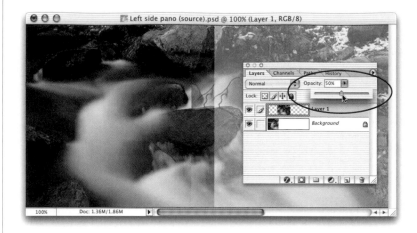

Step Seven:

As the two rocks (your target objects) get closer in alignment, it's easier if you take your hands off the mouse and do the final aligning using the Arrow keys on your keyboard. Start nudging the top layer with the Left Arrow key to line them up. Because the Opacity has been lowered on the top layer, things look kind of blurry (almost out of focus), but as the two target objects get closer to each other, the blur lessens.

Step Eight:

Keep nudging with the Arrow keys, and when the rocks don't look fuzzy anymore and are perfectly clear, your two segments are lined up right on the money (as shown here).

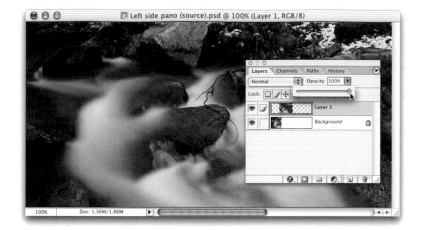

© BRAND X PICTURES

Step Nine:
Now, go to the Layers palette and raise the Opacity of the top layer to 100% (as shown) to see how your stitch looks. The two images should look like one (that is if you shot them using a tripod and didn't bump the camera along the way). If you see a hard edge along the left-hand side of the top layer, switch to the Eraser tool; choose a 200-pixel, soft-edged brush; and lightly erase over the edge. Since the photos overlap, as you erase the edge, the top photo should blend seamlessly into the bottom photo.

Step Ten:
Now, open the third segment of your three-segment pano (as shown here).

Step Eleven:
Repeat the same technique of dragging this photo into your main pano, lowering the Opacity of this layer to 50%, and dragging the segment over your target object. (In this example, we're using overlapping rocks again. Hey, it's not like we've got a lot of other options here, eh?)

Continued

Step Twelve:

Don't forget, as you get close to lining up the rocks, take your hands off the mouse and use the Arrow keys on your keyboard to perfectly align the two segments (as shown here where the two versions of the rocks line up perfectly). Again, after you raise the Opacity of the top layer back to 100%, if you see a hard edge between the two, use a soft-edged Eraser to erase away that seam.

Step Thirteen:

Here are the three segments stitched together in Photoshop. As you can see, by guessing that we'd need 14 inches, I overestimated a bit, and there's some blank canvas space to the right of my pano. No sweat. There's a quick way to get rid of it without even using the Crop tool.

Step Fourteen:

Go under the Image menu and choose Trim to bring up the Trim dialog (shown here). The area we no longer need is on the right-hand side (the extra white area), so in the dialog, under Based On, choose Bottom Right Pixel Color and it will trim away everything outside your photo that is white (which is the color of your bottom-right pixel).

© BRAND X PICTURES

© BRAND X PICTURES

Step Fifteen:

Click OK in the Trim dialog, and the excess Canvas area is trimmed away and your pano is complete (as shown here). Now this was an ideal situation: You shot the panos on a tripod, so the stitching was easy; and you didn't use a fisheye or wide-angle lens, so there wasn't much stretching or distorting to deal with. (Incidentally, we use Free Transform's Distort and Perspective functions to deal with segments that appear to bow upward or outward.)

Step Sixteen:

However, one thing that will absolutely happen from time to time is that the colors of each segment won't precisely match. Technically, they should match—they're shot at the same time, under the same lighting conditions, using the same camera settings, yet—it happens. Luckily, Adobe's own Graphics Guru (and Photoshop Hall of Famer) Russell Preston Brown came up with a great technique for dealing with that common occurrence. Here's how Russell does it: Open the first segment (this will be just a two-segment pano) and add the Canvas size as shown previously.

Step Seventeen:

Open the second segment, drag it on top of the first segment, lower the Opacity, and line up your photo using the common target object (in this case, it's the house in the center).

Continued

Step Eighteen:

After the segments are lined up and the Opacity is raised back to 100% on the top layer, you can see the problem—although the two segments line up perfectly, the tone of the right side differs from the tone of the left side (as shown). Your goal is to make the photo on the right (the top layer) match the tone from the photo on the left (the Background layer). You do this by making simple grayscale edits to the top layer's channels.

Step Nineteen:

Make the Channels palette visible, then click on the Red channel (as shown). Your pano now appears in grayscale (by default, all the channels display as grayscale). As you can see, the tonal difference is very visible here in the grayscale Red channel as well.

Step Twenty:

Next, press Command-L (PC: Control-L) to bring up the Levels dialog (shown here). What you're going to do is drag the midtone Input Levels slider (the center one, directly under the histogram) to the right (as shown) to balance the Red channel of your right image (your top layer) with that of the left image (your bottom layer). When they match, click OK to apply the adjustment.

Step Twenty-One:
Go to the Channels palette, and click on the Green channel (as shown).

Step Twenty-Two:
Press Command-L (PC: Control-L) to bring up the Levels dialog, and drag the midtone Input Levels slider until the two sides match (as shown), and then click OK to apply the adjustment.

Step Twenty-Three:
Go to the Channels palette and click on the Blue channel (as shown).

Continued

Step Twenty-Four:
Press Command-L (PC: Control-L) to bring up the Levels dialog, drag the midtone Input Levels slider until the two sides match (as shown), and then click OK to apply the adjustment.

Step Twenty-Five:
Go to the Channels palette, and click on the RGB channel to see your adjustments. As you can see here, if you matched up each channel, the color image now matches up as well. Here's the final pano after removing the excess Canvas area using the Trim command and using a soft-edged eraser to hide the edge between the two segments.

Automated Pano Stitching with Photomerge

If you've taken the time to get your pano set up right during the shoot (in other words, you used a tripod and overlapped the shots by about 15 to 20% each), then you can have Photoshop CS's new "Photomerge" feature automatically stitch your panoramic images together. If you handheld your camera for the pano shoot, you can still use Photomerge—you'll just have to do most of the work manually.

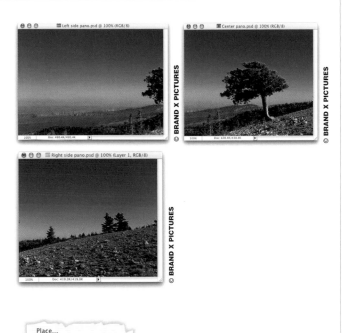

Step One:
Open the photos that you want Photomerge to stitch together as one panoramic image. In the example shown here, I had three shots already open in Photoshop.

Step Two:
There are two ways to access Photomerge: (1) Go under the File menu, under Automate, and choose Photomerge (as shown here), or (2) you can choose Photomerge directly from the mini-menu bar within Photoshop CS's File Browser. In fact, you can save time by selecting the photos in the File Browser that you want to merge, then choosing Photomerge from the Browser's Automate menu (pretty darn convenient).

Continued

Step Three:

If you choose Photomerge from the Automate menu, a dialog appears (shown here) asking which files you want to combine into a panorama. Any files you have open appear in the window, or you can change the Use pop-up menu to Files, then you can choose individual photos or a folder of photos to open. Make sure the Attempt to Automatically Arrange Source Images check box is on if you want Photomerge to try to build your pano for you.

Step Four:

If your pano images were shot correctly (as I mentioned in the introduction of this technique), Photomerge generally stitches them seamlessly together (as shown here). By default, Photomerge creates a flattened image, but if you want a layered file instead (great for creating panoramic video effects), turn on the Keep as Layers check box in the bottom right-hand corner of the dialog.

Step Five:

Click OK and your final panorama appears as one image (as shown here). This is what we call the "best-case scenario," where you shot the panos on a tripod and overlapped them just right so Photomerge had no problems and did its thing right away, making it perfect the first time. But you know, and I know, life just isn't like that.

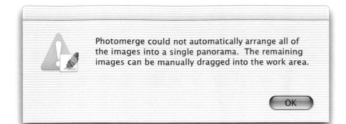

Step Six:

More likely what you'll get (especially if you handheld your camera, or didn't allow enough overlap) is a warning dialog that lets you know that Photomerge "ain't gonna do it for you" (that's a technical phrase coined by Adobe's Alabama tech office). In other words—it's up to you.

Step Seven:

Once you click OK in that warning dialog, Photomerge at least tries to merge as many segments as possible. The segments it can't merge are placed in the "Lightbox" (the horizontal row across the top). Although Photomerge didn't do all the work for you, it can still help—just make sure the Snap to Image check box (in the bottom right-hand corner) is turned on (as shown here).

Step Eight:

Using the Select Image tool (the hollow arrow at the top of the Toolbar), drag a segment from the Lightbox down to your work area near the first image. When you get close, release your mouse button. If Photomerge sees a common overlapping area, it snaps them together, and blends any visible edges. It actually works surprisingly well. If you need to rotate a segment to get it lined up, click on it with the Select Image tool first, then switch to the Rotate Image tool, and click-and-drag within the segment to rotate. See, it's not that hard (especially using "Snap to Image").

If you've ever converted a color photo to a grayscale (black-and-white) photo by going under the Image menu, under Mode, and choosing Grayscale, you were probably pretty disappointed with the results.

Back in Black
from color to grayscale

It probably looked less like Ansel Adams, and more like Anson Williams (the guy who played Potsie on *Happy Days*, which I'm told is a TV show that aired long before I was born, seeing as though I'm just 17 years old, which doesn't really explain how I came up with the chapter title "Back in Black" from AC/DC, which is another band that I guess my parents used to listen to. Freaks). Anyway, Photoshop has a number of different ways to convert from color to black-and-white that can give you dramatically better results than Photoshop's default conversion, which… well…emits a pungent odor not unlike a dachshund that dined on a leftover chalupa. Which method is right for you? Try them and find out which one suits your style.

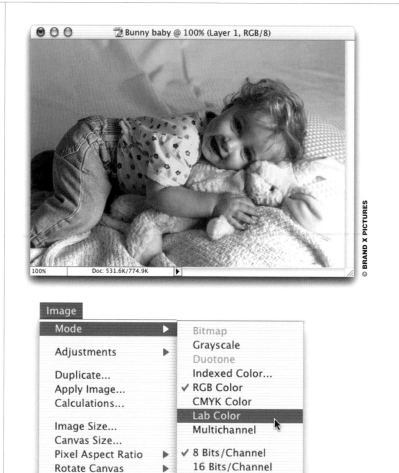

Using the Lightness Channel

This method of converting an RGB image to grayscale lets you isolate just the luminosity in the photo, separating out the color; and by doing so, you often end up with a pretty good grayscale image. However, since this uses the Lightness channel, we also add one little twist that lets you "dial in" a perfect grayscale photo almost every time.

Step One:
Open the color photo that you want to convert to grayscale using the Lightness method.

Step Two:
Go under the Image menu, under Mode, and choose Lab Color to convert your RGB photo into Lab Color mode. You won't see a visual difference between the RGB photo and the Lab Color photo—the difference is in the channels that make up your color photo (as you'll see in a moment).

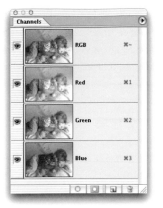

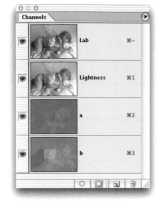

Regular RGB image.   *Converted to Lab Color.*

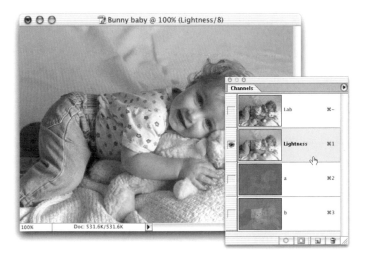

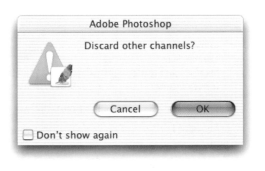

Step Three:
Go to the Channels palette and you'll see that your photo is no longer made up of a Red, a Green and a Blue channel (as shown far left). Instead, the luminosity (the Lightness channel) has been separated from the color data, which now resides in two channels named "a" and "b" (shown at right).

Step Four:
We're interested in the grayscale image that appears in the Lightness channel, so click on the Lightness channel in the Channels palette to make it active. (Your photo now looks grayscale onscreen too, as it displays the current active channel).

Step Five:
Now, go under the Image menu, under Mode, and choose Grayscale. Photoshop asks if you want to discard the other channels. Click OK.

Continued

Step Six:

If you look in the Channels palette, you see just a Gray channel (as shown here).

Step Seven:

Go to the Layers palette, click on the Background layer, then press Command-J (PC: Control-J) to duplicate the Background layer. Switch the Blend Mode of this duplicated layer from Normal to Multiply, and you see the photo become much darker onscreen.

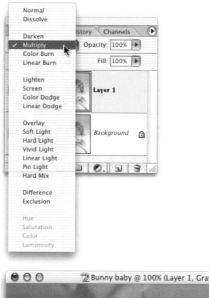

Step Eight:

Chances are, changing that top layer to Multiply made your photo too dark (as shown here). Since you're using a "multiplier" effect (the Multiply Blend Mode), getting a darker result is fairly common, but you fix that in the next step.

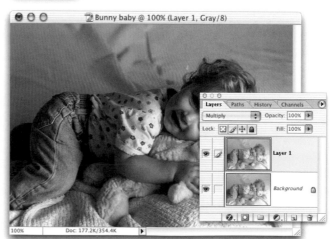

Step Nine:

This is where you get to "dial in" your ideal tone (and fix that "too dark" look from the Multiply layer). Just lower the Opacity of your Multiply layer in the Layers palette until you have the tonal balance you've been looking for. Below, you see the final conversion from color to grayscale, using the Lab color method, which gives you much more control, and depth, than just choosing Grayscale mode from the Image menu.

Standard grayscale conversion.

Lab Lightness Channel conversion.

Custom Grayscale Using Channel Mixer

This has become the favorite of many professionals (and some argue that this is the absolute best way to create grayscale photos from color photos) because it lets you blend all three RGB channels to create a custom grayscale image, and it's easier to use (and more intuitive) than using the Calculations feature that I'll show you later in this chapter. Here's how it works.

Step One:

Open the color photo you want to convert to grayscale. Choose Channel Mixer from the Adjustment Layers pop-up menu at the bottom of the Layers palette (as shown here). Channel mixer is also found under the Image menu, under Adjustments; however, by choosing it as an Adjustment layer, you have the added flexibility of being able to edit your grayscale conversion later in your creative process, or to change your mind altogether and instantly return to a full-color photo.

Step Two:

By default, the Channel Mixer is set to blend color RGB channels. When you're using this tool to create a gray-scale image, you have to turn on the Monochrome check box at the bottom of the dialog to enable the blending of these channels as grayscale.

Step Three:

Now that you're blending the chan-nels as grayscale, you can use the three sliders to combine percentages of each

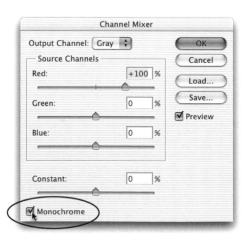

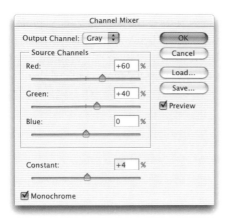

channel to create your grayscale photo. When blending channels, a rule of thumb is to make sure that whatever your percentages are, they add up to a total of no more than 100% (as shown here). You can tweak the overall brightness of your grayscale image using the Constant slider at the bottom of the dialog.

Step Four:
Click OK and the Channel Mixer is applied to your photo to create a grayscale image.

Regular grayscale conversion.

Channel Mixer grayscale conversion.

TIP: After you click OK, if you decide you want to edit your Channel Mixer settings—just double-click on the Channel Mixer layer thumbnail in your Layers palette (as shown here), and the Channel Mixer dialog appears with the last settings you applied to your photo. If you decide that you don't want your photo to be grayscale at all, just click-and-drag the Channel Mixer Adjustment Layer into the Trash icon at the bottom of the Layers palette.

"Ansel Adams-Style" Extreme Grayscale Conversion

Got a great shot of a mountainous landscape and want to convert it to grayscale with an Ansel Adams-style conversion (one with intense contrast and depth)? Try Jim DiVitale's great trick for an instant Ansel-like effect using the Channel Mixer.

Step One:

Open the color photo you want to convert into a high-contrast Ansel Adams-style black-and-white image.

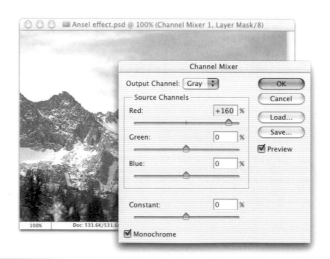

Step Two:

Go to the Layers palette, and from the Adjustment Layer pop-up menu at the bottom of the Layers palette, choose Channel Mixer. When the Channel Mixer appears, first, click on the Monochrome check box in the bottom left-hand corner (this changes your output channel to gray, giving you a black-and-white photo). Then, drag the Red slider to the right until it reads +160. (Note: This is just a starting point, but to add extreme contrast, it takes extreme measures.)

Step Three:
Drag the Green channel slider to the right until it reads around +190 (as shown). This pretty much blows out the photo (giving you extreme highlights) but the next step brings the detail back, and creates extreme shadows.

Step Four:
Last, drag the Blue slider all the way to the left until it reads -200%. When you click OK, you'll have the extreme black-and-white conversion shown below right. Again, these are just starting points—depending on the photo, you might try bringing the Green channel down to +140, or moving the Constant slider up 3 or 4% to add some brightness.

Regular grayscale conversion.

Extreme grayscale conversion.

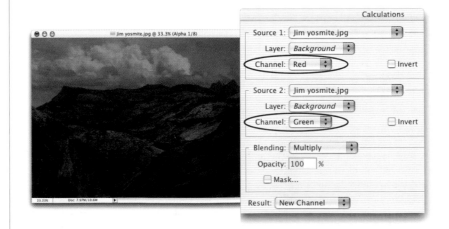

Calculations Method

ADVANCED TECHNIQUES
FOR PROS ONLY!

If there's one dialog in Photoshop that scares the living daylights out of people, it's the Calculations dialog. It's got an awfully intimidating layout for a dialog that simply lets you combine channels, and that's part of the beauty of it—once you learn this technique, you can "name drop" with it to impress other Photoshop users. For example, if you're talking color-to-grayscale conversions, just mention in passing, "Oh, I don't use Channel Mixer. I do my conversions using Calculations," and they'll act like P. Diddy just walked in the room. Bling, bling!

Step One:

Open the color photo that you want to convert to grayscale using Calculations. Go under the Image menu and choose Calculations to bring up the Calculations dialog. This scary-looking dialog lets you choose two channels from your photo that you can blend to create an entirely new channel. That way, if you have one channel that looks too dark, and one that looks too light, you can combine the two into one gloriously perfect channel (at least, that's the theory). Once you realize that's what you're doing in Calculations, the dialog becomes much less intimidating.

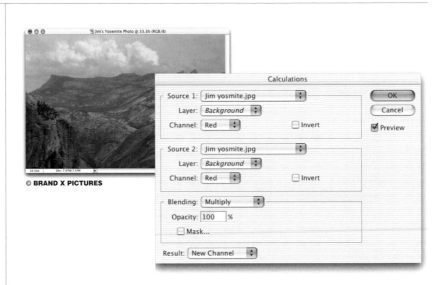

© BRAND X PICTURES

Step Two:

So, your job is to choose two channels from your color photo and blend them (using the Blend Modes in Calculations) to create a new grayscale channel that looks better than if you had used Photoshop's default grayscale conversion. It's easier than it sounds. First, start by choosing the Red channel from the Source 1 Channel pop-up menu. Then, choose Green from the Source 2 Channel pop-up menu, as shown here.

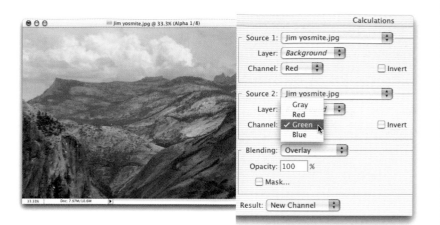

Step Three:

In this case, with the Blend Mode set to Multiply and the Opacity at 100%, the photo looks a little too dark. So, to get a better-looking grayscale photo, you can (a) try different channel combinations (rather than Red and Green, try Red and Red, or Red and Blue, or Red and Gray, or Green and Blue, etc.); (b) change the Blend Mode to something other than Multiply and see how it looks; or (c) lower the Opacity setting just a little (maybe 5% or 10%) and see how a more subtle blending works.

Step Four:

When you've come up with a combination that looks good to you, go to the Result pop-up menu at the bottom of the dialog (by "Result," they mean "what should Photoshop do with this new channel you've created?") and choose New Document. Click OK. A new document appears with your custom-calculated channel as the Background layer. One last thing: In this new document, go under the Image menu, under Mode, and choose Grayscale.

Regular grayscale conversion.

Grayscale conversion using Calculations.

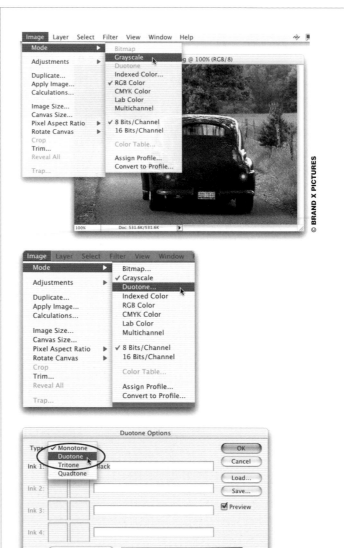

Creating Duotones

For some reason, creating a duotone (a photo that uses just two colors) in Photoshop is immeasurably more complex than creating one with four colors (as in CMYK). You definitely have to jump through a few hoops to get your duotones to look good and separate properly; but the depth added by combining a second, third, or fourth color with a grayscale photo is awfully hard to beat.

Step One:
Open the photo that you want to convert to a duotone. If you're starting with a color photo, you have to convert to grayscale first by going under the Image menu, under Mode, and choosing Grayscale.

Step Two:
Once your photo is grayscale, you can go under the Image menu, under Mode, and choose Duotone.

Step Three:
This may seem weird, but the first time you open the Duotone Options dialog, for some reason, Adobe set the default Type of Duotone to Monotone (I know, it doesn't make sense), so to actually get a duotone, you first have to select Duotone from the Type pop-up menu at the top left of the dialog.

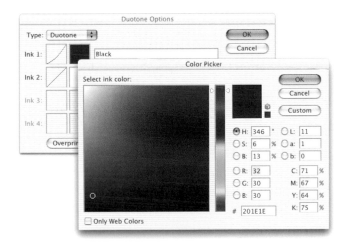

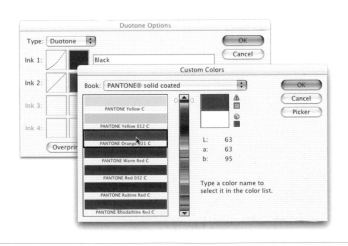

Step Four:

Now that Duotone is your selected Type, you have to choose which two inks you want to use. First, we look at Ink 1. The first box (the one with the diagonal line through it) is called the "Curve Box," and this is where you determine how the color you choose will be distributed within your photo's highlights, midtones, and shadows. You determine this distribution using a Curve. (Now don't stop reading if you don't know how to use Curves—you don't need to know Curves to create a duotone, as you'll soon see.)

Step Five:

The black box to the right of the Curve Box is the Color Box (where you choose the color of Ink 1). By default, Ink 1 is set to the color black (that's actually pretty handy, because most duotones are made up of black and one other color). If you decide you don't want black as your Ink 1 color, just click the Color Box and Photoshop's Color Picker appears so you can choose a different color.

Step Six:

Notice that Ink 2's Color Box is blank. That's because it's waiting for you to choose your second ink color. To do so, click on the box to bring up Photoshop's Custom Colors Picker, where you can choose the color you'd like from the list of PANTONE® colors. (Photoshop assumes you're going to print this duo-tone on a printing press, and that's why it displays the PANTONE coated colors as the default.)

Continued

Step Seven:

When you click OK in the Pantone Custom Colors Picker, the name of your Ink 2 color appears beside the Color Box. Now that you've selected the two colors that will make up your duotone, it's time to determine the balance between them. Do you want more black in the shadows than your spot color? Should Ink 2 be stronger in the highlights? These decisions are determined
in the Duotone Curve dialog for each ink, so click once on the Curves Box next to Ink 2 to bring up the dialog.

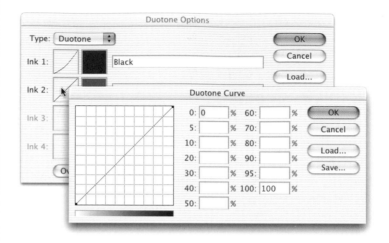

Step Eight:

If you look at the set of fields in the middle of the dialog (as shown in Step Seven's screen capture), the default curve is flat. It mimics your black color, in that equal amounts of orange (Ink 2) appears in the highlights, midtones, and shadows. For example, in the field marked 100%, a value of 100 indicates that 100% shadow areas will get 100% orange ink. However, if you want less orange in the shadows, type in a lower number in the 100% field (for example, in the capture shown here, I entered 80% for the 100% shadow areas, so now the darkest shadow areas will get 20% less orange, and will appear more black).
For 70% ink density areas, I lowered it to 60%, and for the 50% midtone, I entered 35%. When you enter these numbers manually like this, you'll see that Photoshop builds the Curve for you. Vice versa, if you click-and-drag in the Curve—Photoshop fills in the amounts in the corresponding fields.

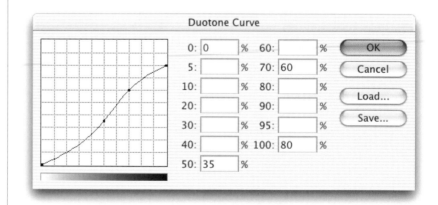

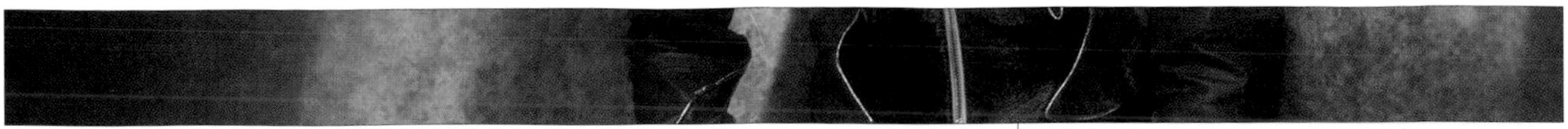

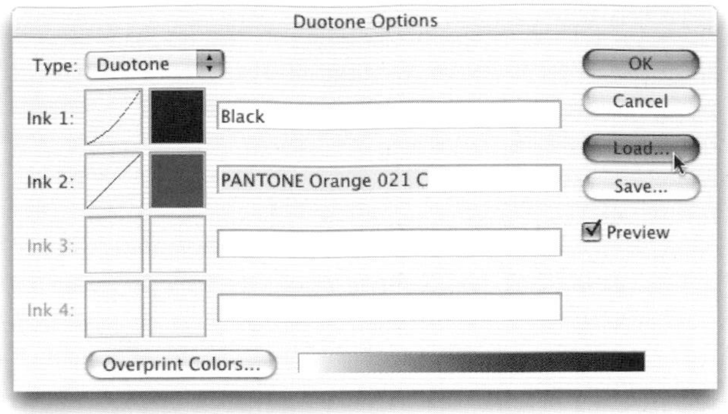

Step Nine:

If the idea of creating your own Curve freaks you out, all is not lost. Adobe figured that first-time duotoners might get the "Willies," so they included a bunch of presets using popular colors and pre-built duotone curves. All you have to do is try some out to find the one that looks good to you, and use it. These duotone presets were loaded on your computer when you first installed Photoshop. To load them into Photoshop's Duotone dialog, first click the Cancel button in the Duotone Curve dialog we've been working in, then click on the Load button in the Duotone Options dialog.

Step Ten:

The Load dialog appears and by default, Photoshop targets the Duotones folder on your drive. If, for some reason, it doesn't (it's been changed, or you don't see the Duotones folder), the search is on—in this Load dialog, navigate to your Photoshop application folder. Look inside for a folder called Presets, and inside that, look for a folder called Duotones. Inside that folder, you find another folder named Duotones (you also see a folder called Tritones for mixing three colors and Quadtones for mixing four).

Continued

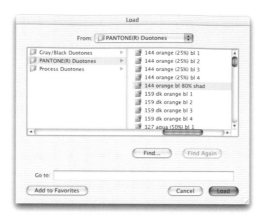

Step Eleven:

In the Load dialog, click on this Duotones folder, and inside that folder is (believe it or not) yet another folder called PANTONE Duotones. This is where Adobe carefully buried the individual presets, which you can choose from. Each color listed gives you four choices. The first one includes a duotone curve that gives you the strongest amount of spot color ink, progressing to the least amount with the fourth choice. Try a couple out by double-clicking on the duotone color that you want to load. You get an instant onscreen preview, so you can decide if the color, and amount, of Ink 2 are right. If they aren't, click Load again and pick another from the list to try.

Step Twelve:

When you've got the combination that looks right to you, click OK and the duotone is applied to your photo , as shown. (Note: In the example shown here, I chose the Duotone Preset "144 Orange 25% bl 1.")

Step Thirteen:

Okay, you've got what looks like a perfect duotone (onscreen anyway), but if it's going to press, before you save your file, you have to do a couple of simple, but absolutely critical, steps to make sure your duotone separates properly. Go under the File menu and choose Print with Preview. When the Print with Preview dialog appears, click on the Show More Options check box (as shown). Make sure the pop-up menu just below the check box is set to Output.

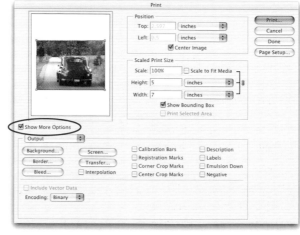

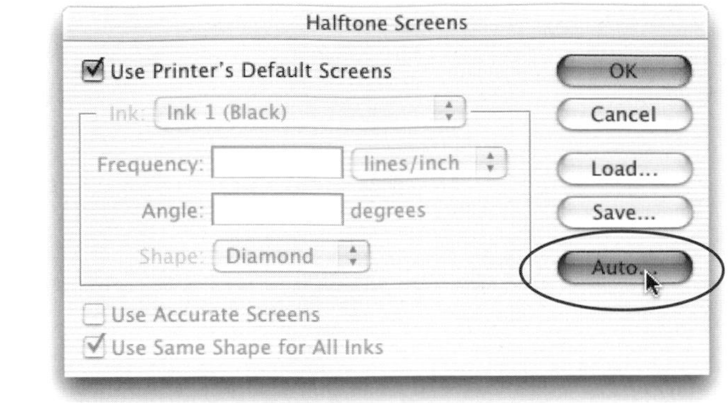

Step Fourteen:

As your duotone sits right now, both colors have the same screen angle. This will likely cause a distracting pattern (called a moiré pattern) to appear across your entire photo when printing on a printing press. To avoid this, you have to make Photoshop assign separate screen angles for your duotone. You do this by clicking on the Screen button in the Print Preview dialog. This brings up the Halftone Screens dialog. Click the Auto button to bring up the Auto Screens dialog.

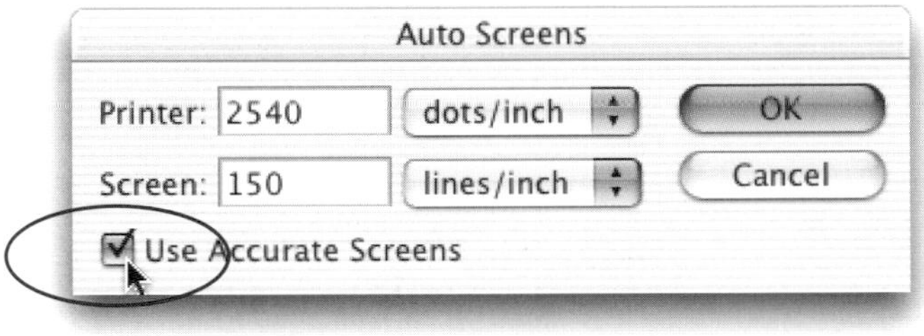

Step Fifteen:

In the Printer field of the Auto Screens dialog, enter the dpi of the device your duotone will be output to. (In this case, I entered 2540, the resolution of the imagesetter that the prepress department of our print shop uses). Then, call the print shop that's printing your duotone, and ask them at what line screen your job will be printed. Enter that number in the Screen field. Also, turn on Use Accurate Screens (it could help, depending on the imagesetter that is used; otherwise, it will be ignored. Either way, no harm done).

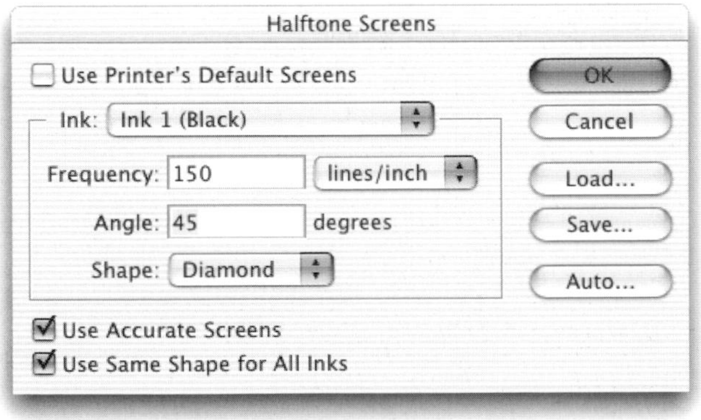

Step Sixteen:

Click OK to close the Auto Screens dialog with your new settings. You see in the Halftone Screens dialog that the screen frequencies have now been set for you. Don't change these settings or you'll undo the "Auto Screens" function you just applied (and risk ruining your print job).

Continued

Step Seventeen:

Click OK in the Halftone Screens dialog and Done in the Print with Preview dialog, and those settings are saved. Now, the trick is how to embed that information into your duotone so it separates and prints properly. Easy—save your duotone as an EPS (choose EPS from the Format pop-up menu in the Save As dialog). This enables you to embed the screen info into your file to make sure it separates properly on press.

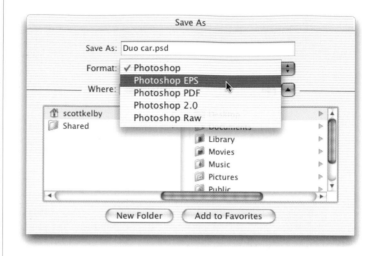

Step Eighteen:

Once you choose EPS as your file format, you are presented with the EPS Options dialog (shown here). You only have to choose one option—Include Halftone Screen. The screen angles that you set earlier are now included with your file. Click OK to save your file, and now your duotone is ready to be imported into your page-layout application.

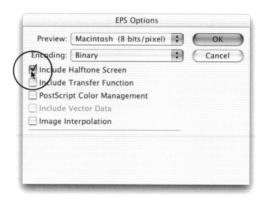

NOTE: When creating duotones, we recommend always printing a test to your color inkjet to make sure it separates correctly (giving you just two plates—one black, and one with your color tint).

ANOTHER NOTE: Again, if you're printing straight from Photoshop to a color inkjet printer, or some other desktop printer, you can skip all this "setting screens, halftone dialogs, etc." and just hit print. These extra steps are only necessary if you're going to output your duotone for reproduction on a printing press.

Original color image.

Final duotone.

Okay, I have to admit, not every sharpening technique in this chapter is a professional technique. For example, the first one, "Basic Sharpening," is clearly not a professional technique, although many professionals sharpen

Sharp-Dressed Man
professional sharpening techniques

their images exactly as shown in that tutorial (applying the Unsharp Mask to the RGB composite—I'm not even sure what that means, but it sounds good). There's a name for these professionals—"lazy." But then one day, they think to themselves, "Geez, I'm kind of getting tired of all those color halos and other annoying artifacts that keep showing up in my sharpened photos," and they wish there was a way to apply more sharpening, and yet avoid these pitfalls. At that point, they're looking for some professional sharpening techniques that will avoid those problems (and the best of those techniques are included in this chapter—the same sharpening techniques used by today's leading digital photographers and retouchers). But as soon as they learn these advanced techniques, they turn around and write Actions for them so they'll be applied with just the touch of one button. But automating this process in this way is not seen as lazy. In fact, now they're seen as being "productive," "efficient," and "smart." Why? Because life ain't fair. How unfair is it? I'll give you an example. A number of leading professional photographers have worked for years to come up with these advanced sharpening techniques, which took tedious testing, experimentation, and research; and then you come along, buy this book, and suddenly you're using the same techniques they are, but you didn't even expend a bead of sweat. You know what that's called? Cool!

Basic Sharpening

After you've color corrected your photos and right before you save your file, you'll definitely want to sharpen your photos. I sharpen every digital-camera photo, either to help bring back some of the original crispness that gets lost during the correction process, or to help fix a photo that's slightly out of focus. Either way, I haven't met a digital camera (or scanned) photo that I didn't think needed a little sharpening. Here's a basic technique for sharpening the entire photo.

Step One:

Open the photo that you want to sharpen. Because Photoshop displays your photo in different ways at different magnifications, it's absolutely critical that you view your photo at 100% when sharpening. To ensure that you're viewing at 100%, once your photo is open, double-click on the Zoom tool in the Toolbox, and your photo jumps to a 100% view (look up in the image window's Title Bar to see the actual percentage of zoom, circled here).

Step Two:

Go under the Filter menu, under Sharpen, and choose Unsharp Mask. (If you're familiar with traditional darkroom techniques, you probably recognize the term "unsharp mask" from when you would make a blurred copy of the original photo and an "unsharp" version to use as a mask to create a new photo whose edges appeared sharper.) Of Photoshop's sharpening filters, Unsharp Mask is the undisputed choice of professionals because if offers the most control over the sharpening process.

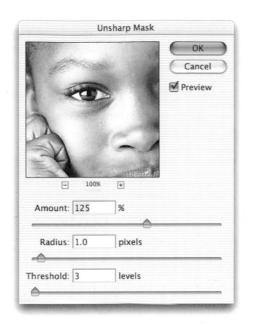

Step Three:

When the Unsharp Mask dialog appears, you'll see three sliders. The Amount slider determines the amount of sharpening applied to the photo; the Radius slider determines how many pixels out from the edge the sharpening will affect; and the Threshold slider works the opposite of what you might think—the lower the number, the more intense the sharpening effect. Threshold determines how different a pixel must be from the surrounding area before it's considered an edge pixel and sharpened by the filter. So what numbers do you enter? I'll give you some great starting points on the following pages, but for now, we'll just use these settings: Amount 125%, Radius 1, and Threshold 3. Click OK and the sharpening is applied to the photo. A before and after is shown below.

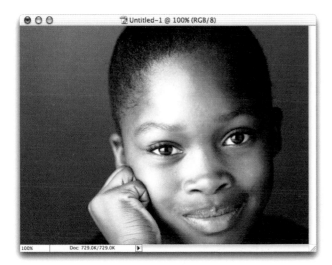

Before sharpening.

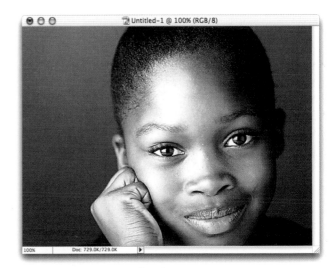

After sharpening.

Continued

Sharpening soft subjects:

Here is an Unsharp Mask setting (Amount 150%, Radius 1, Threshold 10) that works well for images where the subject is of a softer nature (e.g., flowers, puppies, people, rainbows, etc.). It's a subtle application of sharpening that is very well suited to these types of subjects.

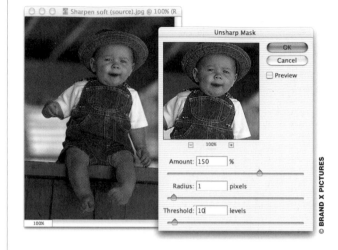

Sharpening portraits:

If you're sharpening close-up portraits (head-and-shoulders type of thing), try this setting (Amount 75%, Radius 2, Threshold 3), which applies another form of subtle sharpening.

Moderate sharpening:

This moderate amount of sharpening works nicely on product shots, photos of home interiors and exteriors, and land-scapes. If you're shooting along these lines, try applying this setting (Amount 225%, Radius 0.5, Threshold 0), and see how you like it (my guess is, you will).

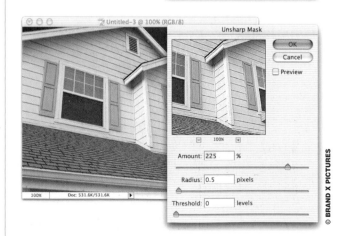

Maximum sharpening:

I use these settings (Amount 65%, Radius 4, Threshold 3) in only two situations: (1) The photo is visibly out of focus and it needs a heavy application of sharpening to try to bring it back into focus. (2) The photo contains lots of well-defined edges (e.g., buildings, coins, cars, machinery, etc.).

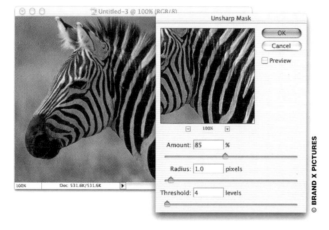

All-purpose sharpening:

This is probably my all-around favorite sharpening setting (Amount 85%, Radius 1, Threshold 4), and I use this one most of the time. It's not a "knock-you-over the-head" type of sharpening—maybe that's why I like it. It's subtle enough that you can apply it twice if your photo doesn't seem sharp enough the first time you run it, but once usually does the trick.

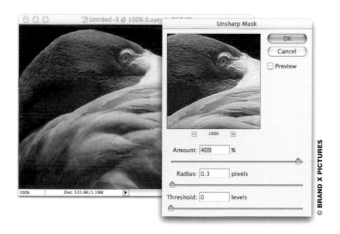

Web sharpening:

I use this setting (Amount 400%, Radius 0.3, Threshold 0) for Web graphics that look blurry. (When you drop the resolution from a high-res, 300-ppi photo down to 72 ppi for the Web, the photo often gets a bit blurry and soft.) If the effect seems too intense, try dropping the Amount to 200%. I also use this same setting (Amount 400%) on out-of-focus photos. It adds some noise, but I've seen it rescue photos that I would have otherwise thrown away.

Continued

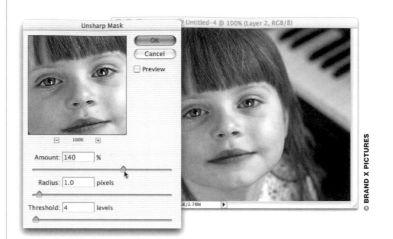

Coming up with your own settings:
If you want to experiment and come up with your own custom blend of sharpening, I'll give you some typical ranges for each adjustment so you can find your own sharpening "sweet spot."

Amount

Typical ranges go anywhere from 50% to 150%. This isn't a rule that can't be broken, just a typical range for adjusting the Amount, where going below 50% won't have enough effect, and going above 150% might get you into sharpening trouble (depending on how you set the Radius and Threshold). You're fairly safe to stay under 150%.

Radius

Most of the time, you'll use just 1 pixel, but you can go as high as—get ready—2. You saw one setting I gave you earlier for extreme situations, where you can take the Radius as high as 4. I once heard a tale of a man in Cincinnati who used 5, but I'm not sure I believe it. (Incidentally, Adobe allows you to raise the Radius amount to—get this—250! If you ask me, anyone caught using 250 as their Radius setting should be incarcerated for a period not to exceed one year, and a penalty not to exceed $2,500.)

Threshold

A pretty safe range for the Threshold setting is anywhere from 3 to around 20 (3 being the most intense, 20 being much more subtle. I know, shouldn't 3 be more subtle and 20 more intense? Don't get me started). If you really need to increase the intensity of your sharpening, you can lower the Threshold to 0, but keep a good eye on what you're doing (watch for noise appearing in your photo).

Lab Color Sharpening

This sharpening technique is probably the most popular technique with professional photographers because it helps to avoid the color halos that appear when you add a lot of sharpening to a photo. And because it helps to avoid those halos, it allows you to apply more sharpening than you normally could get away with.

Step One:

Open the photo you want to sharpen using Lab sharpening.

Step Two:

Go to the Channels palette and you can see that your RGB photo is made up of three channels—a Red, a Green, and a Blue channel. Combining the data on these three channels creates a full-color RGB image (and you can see that repre-sented in the RGB thumbnail at the top of the palette).

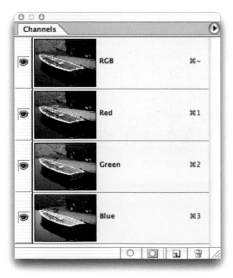

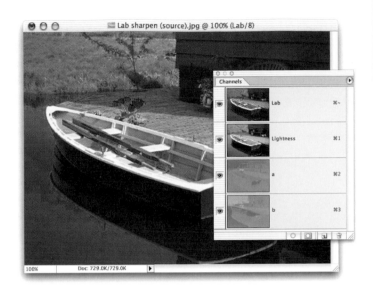

Step Three:

Go under the Image menu, under Mode, and choose Lab Color. Now look in the Channels palette and you see that although your photo still looks the same onscreen, the channels it comprises have changed. There are still three channels (besides your full-color composite channel), but now they're a Lightness channel (the luminosity and detail of the photo), an "a" channel, and a "b" channel, which hold the color data.

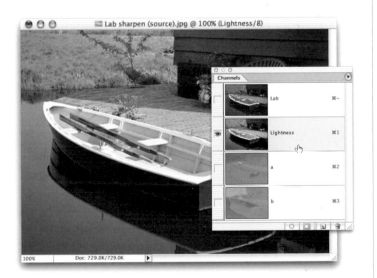

Step Four:

By switching to Lab color, you've separated the detail (Lightness channel) from the color info (the a and b channels), so click on the Lightness channel to select it. Now you'll apply the Unsharp Mask filter to just this black-and-white Lightness channel, thereby avoiding the color halos, because you're not sharpening the color (pretty tricky, eh?).

NOTE: If you need some settings for using Unsharp Mask, look in the "Basic Sharpening" section at the beginning of this chapter.

Continued

Step Five:

Once you sharpen the Lightness channel (and again, you may be able to apply the filter twice here), go under the Image menu, under Mode, and choose RGB Color to switch your photo back to RGB. Now, should you apply this brand of sharpening to every digital-camera photo you take? I would. In fact, I do, and since I perform this function quite often, I automate the process (as you'll see in the next step).

Step Six:

Open a new photo, and let's do the whole Lab sharpening thing again, but this time, before you start the process, go under the Window menu and choose Actions to bring up the Actions palette. The Actions palette is a "steps recorder" that records any set of repetitive steps and lets you instantly play them back (apply them to another photo) by simply pressing one button. You'll dig this.

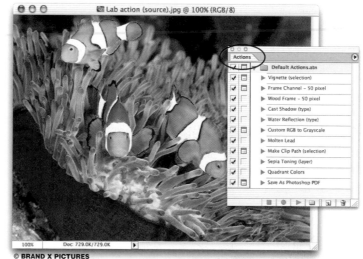

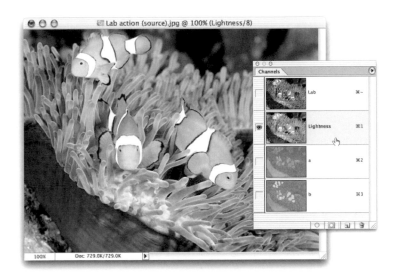

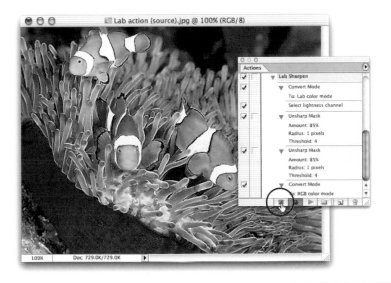

Step Seven:

From the Actions palette's pop-down menu, choose New Action to bring up the New Action dialog (shown here). The Name field is automatically highlighted, so go ahead and give this new Action a name. (I named mine "Lab Sharpen." I know—how original!) Then, from the Function Key pop-up menu, choose the number of the Function key (F-key) on your keyboard that you want to assign to the Action (it's this key that you'll hit to make the Action do its thing). I've assigned mine to F12, but you can choose any open F-key that suits you (but everybody knows F12 is, in fact, the coolest of all F-keys. Just ask anyone).

Step Eight:

You'll notice that the New Actions dialog has no OK button. Instead, there's a Record button, because once you exit this dialog, Photoshop starts recording your steps. So go ahead and click Record, and then convert your photo to Lab color, click on the Lightness channel, and apply your favorite Unsharp Mask setting to it. If you generally like a second helping of sharpening, run the filter again. Then switch back to RGB mode.

Step Nine:

Now, in the Actions palette, click on the Stop button at the bottom of the palette (it's the square button, first from the left). This stops the recording process. If you look in the Actions palette, you'll see all your steps recorded in the order you did them. Also, if you expand the right-facing triangle beside each step, you'll see more detail, including individual settings, for the steps it recorded. *Continued*

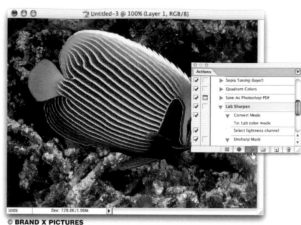

© BRAND X PICTURES

Step Ten:

Open a new photo and press the F-key you assigned to your Action (you chose F12, right? I knew it!). Photoshop immediately applies the sharpening to the Lab channel for you (complete with conversions from RGB to Lab and back) and does it all faster than you could ever do it manually because it takes place behind the scenes with no dialogs popping up.

Step Eleven:

Now that you have an Action written that applies Lab sharpening, let's put this baby to work. Let's say you have a card of photos you took with an underwater camera. The color looks okay, but you want to sharpen the 40+ photos. Certainly, you could open each photo, press F12 to sharpen it quickly, and then close it; but there's a better way—once you've written an Action that does what you want it to do, Photoshop lets you apply that Action to an entire folder of photos; and Photoshop totally automates the whole process. You can literally have it open every photo, apply your Lab sharpening, and then close every photo, all automatically, while you're watching CNN. How cool is that? This is called Batch processing, and here's how it works: First, go under the File menu, under Automate, and choose Batch to bring up the Batch dialog (or you can choose Batch from the Automate "mini-menu" within Photoshop CS's File Browser).

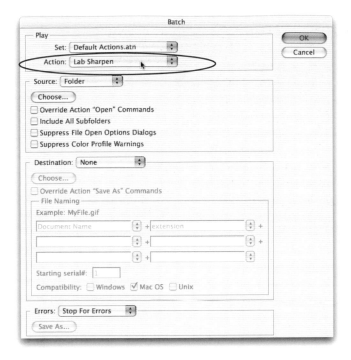

Step Twelve:

Up at the top of the dialog, under the Play section, Photoshop wants you to choose which Action you want to apply to your folder full of photos. From the Action pop-up menu, choose Lab Sharpen. This Action now is applied to the folder.

Step Thirteen:

In the Source section of the Batch dialog, you can tell Photoshop where the folder of photos you want to Lab sharpen is on your hard drive (or CD, or network, etc.). From the Source pop-up menu, you can choose a Folder (which is what we're going to do), or you can have selected photos batched from the File Browser, or you can Import photos from another source. Again, we're doing a folder, so make sure Folder is selected in the Source pop-up menu, then click the Choose button. A standard "Open" dialog appears. Navigate to your desired folder of photos, click on that folder, then click the Choose button.

Continued

Step Fourteen:

In the Destination section of the Batch dialog, you can tell Photoshop where you want it to put these photos once it's finished applying the Lab sharpening to them. If you choose Save and Close from the Destination pop-up menu, it saves the images in the same folder where they started. It just opens them, applies the Lab sharpening, saves the files, then closes them. If you select Folder from the Destination pop-up menu, Photoshop places your Lab sharpened photos into a totally different folder. Which folder? You have to tell Photoshop which folder (or create a new one) by clicking on the Choose button in the Destination section.

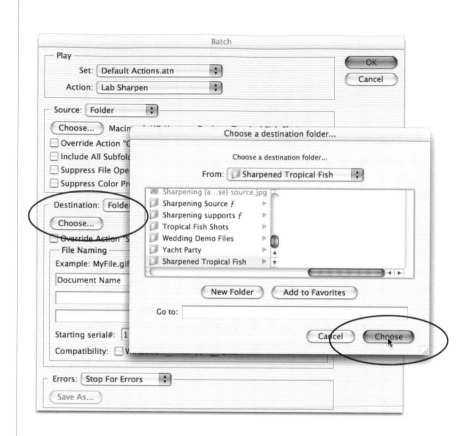

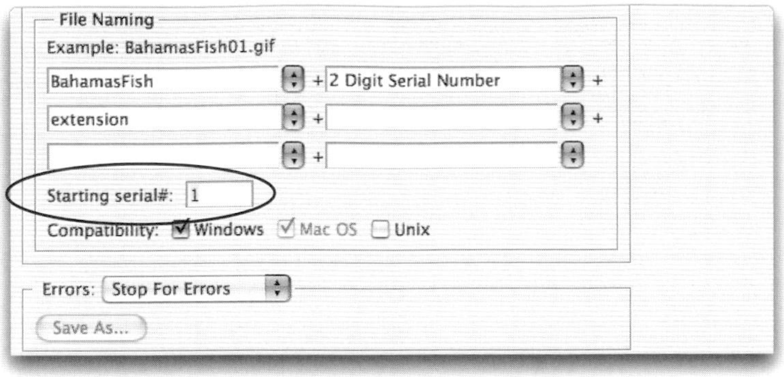

Step Fifteen:

If you choose a folder to save your newly sharpened photos into, you might also want to rename them (you don't have to, but if you want to rename them, now's the time). This is particularly handy if you're opening photos that still have the default names assigned by your camera. The fields under the File Naming section are where you decide how the auto-naming will name your files. (Note: If you want detailed information on how Photoshop's automated file naming works, look in Chapter 1 [File Browser Essentials], for details.) In short, here's how the file naming works: In the first field, you type the basic name you want all the files to have. In the second field, you can choose (from a pop-up menu) the automatic numbering scheme to use (adding a 1-digit number, 2-digit number, date, etc.). (Note: New in Photoshop CS, there's a field where you can choose the starting serial number, as shown here.) In the third field, you can choose the file extension (.jpg, .tif, etc.). Now, Photoshop automatically renames the photos at the same time it applies your Action.

Step Sixteen:

At the bottom of the dialog, there's a row of check boxes for choosing compatibility with other operating systems. I generally turn all of these on, because "ya never know." For example, I often put digital-camera photos on the Web, and you don't always know which kind of server (Mac, Win, UNIX) you might be uploading your files to. When you're finally done, click OK, and Photoshop automatically Lab sharpens and saves all of your photos for you.

Luminosity Sharpening

This is another sharpening technique popular with professionals, and one that sparks debate between photographers who prefer it to the Lab sharpening technique. Both sharpen just the luminosity (rather than the color data), so theoretically, they do the same thing, but you'll hear pros argue that one method produces better results than the other. That's why I'm including both in the book, so you can decide which you like best. (And then argue about it with other photographers. This is what we do for fun.)

Step One:

Open a photo that needs some moderate sharpening.

Step Two:

Go under the Filter menu, under Sharpen, and choose Unsharp Mask. Apply the filter directly to your RGB photo (don't switch to Lab color, etc.).

NOTE: If you're looking for some sample settings for different situations, look at the Basic Sharpening tutorial at the beginning of this chapter, and on page 302, I list some settings that are popular with professionals.

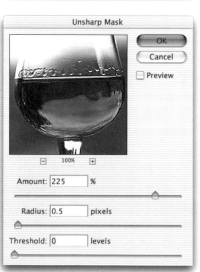

Step Three:
Click OK to apply the Unsharp Mask filter. Then, immediately go under the Edit menu and choose Fade Unsharp Mask. When the Fade dialog appears, change the Mode pop-up menu from Normal to Luminosity (as shown). When you click OK, the sharpening is now applied only to the luminosity of the photo, and not to the color data. This enables you to apply a higher amount of sharpening without getting unwanted halos that often appear. The result is shown below.

Before sharpening.

After luminosity sharpening.

Edge Sharpening Technique

This sharpening technique doesn't use the Unsharp Mask filter, but still leaves you with a lot of control over the sharpening, even after the sharpening is applied. It's ideal to use when you have an image (a photo with a lot of edges) that can hold a lot of sharpening, or one that really needs it.

Step One:

Open a photo that needs edge sharpening. Duplicate the Background layer by pressing Command-J (PC: Control-J). The copy will be named Layer 1 in the Layers palette.

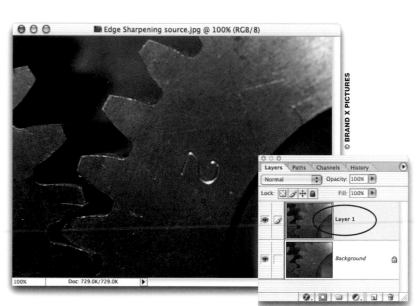

Step Two:

Go under the Filter menu, under Stylize, and choose Emboss. You're going to use the Emboss filter to accentuate the edges in the photo. You can leave the Angle and Amount settings at their defaults (135° and 100%) but if you want more intense sharpening, raise the Height amount from its default setting of 3 pixels to 5 or more pixels. Click OK to apply the filter, and your photo turns gray with neon-colored highlights along the edges.

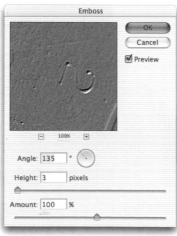

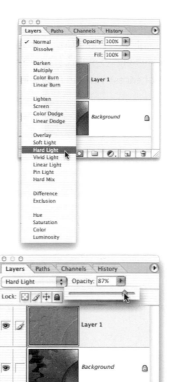

Step Three:
In the Layers palette, change the Blend Mode of this layer from Normal to Hard Light. This removes the gray color from the layer, but leaves the edges accentuated, making the entire photo appear much sharper.

Step Four:
If the sharpening seems too intense, you can control the amount of the effect by simply lowering the Opacity of this layer in the Layers palette. A before and after is shown below.

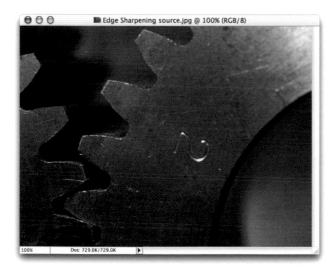

Before sharpening.

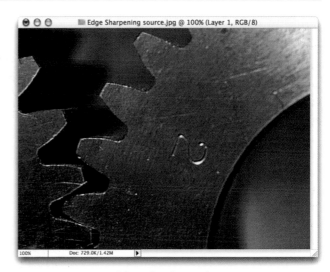

After edge sharpening.

Extreme Edge Sharpening

This edge-sharpening technique is great when you want to apply some intense sharpening to a particular object in your photo, but there are other areas that you don't want sharpened at all. This technique is different because you're going to actually enhance the edge areas yourself by using some tricks to put a selection around only those edges that you want to sharpen.

Step One:

Open the photo to which you want to apply edge sharpening (in this example, I want to sharpen the most prominent feathers, but I don't want to sharpen the soft background). Press Command-A (PC: Control-A) to put a selection around the entire photo, then press Command-C (PC: Control-C) to copy the photo into memory.

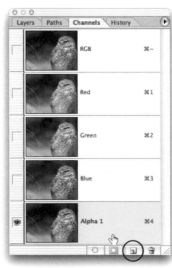

Step Two:

Go to the Channels palette and click on the New Channel icon at the bottom of the palette. When the new channel appears, press Command-V (PC: Control-V) to paste a grayscale version of your photo into this new channel (as shown). Now, deselect by pressing Command-D (PC: Control-D).

Step Three:

Go under the Filter Menu, under Stylize, and choose Find Edges. There's no dialog, no settings to enter—the filter is simply applied and it accentuates any visible edges in your photo. The problem you'll probably encounter is that it accentuates too many edges, so you'll want to tweak things a bit so just the most defined edges remain visible.

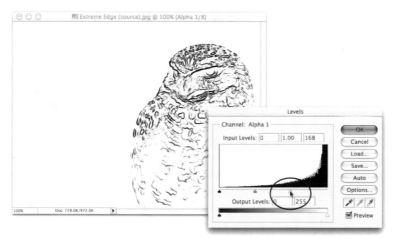

Step Four:

Press Command-L (PC: Control-L) to bring up Levels. When the dialog appears, drag the top-right Input Levels slider (the highlights) to the left. As you do, you'll be "cleaning up" the excess lines: the lines that aren't very well defined and don't need to be sharpened. Defining the edge areas within your photo is very important for this method of sharpening to be effective, so we're going to take another step to define those edges.

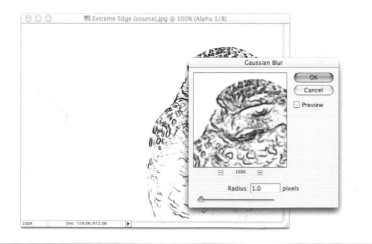

Step Five:

It's going to sound kind of counter-productive, but you're going to blur the existing lines (don't worry, you remove the blur in the next step). Go under the Filter menu, under Blur, and choose Gaussian Blur. Enter a setting of 1 pixel and click OK to slightly blur your channel. Next, press Command-L (PC: Control-L) to bring up the Levels dialog. This time, you're going to use Levels to remove the blurring, and by doing so, further accentuate the edges.

Continued

Professional Sharpening Techniques | Chapter 11 | 319

Step Six:

All you have to do is drag the Input Levels sliders at each end (the left shadow slider and the right highlight slider) toward the middle until the blurring is gone. You'll drag them until they almost meet the center midtone slider, or until the blurring is gone and the lines look much more defined. When it looks good to you, click OK.

Step Seven:

Go to the Channels palette, hold the Command key (PC: Control key), and click on the Alpha 1 channel to load it as a selection. You'll notice that some background areas are selected, so go under the Select menu and choose Inverse to inverse the selection. Then, click on the RGB channel to show the full-color photo (the selection will still be in place). Your selection is only around the well-defined feathers in the photo, so now you can apply the Unsharp Mask filter using some heavy settings, and only the selected areas will be affected, leaving the background unsharpened (as shown in the After photo on the next page).

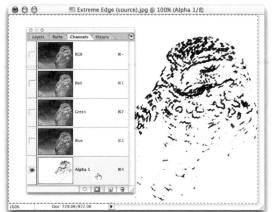

Before sharpening.

After extreme sharpening.

Sharpening with Layers to Avoid Color Shifts and Noise

This is another technique for avoiding noise and color shifts when sharpening, but this one makes use of Layers and Blend Modes. The method shown here is a cross between a technique that I learned from Chicago-based retoucher David Cuerdon, and one from Jim DiVitale, in one of his columns for *Photoshop User* magazine.

Step One:
Open the photo you want to sharpen using this technique. Duplicate the Background layer by pressing Command-J (PC: Control-J).

Step Two:
Change the Blend Mode of this duplicate layer from Normal to Luminosity (as shown).

Step Three:
Apply the Unsharp Mask filter to this duplicate layer. (If you've read this far, you already know which settings to use, so have at it.)

Step Four:
Now, duplicate this sharpened Luminosity layer by pressing Command-J (PC: Control-J).

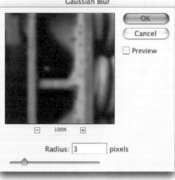

Step Five:
Go under the Filter menu, under Blur, and choose Gaussian Blur. When the dialog appears, enter 3 pixels to add a slight blur to the photo. If this setting doesn't make your photo look as blurry as the one shown here, increase the amount of blur until it does. This hides any halo, or noise, but obviously, it makes the photo really blurry.

Step Six:
To get rid of the blur on this layer, but keep the good effects from the blur-ring (getting rid of the noise and halos), change the Blend Mode of this blurred layer from Luminosity to Color. Zoom in on edge areas that would normally have halos or other color shifts and you'll notice the problems just aren't there. Now you can flatten the photo and move on.

NOTE: In some cases, this technique mutes some of the red in your photo. If you notice a drop-out in red, lower the Opacity of the blurred layer until the color is restored.

Before.

After.

Sharpening Close-Up Portraits of Women

If you need to sharpen a close-up portrait but want to keep your subject's skin as smooth as possible, here's a technique used by fashion photographers and retouchers that enables them to apply sharpening without overly enhancing pores, wrinkles, or any imperfections in the skin. It's simple, but it works.

Step One:

Open the close-up portrait you want to sharpen using this technique.

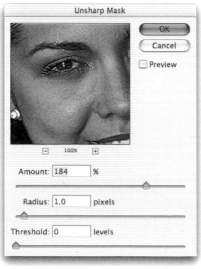

Step Two:

If you apply sharpening to the RGB composite, or even the luminosity of the image, you wind up accentuating the texture of the skin (which is a bad thing if your goal is to keep the skin looking smooth).

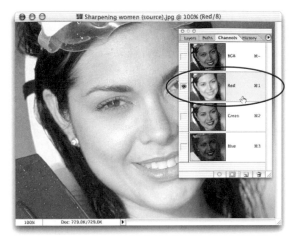

Step Three:

To avoid accentuating the skin texture, go to the Channels palette and click on the Red channel to make it active. Now when you apply the Unsharp Mask filter, the sharpening only is applied to this channel.

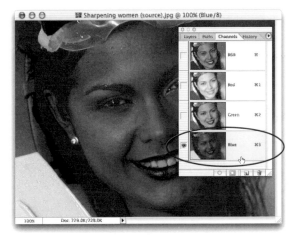

Step Four:

Why only the Red channel? In portraits, the Red channel usually contains the least amount of edge detail and definition, and sharpening just this channel sharpens the areas you want (the eyes, lips, etc.) without having too much effect on the skin (leaving it smooth). In the capture shown here, the Blue channel is selected, and you can see her skin texture clearly. Sharpen this channel, and you intensify that texture.

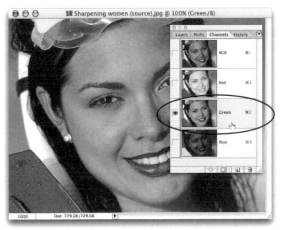

Step Five:

In the capture shown here, the Green channel is selected, and although the texture isn't as pronounced as in the Blue channel, it's still more distinct than in the Red channel.

Continued

Step Six:

Here's the final portrait (below right), using the Unsharp Mask filter on the Red channel only. The original image (below left) is also shown for reference.

The original portrait.

The portrait sharpened on just the Red channel to avoid overly accentuating the skin texture.

This is a more advanced technique for sharpening portraits of women that I learned (not surprisingly) from fashion photographer Kevin Ames. It does a great job of enabling you to create an overall feeling of sharpness, without emphasizing the texture of the skin. It takes a few extra steps, but the final effect is worth it.

Advanced Sharpening for Portraits of Women

Step One:
Open the portrait you want to sharpen without accentuating the skin texture.

Step Two:
Duplicate the Background layer by pressing Command-J (PC: Control-J).

Continued

Step Three:

Now, you can go under the Filter menu, under Sharpen, and apply the Unsharp Mask filter to this layer. Although you'll see the texture in the skin appear to be accentuated as a result of the sharpening, it's okay, because we fix that in the next step.

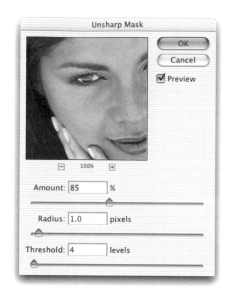

Step Four:

Hold the Option key (PC: Alt key) and click on the Layer Mask icon at the bottom of the Layers palette. Holding the Option/Alt key fills the Layer Mask with black, hiding the Unsharp Mask filter you just applied. Get the Brush tool and choose a medium-sized, soft-edged brush. Press the letter "d" to switch your Foreground color to white, then begin to paint over the areas on her face that you want to have detail (lips, eyes, eyelashes, eyebrows). As you paint, it paints the sharpening back in, so avoid any skin areas (that's the whole point of sharpening using this method), and only paint over detail areas. You can also paint over hair and other areas outside the face that you want to sharpen. The final sharpened image is on the opposite page.

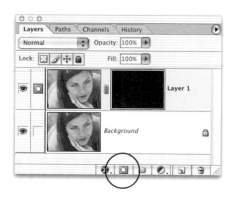

Before sharpening.

After advanced sharpening.

Okay, you've sorted and categorized the photos from the shoot; you've backed up your digital negs to CD; and you've color corrected, tweaked, toned, sharpened, and otherwise messed with your photo until it

The Show Must Go On

showing it to your clients

is, in every sense of the word, a masterpiece. But now it's time to show it to the client. Hopefully, you'll get to show it to the client in person, so you can explain in detail the motivation behind collaging a 4x4 monster truck into an otherwise pristine wedding photo. (Answer: Because you can.) There's a good chance they'll see the photo first on your screen, so I included some cool tricks on how to make your presentation look its very best (after all, you want those huge 122" tires to look good), and I even included some techniques on how to provide your own online proofing service using Photoshop (in case your clients smell bad, and you don't want them coming back to your studio and stinkin' up the place). This is the last chapter in the book, so I want you to really sop up the techniques (like you're using a big ol' flaky biscuit) because once you're done with this chapter, once you've come this far, there's no turning back. At this point, some people will start to scour their studio, searching for that one last roll of traditional print film, probably knocking around at the bottom of some drawer (or hidden in the back of the refrigerator, behind some leftover Moo Shoo Pork), so they can hold it up toward the light, smile, and begin laughing that hysterical laugh that only people truly on the edge can muster. These people are not Kodak shareholders.

Watermarking and Adding Copyright Info

This two-part technique is particularly important if you're putting your proofs on the Web for client approval. In the first part of this technique, you add a see-through watermark, so you can post larger proofs without fear of the client downloading and printing them; and secondly, you embed your personal copyright info so if your photos are used anywhere on the Web, your copyright info goes right along with the file.

Step One:

First, the see-through watermark: Open the image for watermarking.

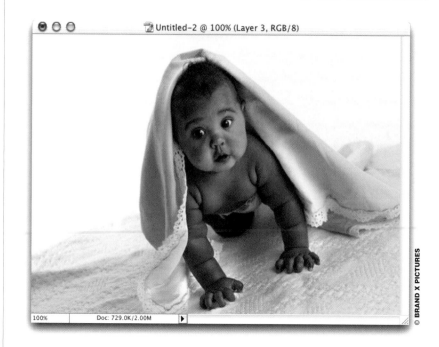

Step Two:

Choose the Custom Shape tool from the Toolbox as shown.

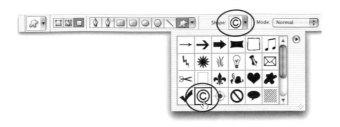

Step Three:
Once you have the Custom Shape tool, go up to the Options Bar and click on the Shape thumbnail to bring up the Custom Shape Picker. Choose the Copyright symbol (as shown), which is included in the default set of the Custom Shape library.

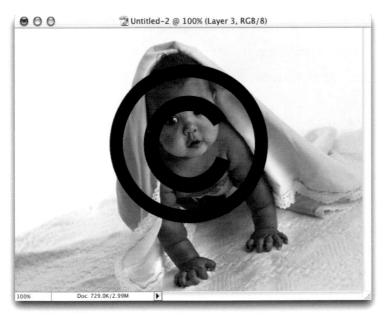

Step Four:
Create a new blank layer by clicking on the Create New Layer icon at the bottom of the Layers palette. Press the letter "d" to set your Foreground color to black, and drag out the Copyright symbol over your photo (use your own judgement as to size and placement).

NOTE: If you end up with a Shape Layer or a path, go to the Options bar and make sure that you have Fill Pixels selected (third icon from the left in the first group of icons on the left) before you draw the Copyright symbol.

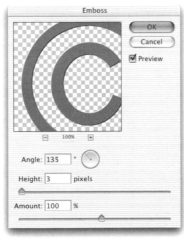

Step Five:
Go under the Filter menu, under Stylize, and choose Emboss. Apply the Emboss filter with the default settings of Angle 135°, Height 3 pixels, and Amount 100% (you can increase the Height setting to 5 if you want the effect to be more pronounced), then click OK.

Continued

Step Six:

To smooth the edges of the Copyright symbol, go to the Layers palette, turn on Lock Transparent Pixels (the first icon from the left in the Lock section at the top of the palette), and add a 2- or 3-pixel Gaussian Blur (Filter> Blur>Gaussian Blur).

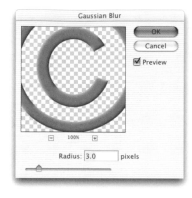

Step Seven:

Go to the Layers palette and change the Blend Mode of this Copyright symbol layer from Normal to Hard Light, to make the watermark transparent (as shown).

Step Eight:

Switch to the Type tool, enter the name of your studio, and position it where you think it looks best.

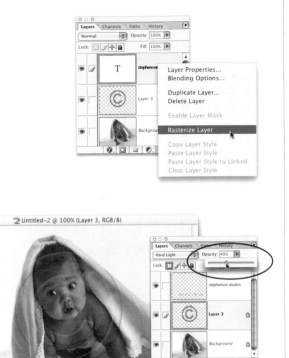

Step Nine:
You're going to apply the same filter to your type that you applied to the Copyright logo. But to apply a filter to type, you first have to convert your Type layer into a regular Photoshop image layer by Control-clicking (PC: right-clicking) on the Type layer (in the Layers palette) and choosing Rasterize Layer from the resulting pop-up menu (as shown).

Step Ten:
Apply the Emboss filter to your raster-ized type layer, then change the Blend Mode from Normal to Hard Light to make the type see-through; then, lower the Opacity of both of these layers to 40% (as shown here) so the watermark isn't overwhelming. That completes the first part of this two-part technique. The next part is embedding the copyright info into the file.

Step Eleven:
Go under the File menu and choose File Info to bring up the File Info dialog (shown here). This is where you enter information that you want embedded into the file itself. This embedding of info is supported by all Macintosh file formats, but on Windows, only the major file formats are supported, such as TIFF, JPEG, EPS, PDF, and Photoshop's native file format.

Continued

Step Twelve:

In the File Info dialog, change the Copyright Status pop-up menu to Copyrighted (as shown). In the Copyright Notice field, enter your personal copyright info, and then under Copyright Info URL, enter your full Web address. That way, when people open your file in Photoshop, they can go to File Info, click the Go To URL button, and it launches their browser and takes them directly to your site.

Step Thirteen:

Click OK and the info is embedded into the file. Once copyright info has been added to a file, Photoshop automatically adds a Copyright symbol before the file's name which appears in the photo's Title bar (as shown here). It also adds the symbol before the Document Size in the Info Bar at the bottom left of the document window. Last, flatten the image by choosing Flatten Image from the Layers palette's pop-down menu.

Step Fourteen:

Now, you can automate the entire process with the click of one button. Start by opening a new photo, then go to the Actions palette and click on the Create New Action icon at the bottom of the palette. When the New Action dialog appears (shown here), name the Action, and choose the Function Key (F-key) that you want to use to apply the Action.

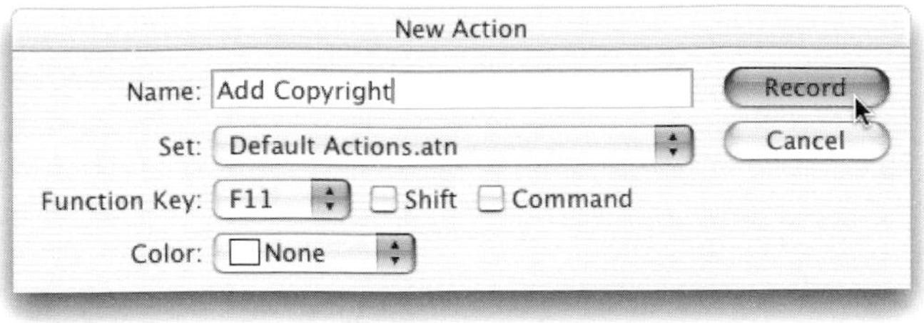

Step Fifteen:

Click the Record button (as shown) and repeat the whole process of adding the Copyright symbol and File Info, starting at Step One, and Photoshop records all your steps. (I know, you're thinking, "Shouldn't you have told me this in Step One?" Probably, but it wouldn't be as much fun as telling you now.)

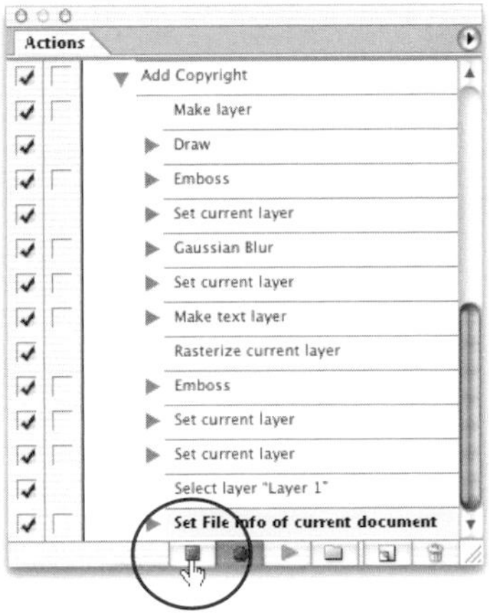

Step Sixteen:

When you're done, click the Stop button at the bottom of the Actions palette (as shown). You can close the Actions palette now, because you can apply the watermark, studio name, and copyright info just by pressing the F-key you chose in the New Action dialog box.

Step Seventeen:

If you want to apply this Action to a whole folder full of photos, just go under the File menu, under Automate, and choose Batch to bring up the Batch dialog (which lets you pick one Action and automatically apply it to a whole folder of photos). In the Play section (at the top), for Action, choose "Add Copyright" (as shown). Under Source, click the Choose button and navigate to your folder full of photos, then under Destination, choose Save and Close. This applies the watermark, studio name, and copyright info to your images, and then save and close the documents. If you want to save them to a different folder, or rename them, under Destination, choose "Folder."

Creating Your Own Custom Copyright Brush

If you want a quick way to apply your Copyright watermark to an image, check out this trick I learned from portrait photographer (and Photoshop guru) Todd Morrison. He showed me how to turn your copyright info into a brush so you're only one click away from applying your mark to any photo. My thanks to Todd for letting me share his ingenious technique.

Step One:

Create a new document, then click on the New Layer icon at the bottom of the Layers palette to create a new blank layer. Get the Custom Shape tool (it's in the flyout menu of Shape tools right below the Type tool in the Toolbox), then go up to the Options bar and click on the third icon from the left (which creates your custom shape using pixels, rather than paths). Then, press the Enter key to bring up the Shape Picker, and choose the Copyright symbol from the default set of shapes (as shown here). Press the letter "d" to set black as your Foreground color and drag out a copyright symbol in the center of your document (as shown).

Step Two:

Switch to the Type tool, then type in your copyright info. The Type tool should create a new layer above the copyright symbol. (Note: When you set your type, go up to the Options bar and make sure your justification is set to "Center Text" [click the center of the three align icons]). Then, type a few spaces between the copyright date and the name of your studio. This enables you put the large copyright symbol in the center of your type (as shown here).

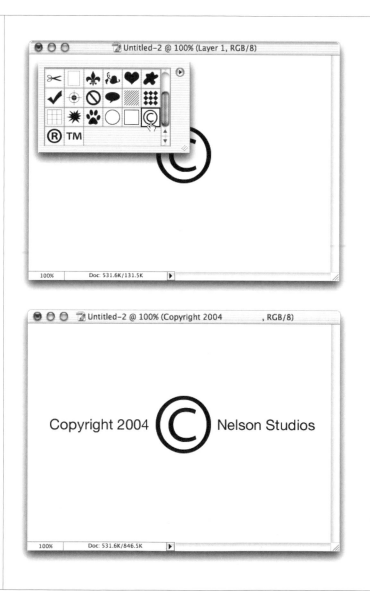

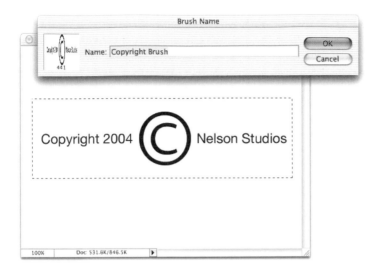

Step Three:
Get the Rectangular Marquee tool and drag out a selection around your type and your copyright symbol (as shown here). Then, go under the Edit menu and choose Define Brush Preset. When the Brush Name dialog appears (shown here), name your brush, then click OK. This adds your type as a custom brush in your Brush Presets library.

NOTE: The preview of the brush that appears in the Brush Name dialog may make the brush look squished. Don't worry, the preview looks squished, but

Step Four:
Get the Brush tool, then go up to the Brush Picker in the Options bar and scroll to the bottom of the brushes. The last brush in the set is the custom logo brush you just created. Click on this brush to make it your current brush.

Step Five:
Now that you've created your copyright brush, it's time to put it to use. Open a photo that you want to use as a client proof. Add a new blank layer, then get the Brush tool, choose your copyright brush, and click once where you want your copyright info to appear. Then, lower the Opacity in the Layers palette to around 20% so you can see through the copyright (as shown here). Two things to keep in mind: (1) If the photo is dark, try white as your Foreground color; (2) You can use the Brush palette's or Brush Picker's Master Diameter slider to change the size of your brush.

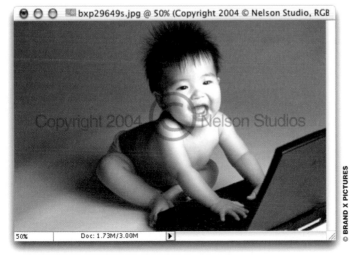

Embedding Digimarc Digital Copyright Info

ADVANCED TECHNIQUES FOR PROS ONLY!

Digimarc is a digital copyright watermarking system that is applied to your photos from right within Photoshop using the Digimarc filter, which appears at the bottom of the Filter menu. (You always wondered what that filter was for, didn't you?) The system is pretty ingenious, and although it requires an annual subscription to the Digimarc service, you can do that online right from within the filter dialog. Here's how the process is done (and how to prepare your files for digital watermarking).

Step One:

Open a photo for digital watermarking. This watermark is applied directly to your photo, and as long as the photo isn't one big solid color (there are some variations in color and detail in the image) the digital watermark is imperceptible to the human eye (however, dogs can see it, no sweat, but they see it in black-and-white).

Step Two:

The embedding should take place right before you save the file, so do all your color correction, retouching, sharpening, and special effects before you get ready to embed the watermark. Also, this Digimarc embedding only works on a flattened photo, so if you have a layered document, duplicate it (by going under the Image menu and choosing Duplicate) then flatten the duplicate layered document by choosing Flatten Image from the Layers palette's pop-up menu (as shown).

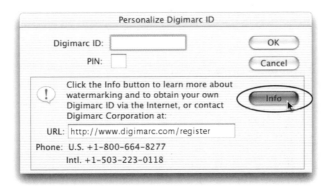

Step Three:
Go under the Filter menu, under Digimarc, and choose Embed Watermark.

Step Four:
This brings up the Embed Watermark dialog. I'm assuming at this point you don't have a Digimarc account set up, so click the Personalize button (as shown). If you do have a Digimarc account, click the same button, and it will ask for your Digimarc ID and PIN. If not, you'll have a chance to get yours in the next dialog.

Step Five:
The Personalize Digimarc ID dialog is where you enter your Digimarc ID and PIN. If you don't have one, click on the Info button (as shown), and as long as you have an Internet connection, it launches your browser and take you to Digimarc's Web site where you can choose which subscription plan best suits your needs. At the time of this writing, the service started at $49 for a one-year basic subscription and went up from there based on how many photos you want to protect, and other options you might want to purchase. See the site for details.

Continued

Step Six:

At the Digimarc site, the registration process is very simple (pretty much like any other e-commerce site these days) and immediately after you hit the Submit button (with your payment info) you're presented with your Digimarc ID and PIN. Enter these in the Personalize Digimarc ID dialog (as shown). Needless to say, that's not my real Digimarc ID number and PIN. Or is it? Hmmmm.

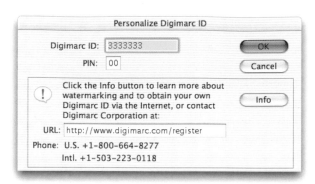

Step Seven:

Click OK to return to the Embed Watermark dialog. In the Image Information: Copyright Year field, enter the year the photo is copyrighted. For Image Attributes, enter the information you'd like to appear on the file. You also need to choose a Target Output. This helps determine how strongly the watermark should be applied to your photo (for example, Web images that will go through compression will need more durability than photos saved in lossless formats like TIFF or PSD). Look under the Watermark Durability slider in the dialog to see the relationship between visibility and durability (kind of like the compression relationship in JPEG images where higher quality means larger file sizes, and lower quality means smaller file sizes).

Step Eight:

Click the Verify check box at the bottom left of the dialog if you want to check the strength of the watermark immediately after you apply it.

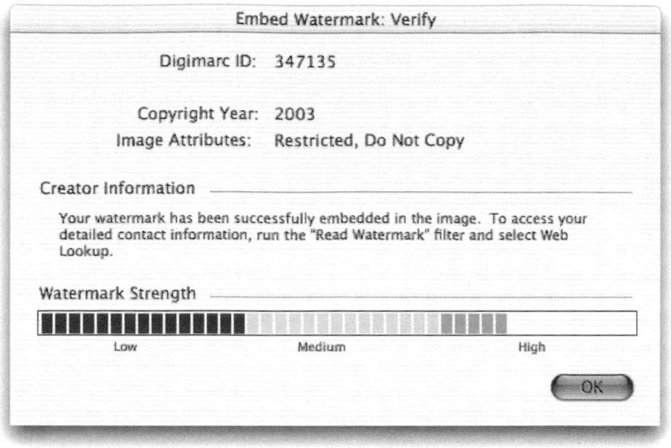

Embed Watermark: Verify

Digimarc ID: 347135

Copyright Year: 2003
Image Attributes: Restricted, Do Not Copy

Creator Information

Your watermark has been successfully embedded in the image. To access your detailed contact information, run the "Read Watermark" filter and select Web Lookup.

Watermark Strength

| Low | Medium | High |

OK

Noise ▶
Pixelate ▶
Render ▶
Sharpen ▶
Sketch ▶
Stylize ▶
Texture ▶
Video ▶
Other ▶
Digimarc ▶ Embed Watermark...
Read Watermark

Watermark Information

Digimarc ID: 333333 (This is your Digimarc ID.)

Copyright Year: 2003
Image Attributes: Restricted, Do Not Copy

Creator Information

For information about the creator of this image, click the Web Lookup button to connect to Digimarc's MarcCentre® locator service.

Watermark Strength

| Low | Medium | High |

Web Lookup   OK

Step Nine:

When you click OK (with Verify turned on), Digimarc immediately verifies the strength of the watermark, and whether it was successful. Click OK in this dialog, and the process is complete—a copyright symbol appears next to your file's name when viewed in Photoshop. Also, your Web site URL, your contact info, and your copyright info are embedded into the file. Now it's okay to save the file. (Note: If you're saving as a JPEG, to preserve the watermark, it's recommended that you don't use a compression quality lower than 4.)

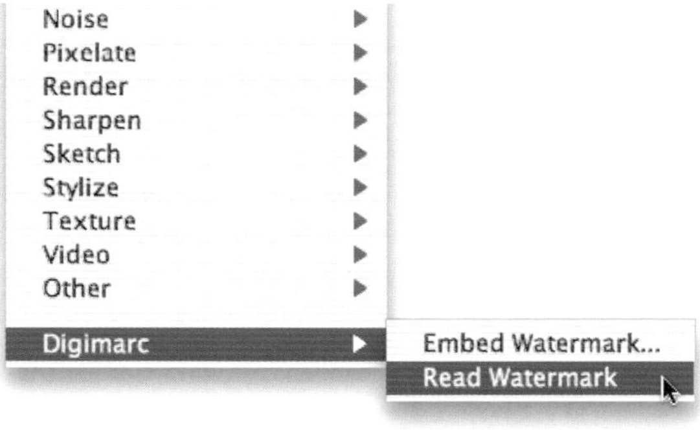

Step Ten:

Now that the info is embedded, if somebody opens your copyrighted photo in Photoshop, the watermark will be detected. You can check the watermark manually by going under the Filter menu, under Digimarc, and choosing Read Watermark (as shown).

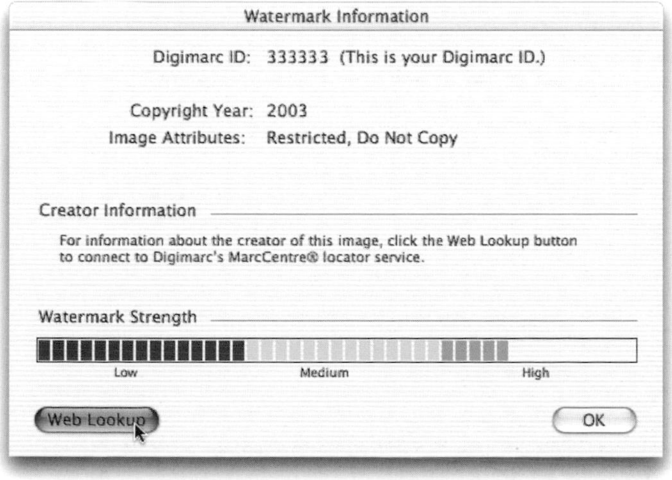

Step Eleven:

This brings up the Watermark Information dialog that shows that the photo is copyrighted and whether the image is restricted. At the bottom left-hand corner of the dialog is a button called "Web Lookup," and if someone who downloaded your photo clicks on this button, it will launch their Web browser and take them directly to your copyright info and your contact info. Pretty slick stuff!

Showing a Client Your Work on Your Computer

Any time I'm showing a client my work on screen, I use this technique because it quickly tucks Photoshop out of the way so the client isn't distracted by the palettes, menus, etc. They can focus on just the image, and not on the software I'm using. Also, it does a nice job of presenting each photo in almost a museum setting—perfectly centered on a black background with no distractions.

Step One:

Open the Photo you want to show to your client in Photoshop.

© BRAND X PICTURES

Step Two:

Press f, f, Tab (that's the letter "f" twice, then the Tab key). The first "f" centers your photo on the screen, surrounded by gray canvas area. The second time you press "f," the background changes to black, and Photoshop's Menu Bar is hidden. Then, when you press Tab, it hides the Toolbox, Options bar, and any open palettes, presenting your photo onscreen as shown here.

Step Three:
To return quickly to your normal display layout, just press f, then Tab. Now that you know these two shortcuts, you can use a variation of them to create a slide-show from right within Photoshop.

Step Four:
Go under the File menu and choose Open. In the Open dialog, click on the first photo you want to open, hold the Command key (PC: Control key), then click on all the other photos you want to open. If the images that you want to open are contiguous, simply hold the Shift key and then click on the first and last image in the Open dialog to select them all.

Continued

Step Five:

Click the Open button and Photoshop opens all the photos, one right after the other (as shown here).

© BRAND X PICTURES

Step Six:

Now that all the photos you want in your slideshow are open, hold the Shift key and click on the Full Screen Mode button at the bottom of the Toolbox (as shown here).

Step Seven:

This centers the first photo in your stack of photos on a black background, but your palettes will still be visible, so press the Tab key to hide them.

© BRAND X PICTURES

© BRAND X PICTURES

© BRAND X PICTURES

Step Eight:

Once your palettes are hidden, your slideshow is ready. To view the next "slide," just press Control-Tab and the next photo in the stack opens. Because you held the Shift key when you switched to Full Screen Mode, the previous picture will automatically be hidden when the next photo appears. Continue through the stack by pressing Control-Tab. The slideshow automatically loops, so scroll through as many times as you'd like.

Step Nine:

When you're done with your slideshow and want to return to Standard Screen Mode, press the Tab key to make the Toolbox visible again, hold the Shift key, then click on the Standard Screen Mode button at the bottom of the Toolbox (as shown here).

Showing Your Clients Different Versions of Your Work

I think Adobe had graphic designers in mind when they added the Layer Comps feature to Photoshop, but my guess is photographers will use it as much, if not more, because it's a great tool for showing off things like different wedding photo layouts, sports template layouts, and photos with different amounts of retouching or effects applied. Here's how to use new Layer Comps feature in your work.

Step One:

While you're working, once you have a layout that you think is fairly decent, go under the Window menu and choose Layer Comps to bring up the Layer Comps floating palette (shown here). Then, click on the New Layer Comp button at the bottom of the Layer Comps palette (which looks surprisingly like the New Layer icon in the Layers palette).

© BRAND X PICTURES

Step Two:

When you click this button, the New Layer Comp dialog (shown here) appears. Give your Layer Comp a descriptive name, then choose which attributes you want Photoshop to remember (it can remember which layers are visible, where your layers are positioned, and whether or not Layer Styles applied to your layers are visible). At the bottom is a Comment field, which is particularly important if you have multiple people working on the same document creating their own versions of the image.

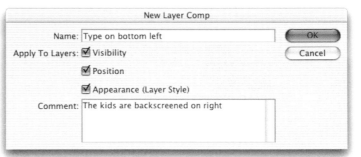

Step Three:
Click OK and your Layer Comp is added to the Layer Comps palette. This isn't just a still snapshot, because if you make changes, and then click on the Comp you just saved, the Layers palette itself actually reverts to what it looked like when you saved the comp. That way, you can pick up right where you left off, without having to recreate anything. You can continue to work, and each time you have a layout you like, click that New Layer Comp icon at the bottom of the palette.

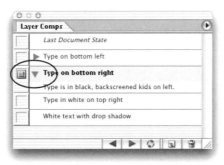

Step Four:
It won't be long before you'll have a number of different versions of your document, all within the same document. The comments you added when creating Layer Comps are helpful, and you can view them by clicking on the gray right-facing triangle beside your Layer Comp (these comments appear directly below your Layer Comp in the palette as shown).

Step Five:
Now, it's time to show the client your different layouts: Just use the left and right arrow buttons at the bottom of the Layer Comps palette to cycle through your different saved layouts (kind of like a slide show). Also, if you click one of the Layer Comps and then make a change to the layer (adjust opacity, change position, edit a Layer Style, etc.), you can update that comp to reflect your changes by clicking on the circular arrows icon at the bottom of the Layer Comps palette.

Letting Your Clients Proof on the Web

Giving your clients the ability to proof online has many advantages, and that's probably why it's become so popular with professionals. Luckily, Photoshop has a built-in feature that not only automatically optimizes your photos for the Web, it actually builds a real HTML document for you, with small thumbnail images, links to large full-size proofs, e-mail contact back to you, and more. All you have to do is upload it to the Web, and give your client the Web address for your new site. Here's how to make your own.

Step One:
Put all the proofs you want your client to view on the Web into one folder.

Step Two:
Open the File Browser (either choose Browse from the File menu, or click on the File Browser button in the far right side of the Options bar, right before the Palette Well). Go under Automate, and choose Web Photo Gallery (as shown).

Step Three:

This brings up the Web Photo Gallery dialog. At the top is a pop-up list of Styles (presets) where you can choose from different Web page layouts. A thumbnail preview of each template appears in the far right column of the dialog (below the Cancel button) as you choose the different Styles. In this example, I chose Centered Frame 1—Feedback, which creates a Web site with small thumbnails down the left side of the page that can be clicked on to display full-size photos on the right side of the page. Just below the Styles pop-up menu is a field for entering your e-mail address (which will appear prominently on your Web page) so your client can easily contact you with their choice made from the online proofs.

Step Four:

In the Source Images section of the Web Gallery dialog, specify the location of the folder of photos you want to put on the Web, and determine which folder these Web-optimized images will reside in for uploading. When you click the Choose button, a dialog appears prompting you to Select Image Directory (the folder full of photos). Locate them and click the Choose button. (Note: Although we're using a folder of images for this technique, in CS, you can also create a Web Photo Gallery using selected photos in the File Browser. Just Command-click [PC: Control-click] on the photos you want to use before you open the Web Photo Gallery, and then under Source Images choose Selected Images from File Browser instead of Folder.)

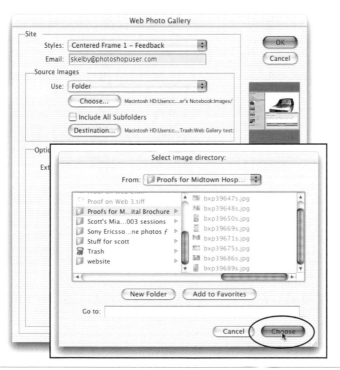

Continued

Step Five:

In the Options section of the dialog, choose Banner from the pop-up menu to enter the headlines and subheads for the site (as shown here). Next, from the Options pop-up menu, choose Large Images (shown in the capture in Step Six).

Step Six:

The Large Images Options area is where you choose the final size and quality of the full-size photos displayed on your Web page. You can also choose titles to appear under each photo in the Titles Use section. I recommend checking the Copyright check box, which will display your copyright info under each photo. Note: For this to work, you have to embed your copyright info in the photo first, by going under the File menu, choosing File Info, and entering your copyright text in the Copyright field.

Step Seven:

Change the Options pop-up menu to Security, then in the Content pop-up menu, choose Custom Text. This makes available the Custom Text field where you can enter text that will appear right across your large size photo. This is where you might add things like "Proof Copy," "Not for Printing," or "Not for Duplication." You can also specify the Font Size, Font Color, Opacity, and Position in this section.

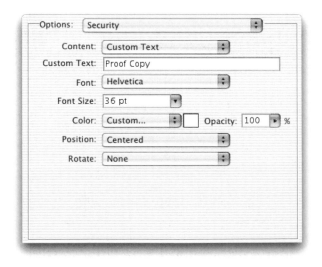

© BRAND X PICTURES

© BRAND X PICTURES

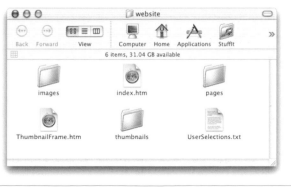

Step Eight:
When you add custom text, here's how that text appears over your photo.

Step Nine:
Click OK and Photoshop will do its thing—resizing the photos, adding custom text, making thumbnails, etc. Then, it automatically launches your Web browser and displays the HTML Web page it created for you. Here, you can see the site name in the top left-hand corner (which you entered in the Banner Options). Your e-mail address appears with a live link (if your client clicks it, it will open their e-mail client with your e-mail address already entered in the To: field). Under the full-size proof (with your custom text appearing over it) on the right, the client can click on the Image Info tab which will reveal the file's name and the Copyright info (taken from the embedded File Info). The client can also click on the Image Feedback tab, enter comments and e-mail them directly to you.

Step Ten:
Photoshop automatically creates all the files and folders you need (shown here) to put your Web Gallery up live on the Web, including your home page (index.htm), and places them neatly in your destination folder ready for uploading.

Getting One 5"x7", Two 2.5"x3.5", and Four Wallet Size on One Print

When it's time to deliver final prints to your client, you can save a lot of time and money by creating a "Picture Package," which lets you gang-print common final sizes together on one sheet. Luckily, Photoshop does all the work for you. All you have to do is open the photo you want ganged and then Photoshop will take it from there, except the manual cutting of the final print, which is actually beyond Photoshop's capabilities. So far.

Step One:

Open the photo you want to appear in a variety of sizes on one page, then go under the File menu, under Automate, and choose Picture Package. (In Photoshop CS, you can also choose Picture Package from the Automate mini-menu from right within the File Browser.) At the top of the dialog, the Source block asks which photo you want to use as your Source photo. By default, if you have a photo open, it assumes that's the one you want to use (your Frontmost Document), but you can choose from the Use: pop-up menu to use photos in a folder, or an individual file on your drive. By default, Picture Package chooses an 8x10 Page Size for you, but you can also choose either a 10x16 or 11x17 Page Size.

Step Two:

You choose the sizes and layout for your Picture Package from the Layout pop-up menu (shown here). In this example, I chose (1) 5x7 (2) 2.5x3.5 and (4) 2x2.5, but you can choose any combination you like.

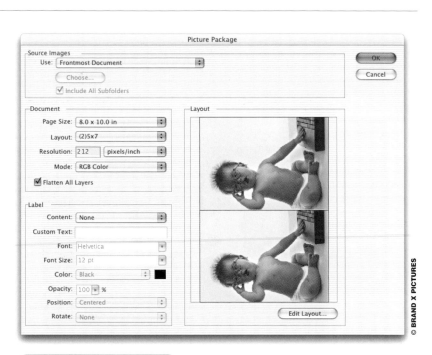

© BRAND X PICTURES

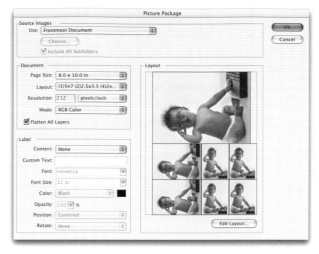

Step Three:
When you choose a layout, a large preview of that layout appears in the right column of the dialog. You can also choose the final output resolution in the Resolution field, and the Color Mode you'd like for your final output (in this case, I chose RGB because I'll be printing them to a color inkjet printer).

Step Four:
The bottom left section of the dialog is for labeling your photos, but be fore-warned—these labels appear printed right across your photos, so use them only if you're creating client proof sheets—not the final prints. Like the Web Photo Gallery, with the exception of adding your own custom text, this informa-tion is pulled from embedded info you enter in the File Info dialog, found under the File menu.

Step Five:
Click OK and Photoshop automatically resizes, rotates, and compiles your photos into one document (as shown). The one thing many photographers have complained about is that Picture Package doesn't offer you a way to add a white border around each photo in the package, but we've got a workaround for that in Step Six.

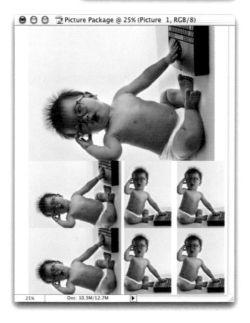

Continued

Step Six:

To have a white border appear around your photo in Picture Package, you have to first add it manually. So, start by pressing the letter "d" to set your Background color to white, then open your photo. Go under the Image menu and choose Canvas Size. Make sure the Relative Box is checked and then enter the amount of white border you'd like in the Width and Height fields (I used ¹/₄ inch).

Step Seven:

When you click OK in the Canvas Size dialog, it adds a white border around your photo. Now, you're ready to go under the File menu, under Automate, and choose Picture Package.

Step Eight:

Here's how your final Picture Package output will look with a border added around each photo (compare it with the Picture Package output on the previous page with no border). Remember, although the final print sizes will be correct (a 5x7 will still measure 5x7 including the border), adding this white border does make the photo itself a little bit smaller in order to compensate.

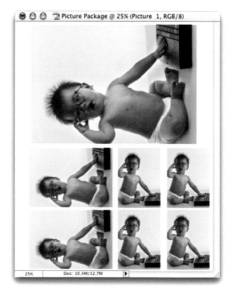

Step Nine:
Another feature of Picture Package is that you can have picture packages that use more than one photo. For example, to change one of the 2.5x3.5 prints to a different photo (while keeping the rest intact), just click on the preview of the image that you want to change.

Step Ten:
When you click on this photo, a dialog appears prompting you to Select an Image File. Navigate to the photo you want to appear here.

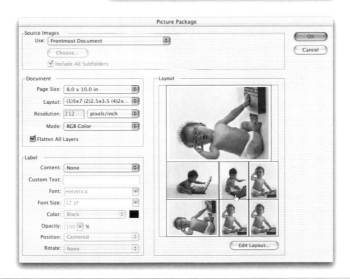

Step Eleven:
Click the Open button and that photo now appears within your Picture Package (as shown here in the dialog's Preview column). You can replace any other photo (or all the photos) using the same method.

Creating Your Own Custom Picture Package Layouts

As cool as Picture Package is, I don't think there's a Photoshop user alive who hasn't used it and thought, "This is cool, I just wish there was a layout that had...." In other words, although most of the popular layout choices are already there as presets, the one you really want isn't there, because that's just the way life works. Although technically, you could edit the text file that controlled these presets back in Photoshop 7, it was a tricky, tedious task. Not so in Photoshop CS, thanks to a clever visual layout editor.

Step One:

Open a photo (it doesn't matter which one, you're just using it as a placeholder to build your template) then go under the File menu, under Automate, and choose Picture Package. (Note: You can also access Picture Package from directly within the File Browser's mini-menu, under Automate.) When the Picture Package dialog opens, click on the Edit Layout button, located under the right corner of the layout preview window (as shown here).

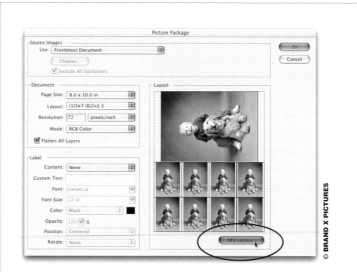

Step Two:

When the Picture Package Edit Layout dialog opens (shown here), go to the Layout Section in the top left corner and give your new custom layout a name (this name will appear in the pop-up list of preset layouts within Picture Package itself). Choose your Page Size and your desired ruler units from this Layout section (as shown).

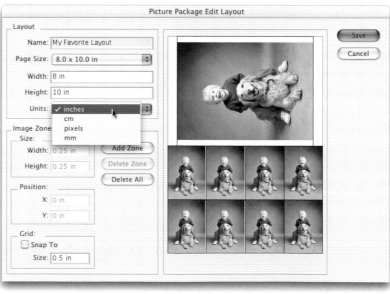

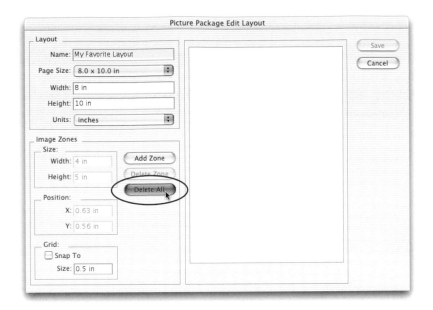

Step Three:

You'll probably find it easier to create your custom layout if you start from scratch (unless the layout you're creating is very similar to an existing layout, in which case, choose that layout before you enter the Edit Layout mode). To start from scratch, click the Delete All button (as shown here) to remove all the existing photo boxes from the preview window. (Note: Adobe calls these areas "Zones," so we might as well get used to calling them that too so we sound cool at Photoshop parties.)

Step Four:

Click the Add Zone button to add your first Zone (as shown here). A bounding box appears around your photo, and you can resize your Zone by dragging the adjustment handles that appear on the corners and sides of the bounding box. To move the Zone around within the preview area, just click inside the bounding box and drag it.

Continued

Step Five:

Since the idea behind Picture Package is "multiple copies of the same image on one page," they make it easy to create duplicate Zones. Just Option-click (PC: Alt-click) within a Zone's bounding box and a pop-up menu appears (shown here), where you can choose to Duplicate the Zone, Delete the current Zone, or create a duplicate of a Zone in one of three preset sizes (as shown here). Choosing one of these sizes from the pop-up menu does not affect the current Zone, it makes a duplicate in the size chosen from the pop-up menu.

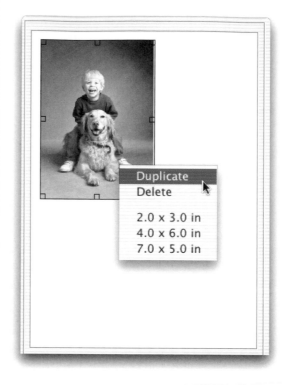

Step Six:

Another thing you might find helpful when creating your layout is to turn on a placement grid. You do this at the bottom of the Image Zones areas of the dialog (in the bottom left corner) by turning on the Snap To option. This also makes your Zones snap to the grid, which makes precise positioning much easier.

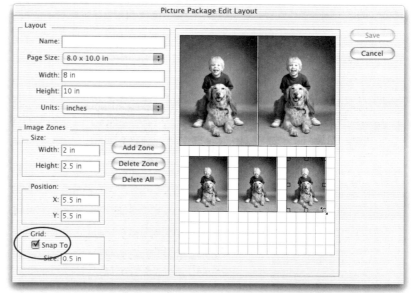

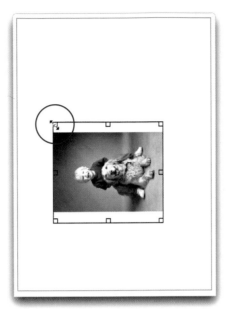

Step Seven:

If you've been looking in the dialog for a button called "make horizontal" or "flip on side," forget it—those are too descriptive, and if Adobe named buttons with names like that, you'd easily figure it out, and then where would we be? Instead, when you want to change the orientation of a photo from portrait to landscape, just click a corner point and drag the box until it's wider than it is tall. When you do this, the Layout Editor automatically flips your photo over on its side. It sounds clunky, but try it once and you'll see it's really not.

Step Eight:

When you click OK, a standard Save dialog appears, asking you to name your new layout. (This is just the name of the file on your hard drive, not the name that will appear in the Layout pop-up menu within Picture Package, so just give it a name that you'll recognize if you decide to delete this layout one day.) Click Save, and your newly named layout now appears in the Layout pop-up list (as shown here) where you can access it anytime from this list.

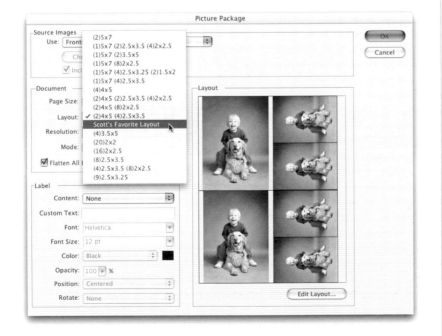

How to E-Mail Photos

Believe it or not, this is one of those "most-asked questions," and I guess it's because there are no official guidelines for e-mailing photos. Perhaps there should be, because there are photographers who routinely send me high-res photos that either (a) get bounced back to them because of size restrictions, (b) take all day to download, or (c) never get here at all because "there are no official guidelines on how to e-mail photos." In the absence of such rules, consider these the "official unofficial rules."

Step One:

Open the photo that you want to e-mail. Before you go any further, you have some decisions to make based on whom you're sending the photo to. If you're sending it to "friends and family," you want to make sure the file downloads fast, and (this is important) can be viewed within their e-mail window. I run into people daily (clients), who have no idea how to download an attachment from an e-mail. If it doesn't show up in the window of their e-mail client, they're stuck, and even if they could download it, they don't have a program that will open the file, so basically, they're stuck. So in short, make it fit in their e-mail browser.

Step Two:

Go under the Image menu and choose Image Size. To play it safe, for "friends and family," use a resolution of 72 ppi and a physical dimension no wider than 8 inches and no higher than 5 inches (but the height isn't the big concern, it's the width, so make sure you stay within the 8" width). By limiting your e-mailed photo to this size, you ensure that friends and family will be able to download it quickly, and it will fit comfortably within their e-mail window.

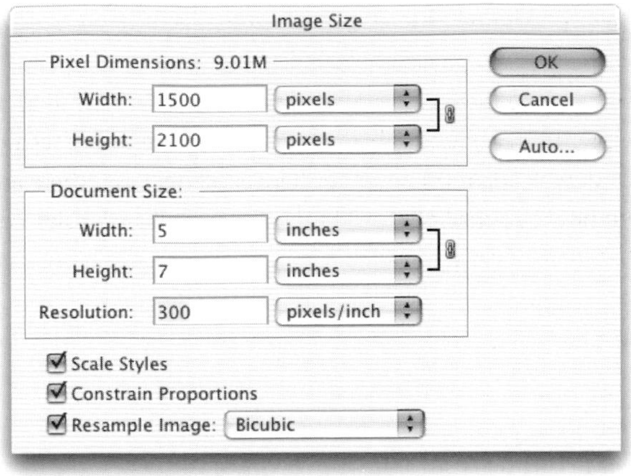

Image Size

Pixel Dimensions: 9.01M

Width: 1500 pixels
Height: 2100 pixels

Document Size:

Width: 5 inches
Height: 7 inches
Resolution: 300 pixels/inch

☑ Scale Styles
☑ Constrain Proportions
☑ Resample Image: Bicubic

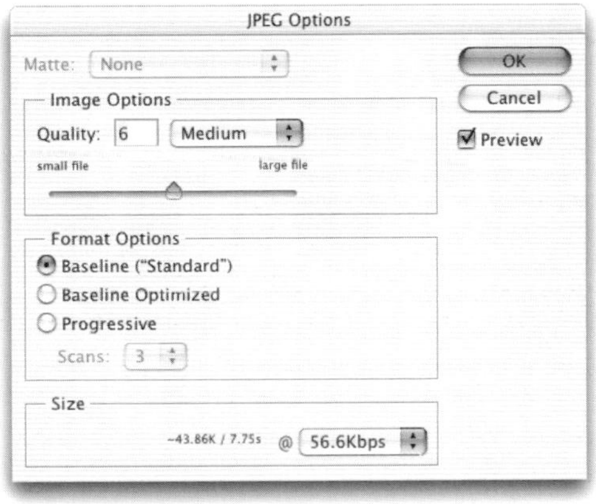

[OK] [Cancel] [Auto...]

JPEG Options

Matte: None

Image Options
Quality: 6 Medium
small file ——————— large file

Format Options
⦿ Baseline ("Standard")
○ Baseline Optimized
○ Progressive
Scans: 3

Size
~43.86K / 7.75s @ 56.6Kbps

[OK] [Cancel] ☑ Preview

5x7 photo @ 300 Resolution
Saved as a JPEG with 12 Quality
= 2.2MB (download time: nearly 7 minutes)

5x7 photo @ 150 Resolution
Saved as a JPEG with 12 Quality
= 656K (download time: Less than 2 minutes)

5x7 photo @ 300 Resolution
Saved as a JPEG with 6 Quality
= 253K (download time: Less than 1 minute)

5x7 photo @ 150 Resolution
Saved as a JPEG with 6 Quality
= 100K (download time: 18 seconds)

Step Three:

If you're sending this to a client who does know how to download the file and print it, you'll need a bit more resolution (at least 150 and as much as 300, depending on how picky you are), but the photo's physical dimensions are no longer a concern because the client will be downloading and printing out the file, rather than just viewing it onscreen in their e-mail program (where 72 ppi is enough resolution).

Step Four:

As a general rule, the file format for sending photos by e-mail is JPEG. To save the file as a JPEG, go under the Edit menu and choose Save As. In the Save As dialog box, choose JPEG, then click Save. This brings up the JPEG Options dialog (shown here). This format compresses the file size, while maintaining a reasonable amount of quality. How much quality? That's up to you, because you choose the Quality setting in the JPEG Options dialog. Just remember the golden rule: the higher the quality, the larger the file size, and the longer it will take your client to download it.

Step Five:

Your goal is to e-mail your client a photo that is small in file size (so it downloads quickly), yet still looks as good as possible. (Remember, the faster the download, the lower the quality, so you have to be a little realistic and flexible with this.) The chart shown here gives you a breakdown of how large the file size and download time would be for a 5x7 saved with different resolutions and different amounts of JPEG compression. It's hard to beat that last one—with an 18-second download on a standard dial-up modem.

Sending a Portfolio Presentation to a Client

In Photoshop CS, there's a new feature that takes a folder full of images, creates a slide show (complete with transitions), and compresses it into PDF format so you can e-mail it easily to a client for proofing. This is perfect for showing your portfolio to clients, sending clients proofs of wedding shots or portrait sittings, and any of a dozen other uses, none of which I can happen to think of right at this particular moment, but I'm sure later today, when I'm at the mall or driving to the office, they'll come to me.

Step One:

Open the photos you want to use in your PDF presentation (you actually have the choice of using photos you have open in Photoshop CS, or choosing a folder, but for this example, we'll start by simply opening a few photos).

© BRAND X PICTURES

Step Two:

There are two ways to access PDF Presentation: (1) Go under the File menu, under Automate, and choose PDF Presentation (as shown here), or (2) choose PDF Presentation from right within the File Browser's mini-menu, under Automate.

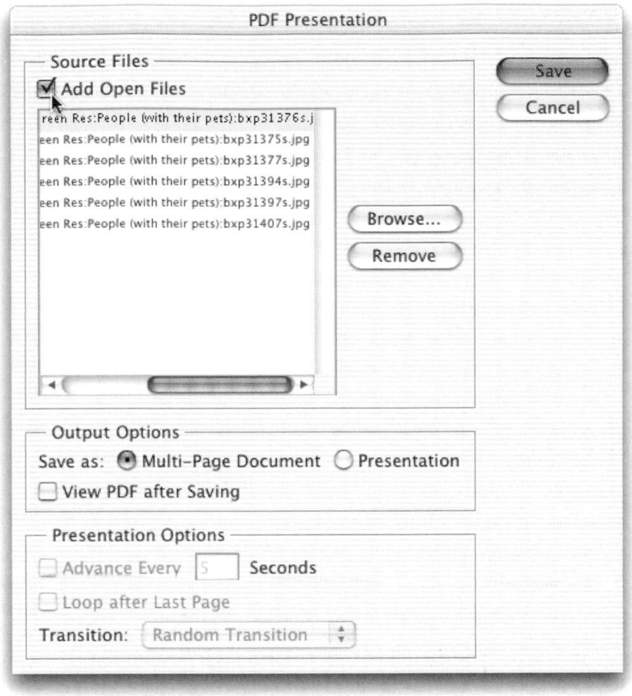

Step Three:

This brings up the PDF Presentation dialog. To create a presentation using the photos you already have open in Photoshop, click the "Add Open Files" check box (as shown) and a list of your open files appears in the window. By default, it will use all the files which appear in this window. If you have a photo open that you don't want in your presentation, just click on the photo (in the list) and then click the Remove button.

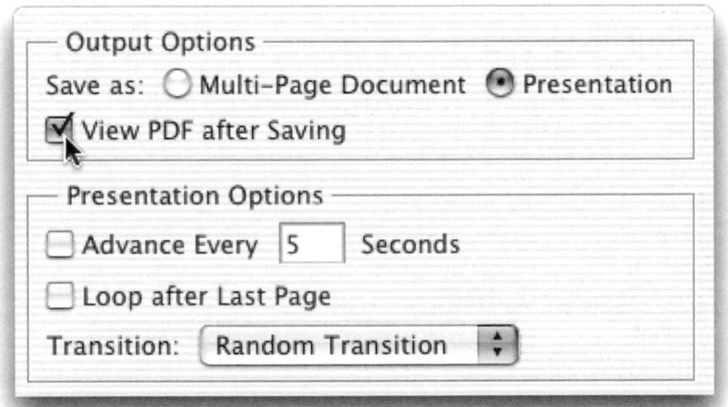

Step Four:

In the Output Options section of the dialog, click the Presentation button, and then check the View PDF After Saving (you don't have to view the PDF after saving, but it's always a good idea to see exactly what you're sending the client before you send it, just in case something didn't come out the way you wanted it to).

Continued

Step Five:

Under the Presentation Options section of the dialog lies one of the coolest things about the PDF Presentation: you can choose a transition between slides, and they've got a pretty decent selection. The best way to find out which ones you like best is to create a test presentation and choose the Random Transition from the Transition pop-up menu (shown here). That way, once you take a look at your test presentation, you'll quickly know which ones fit your style. In this Options section, you can also choose how many seconds you want each image to appear onscreen before it advances to the next image, and you can choose whether you want the presentation to loop (repeat) when it reaches the end.

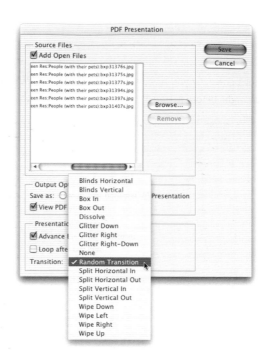

Step Six:

When you click the Save button, a standard Save dialog appears, but when you click OK, the PDF Options dialog (shown here) appears, where you can choose to encode your PDF as ZIP or JPEG. (I usually choose JPEG because it gives me the option of choosing a Quality setting for my photos, which gives me control over the look, and final file size, of the PDF.)

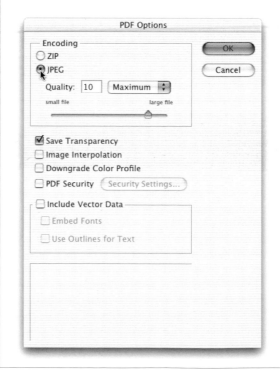

Step Seven:

Once you click OK, Photoshop CS creates a PDF file for you, ready to e-mail to your client. When your client opens your e-mailed PDF, it launches the Adobe Reader, goes into Full Screen Mode (your photos on a black background), and the presentation begins. (Note: To view the transitions correctly you have to view the PDF in Adobe Reader 6 or later.) The capture below shows the first slide in a PDF Presentation, right before it transitioned to the next photo.

contributing
Photographers

JULIEANNE KOST

Joining Adobe in 1993, Julieanne has learned her craft through hands-on experience and now serves as the Senior Digital Imaging Evangelist. Spanning digital imaging and illustration, her role includes customer education, product development, and market research. She is a frequent contributor to several publications, a speaker at numerous design conferences and tradeshows, and a teacher at distinguished photography workshops and fine-art schools around the world. Herself a passionate photographer, she combines her background in psychology in creating artwork, seen in several showings and published in several magazines. She is also the author behind the Photoshop Quickstart and Advanced Photoshop Techniques training CDs published by Dean Collins.

TODD MORRISON

Todd Morrison, a leader in the digital-photography revolution, specializes in timeless portraits of infants and children. Todd's consulting company, Zero2Digital.com, offers training and support for portrait studios making the transition to a digital-capture environment. He's also the owner of Morrison Photography (www.morrisonphotography.com) and has acquired more than 13 years of experience in the professional photographic industry. Todd's experience includes commercial, editorial, stock and portrait photography, as well as managing all aspects of a professional photo lab. Todd brings real-world experience and advanced Photoshop techniques to digital photographers. Clients include Epson America and Apple Computer. Todd also serves as a contributing writer for *Photoshop User* and *Digital Capture* magazines.

JEANNIE THERIAULT

Jeannie Theriault is a photographer/editor/educator based in Jacksonville, Florida. She began her photographic career as a private detective in Boston and has since exhibited her work in Boston, Puerto Rico, and Jacksonville. Special places and people have always inspired her work, but she also enjoys capturing the beauty that unusual aspects and lighting create in ordinary objects. Her images have been published in Jacksonville and internationally and her work also appears in *The Photoshop Elements Book for Digital Photographers.* Most recently, TeNeues published her *Great Escapes* box of greeting cards with worldwide distribution. Jeannie lives in Jacksonville with her husband and two young sons.

CAROL FREEMAN

Carol Freeman is a gifted photographer who combines her graphic design and photographic skills with her love and appreciation for the natural world. She has been published in many publications including *The 2002 Audubon Wildflower Calendar, Kew Magazine, Nikon World Magazine*, and others. She is a Nikon-sponsored photographer and a guest speaker for Fuji Photo Film USA, conducting seminars on the many intriguing and mystifying aspects of nature photography. Carol's work has won numerous awards, most recently the Graphic Design USA award and the Bronze Summit award for her *In Beauty, I Walk* 2002 calendar. Carol is happiest when she is out in nature looking for her next photograph. She can be reached at 847-404-8508.

DAVE CUERDON

David Cuerdon has been a commercial photographer for over 20 years. He was one of the first photographers to begin shoot-ing digital fashion photography full time beginning in 1995. David has photographed models in all the major U.S. markets including Chicago, L.A., Miami, and New York for clients such as Bloomingdale's, *Glamour*, Marshall Field's, Neiman Marcus, *Playboy*, and Spiegel. Currently, David is heading up one of the most advanced digital photography studios in the country for Value City Department Stores in Columbus, Ohio, where he now resides with his lovely wife, collaborator, and make-up artist Lisa and his wonderful son Ian.

KEVIN AMES

Kevin Ames is a commercial photographer who holds the PPA Craftsman degree and is an Approved Photographic Instructor. He has served as Co-Chairman of the Digital Imaging and Advanced Imaging Technology Committee of PPA and Chairman of the Commercial Advertising Group. He's a digital photography instructor on the PhotoshopWorld "Dream Team," and writes the "Digital Photographer's Notebook" for *Photoshop User* magazine. Kevin specializes in creating evocative images that promote his customers' products, services, and ideals. www.amesphoto.com (e-mail: kevin@amesphoto.com)

DAVID MOSER

Dave got his start in professional photography doing equestrian photography, and had his work published in numerous equestrian magazines. He then studied biomedical photography at RIT, before becoming a pioneer in Internet news delivery as one of the founders of Web portal MacCentral.com. Today, Dave acts as Chief Operating Officer of KW Media Group, and as Publisher of Nikon's *Capture User* magazine. Photography still remains an important part of his life where he now primarily shoots nature and concert shots, and his work appears in numerous Photoshop books.

Index

Symbols

COLOPHON

The book was produced by the author and the design team using all Macintosh computers, including a Power Mac G4 733-MHz, a Power Mac G4 Dual Processor 1.25-GHz, a Power Mac G4 Dual Processor 500-MHz, a Power Mac G4 400-MHz, and an iMac. We use LaCie, Sony, and Apple monitors.

Page layout was done using InDesign 2.0.2. Our graphics server is a Power Mac G3, with a 60-GB LaCie external drive, and we burn our CDs to a TDK veloCD 32X CD-RW.

The headers for each technique are set in 20 point CronosMM700 Bold with the Horizontal Scaling set to 95%. Body copy is set using CronosMM408 Regular at 10 points on 13 leading, with the Horizontal Scaling set to 95%.

Screen captures were made with Snapz Pro X and were placed and sized within InDesign. The book was output at 150 line screen, and all in-house proofing was done using a Tektronix Phaser 7700 by Xerox.

ADDITIONAL PHOTOSHOP RESOURCES

ScottKelbyBooks.com
For information on Scott's other books, visit his book site. For background info on Scott, visit www.scottkelby.com.

http://www.scottkelbybooks.com

National Association of Photoshop Professionals (NAPP)
The industry trade association for Adobe® Photoshop® users and the world's leading resource for Photoshop training, education, and news.

http://www.photoshopuser.com

KW Computer Training Videos
Scott Kelby is featured in a series of more than 20 Photoshop training videos and DVDs, each on a particular Photoshop topic, available from KW Computer Training. Visit the Web site or call 813-433-5000 for orders or more information.

http://www.photoshopvideos.com

Adobe Photoshop Seminar Tour
See Scott live at the Adobe Photoshop Seminar Tour, the nation's most popular Photoshop seminars. For upcoming tour dates and class schedules, visit the tour Web site.

http://www.photoshopseminars.com

PhotoshopWorld Conference & Expo
The convention for Adobe Photoshop users has now become the largest Photoshop-only event in the world. Scott Kelby is technical chair and education director for the event, as well as one of the instructors.

http://www.photoshopworld.com

PlanetPhotoshop.com
"The Ultimate Photoshop Site" features Photoshop news, tutorials, reviews, and articles posted daily. The site also contains the Web's most up-to-date resource on other Photoshop-related Web sites and information.

http://www.planetphotoshop.com

Photoshop Hall of Fame
Created to honor and recognize those individuals whose contributions to the art and business of Adobe Photoshop have had a major impact on the application or the Photoshop community itself.

http://www.photoshophalloffame.com

Kelby's Notes
Now you can get the answers to the top 100 most-asked Photoshop questions with Kelby's Notes, the plug-in from Scott Kelby. Simply go to the How Do I? menu while in Photoshop, find your question, and the answer appears in an easy-to-read dialog box. Finally, help is just one click away.

http://www.kelbysnotes.com

Mac Design Magazine
Scott is Editor-in-Chief of *Mac Design Magazine*, "The Graphics Magazine for Macintosh Users." It's a tutorial-based print magazine with how-to columns on Photoshop, Illustrator, InDesign, Dreamweaver, GoLive, Flash, Final Cut Pro, and more. It's also packed with tips, tricks, and shortcuts for your favorite graphics applications.

http://www.macdesignonline.com

Photoshop CS Down & Dirty Tricks
Scott is also author of the best-selling book *Photoshop CS Down & Dirty Tricks*, an amazing new collection of Photoshop techniques, including how to create the same exact effects you see every day in magazines, on TV, at the movies, and on the Web. It's available now at bookstores around the country.

http://www.scottkelbybooks.com

PROFESSIONAL PHOTOGRAPHERS, TAKE NOTE:
This groundbreaking NEW digital SLR is the world's fastest.

8 Frames/Sec for up to 40 Consecutive Shots

4.1 Effective Megapixels

Fast and Accurate 11-Area AF System

Nikon's Exclusive JFET Image Sensor LBCAST

Available Wi-Fi Transmission Capabilities

Motivated by Nikon's heritage in sports/action photography and photojournalism, the D2H is introduced to set a new standard for high-speed digital photography. Every function within the D2H system is optimized for fast, accurate and extreme performance with Total Image Quality. Using a newly developed original Nikon imaging sensor, the D2H is able to produce data-rich files that are compact enough for immediate transmission and rapid workflow, yet yield dramatically high image quality. Learn more at www.nikonusa.com.

All specifications effective July 22, 2003

Adobe® Photoshop® with a Wacom® Pen

Take advantage of Photoshop's 21 pressure-sensitive tools

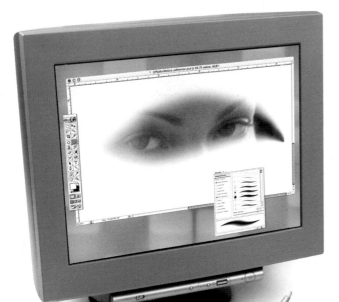

Pressure sensitivity opens up a new world of powerful options in Photoshop. Using a Wacom pressure-sensitive pen you can dynamically control things like brush size, opacity, color, texture, and more!

Pressure-sensitive control

Wacom pens are pressure-sensitive so you can control the amount of a software tool's effect by varying how firmly you press the pen tip to the tablet. Photoshop has 21 customizable tools that are specifically designed for use with a Wacom pen. You paid for them, why not use them properly?

Natural comfort

The Wacom Grip Pen is built for comfort. It has a cushioned, contoured grip-area and features Wacom's patented cordless, battery-free technology. Once you've experienced the natural comfort and superior performance of a Wacom pen, you'll wonder how you ever worked without one.

Time saving productivity

With more control and comfort you'll be more productive. Using a Wacom pen on your PC or Mac® is a very efficient way to work. Many Wacom customers tell us that switching to a pen has doubled their productivity. Try a Wacom pen for yourself and join more than 2,000,000 satisfied Wacom customers.

Call today 1-800-922-6613

Work Directly On Screen!
Cintiq starts at $1899

intuos2
Turn on Photoshop's power!
Intuos2 starts at $199

www.wacom.com

www.informit.com

YOUR GUIDE TO IT REFERENCE

New Riders has partnered with **InformIT.com** to bring technical information to your desktop. Drawing from New Riders authors and reviewers to provide additional information on topics of interest to you, **InformIT.com** provides free, in-depth information you won't find anywhere else.

Articles

Keep your edge with thousands of free articles, in-depth features, interviews, and IT reference recommendations—all written by experts you know and trust.

Online Books

Answers in an instant from **InformIT Online Books'** 600+ fully searchable online books.

POWERED BY

Catalog

Review online sample chapters, author biographies, and customer rankings and choose exactly the right book from a selection of more than 5,000 titles.

VISIT OUR WEB SITE

WWW.NEWRIDERS.COM

On our Web site you'll find information about our other books, authors, tables of contents, indexes, and book errata. You will also find information about book registration and how to purchase our books.

EMAIL US

Contact us at this address: **nrfeedback@newriders.com**

- If you have comments or questions about this book
- To report errors that you have found in this book
- If you have a book proposal to submit or are interested in writing for New Riders
- If you would like to have an author kit sent to you
- If you are an expert in a computer topic or technology and are interested in being a technical editor who reviews manuscripts for technical accuracy
- To find a distributor in your area, please contact our international department at this address. **nrmedia@newriders.com**

- For instructors from educational institutions who want to preview New Riders books for class-room use. Email should include your name, title, school, department, address, phone number, office days/hours, text in use, and enrollment, along with your request for desk/examination copies and/or additional information.
- For members of the media who are interested in reviewing copies of New Riders books. Send your name, mailing address, and email address, along with the name of the publication or Web site you work for.

BULK PURCHASES/CORPORATE SALES

The publisher offers discounts on this book when ordered in quantity for bulk purchases and special sales. For sales within the U.S., please contact: Corporate and Government Sales (800) 382-3419 or **corpsales@pearsontechgroup.com**.
Outside of the U.S., please contact: International Sales (317) 428-3341 or **international@pearsontechgroup.com**.

WRITE TO US

New Riders Publishing
800 East 96th Street, 3rd Floor
Indianapolis, IN 46240

CALL US

Toll-free (800) 571-5840. Ask for New Riders.
If outside U.S. (317) 428-3000. Ask for New Riders.

FAX US

(317) 428-3280

Voices that Matter™

OUR AUTHORS

PRESS ROOM

| web development | design | photoshop | new media | 3-D | server technologies |

EDUCATORS

ABOUT US

CONTACT US

You already know that New Riders brings you the **Voices that Matter**. But what does that mean? It means that New Riders brings you the Voices that challenge your assumptions, take your talents to the next level, or simply help you better understand the complex technical world we're all navigating.

Visit **www.newriders.com** to find:

- ▶ *Discounts* on specific book purchases
- ▶ Never before published chapters
- ▶ Sample chapters and excerpts
- ▶ Author bios and interviews
- ▶ Contests and enter-to-wins
- ▶ Up-to-date industry event information
- ▶ Book reviews
- ▶ Special offers from our friends and partners
- ▶ Info on how to join our User Group program
- ▶ Ways to have your Voice heard

New Riders

WWW.NEWRIDERS.COM